T0105559

THE MASTERPIECE WITHIN

FIVE KEY LIFE SKILLS TO BECOMING A LIVING WORK OF ART

GUY SCHOLZ AND CLAUDIA CHURCH

BALBOA.
PRESS
A DIVISION OF HAY HOUSE

Copyright © 2014 Guy Scholz and Claudia Church.

All rights reserved. No part of this book may be used or reproduced by any means, graphic, electronic, or mechanical, including photocopying, recording, taping or by any information storage retrieval system without the written permission of the publisher except in the case of brief quotations embodied in critical articles and reviews.

Balboa Press books may be ordered through booksellers or by contacting:

Balboa Press
A Division of Hay House
1663 Liberty Drive
Bloomington, IN 47403
www.balboapress.com
1 (877) 407-4847

Because of the dynamic nature of the Internet, any web addresses or links contained in this book may have changed since publication and may no longer be valid. The views expressed in this work are solely those of the author and do not necessarily reflect the views of the publisher, and the publisher hereby disclaims any responsibility for them.

The author of this book does not dispense medical advice or prescribe the use of any technique as a form of treatment for physical, emotional, or medical problems without the advice of a physician, either directly or indirectly. The intent of the author is only to offer information of a general nature to help you in your quest for emotional and spiritual well-being. In the event you use any of the information in this book for yourself, which is your constitutional right, the author and the publisher assume no responsibility for your actions.

Any people depicted in stock imagery provided by Thinkstock are models, and such images are being used for illustrative purposes only. Certain stock imagery © Thinkstock.

Printed in the United States of America.

ISBN: 978-1-4525-2342-2 (sc)
ISBN: 978-1-4525-2343-9 (e)

Library of Congress Control Number: 2014918129

Balboa Press rev. date: 12/17/2014

CONTENTS

Life Skill #4

Life Skill #5

ACKNOWLEDGEMENTS

We would especially like to thank Sonya Stricklin for encouraging us to meet, and for her continuous support throughout the writing of this book.

Jackie Chapman-Brown for her hours upon hours of editing, as well as her enthusiasm and belief in our vision for this book over the entire writing process.

Rodney Crowell for his support, patience, and understanding of the long hours and days spent writing over the phone, via fax and emails, at the kitchen table, and in various North American cities.

Jack and Pia Biensch for their friendship and Medici-like support by providing airmiles, encouragement, and belief in the masterpiece project every step of the way.

Our parents, Mary and Claude Church, and Arni and Herb Scholz, for their love and lifelong belief in our dreams.

We would also like to acknowledge the kindness of our family and friends, for without their encouragement, feedback, and support this book would not have been possible.

Every morning you have two choices; continue to sleep with your dreams, or wake up and chase them.

INTRODUCTION

A LIVING WORK OF ART

Every child is an artist. The problem is how to remain an artist once he grows up.
Pablo Picasso

E very child born into this world is a work of art. As children we learn from our surroundings. Some have the advantage of being reminded they are special and are exposed to a positive, joyful, and loving environment, while others are not as fortunate. Parents do the best they can, but no matter the circumstances in which we were exposed, none of us have the privilege of a picture perfect upbringing void of sadness, heartache, loneliness, discouragement, disappointment, and anger.

Once we leave our family home and strike out in the world to make lives of our own, many of us have no concept of how hard life can be as relationship, career, and monetary pressures begin to mount. So where do we attain the skills needed to balance these pressures? Some of us seek out a friend, some a counselor, some a parent, some a minister, some find books on the subject, some resort to drug and alcohol abuse, some choose rage, and some choose to retreat inward. *The Masterpiece Within* was born out of the need for a comprehensive, yet reader-friendly life skills manual to help us through the struggles we all encounter.

Written from combined female and male viewpoints, we have filled *The Masterpiece Within* with stories from our own personal experiences, both successes and failures. We have incorporated motivational anecdotes and wisdom from the lives of the famous, to the not so famous. We integrate pop culture references, themes, and messages from the sports, film, and music worlds, alongside time-tested principles from ancient masters. We end each major section with thought provoking questions, projects, tasks, and affirmations to better comprehend, retain, and apply key masterpiece tools and principles to everyday life.

Each and every one of us possesses the potential to become a *living work of art* during our lifetime. The responsibility lies in our own hands to unearth the masterpiece within. No one else can do the work for us. Imagine if there were a life museum, and in this museum the lives of each person ever to grace the planet were on display. What an inspiration the museum would be if each of us had been given the proper life skills, and consistently applied these skills, allowing us to become living works of art as priceless as Leonardo da Vinci's *Mona Lisa*, or as stunning as Michelangelo's *David*. Consider for a moment the possibilities on a global scale if every man, woman, and child received the following imprint throughout their lives, "You have the potential to be a living masterpiece!" What a changed world in which we all would live.

CHAPTER 1

DISCOVERING THE MASTERPIECE WITHIN

You can have a paint-by-numbers version of your life, or you can
start with a blank canvas and create a masterpiece.

Jim Collins

One of the most respected artists of the Renaissance period is Michelangelo Buonarroti. In 1501, the Italian artist was commissioned to create a statue of the biblical David, the symbol for strength and courage adopted by the city of Florence. Thirty-eight years earlier, an artist by the name of Agostino di Duccio had begun work on the statue, but he mistakenly blocked the marble and soon after deemed the stone unusable. Thirteen years after Agostino's failed attempt, artist Antonio Rosselli was commissioned to salvage something of the marble, but he too believed it to be flawed. This same block of marble, nicknamed "The Giant," which had been stored for many years in the courtyard of a church, was presented to Michelangelo. He deemed the Carrara marble "spoilt" but still believed he could make use of the discarded Giant and create a masterpiece for the city of Florence to embrace. He worked night and day for nearly three years perfecting the piece.

Michelangelo chose to portray David as a muscular young man whose consummate beauty made him reminiscent of a magnificently structured Apollo from antiquity. David's facial expression showed a quiet confidence and intensity, while his body reflected a relaxed stance, poised and ready for his battle to begin. This depiction of the *David* was different from past portrayals, which focused on the young warrior's post-victory pose of serenity and pride, as he stood over a conquered Goliath. Michelangelo's intent was to capture David's overall character, strength, and courage, which he felt was a more inspiring portrayal than focusing on the end result of the battle.

Upon completion, the seventeen-foot, eleven thousand-pound statue was placed in the Palazzo Vecchio. Because of its magnificent perfection, Michelangelo was viewed as the greatest sculptor of his time by the Florentine people. He was only twenty-nine years old. When the brilliant artist was asked how he could have created such an amazing work of art out of a flawed, "unusable" block of marble, he replied, *"David was underneath the excess marble all along; I simply had to free him. In every block of marble I see a statue, see it as plainly as though it stood before me, shaped and perfect in attitude and action. I have only to hew away the rough walls which imprison the lovely apparition to reveal it to other eyes, as mine already see it."*

Michelangelo's vision for and creation of the *David* serves as a pertinent example of the immense potential we all possess. In the same way the master sculptor was able to visualize the masterpiece within the stone, we as human beings must be able to envision a masterpiece within ourselves. The work of art Michelangelo was able to free from the marble represents the masterpiece each of us is capable of becoming. The flawed excess marble and rough walls from which David was freed can be viewed as the negative belief patterns of self-doubt, guilt, shame, regret, and fear that hold us prisoner at various times in our lives. When we are provided with the correct tools, we are able to free ourselves from negative belief patterns and build into our lives the essential elements required to become a living masterpiece. Making the commitment to discover and develop our masterpiece within should be seen as one of the most loving, personal gifts we can ever give to ourselves. The fact that the marble was left discarded for nearly forty years, also reminds us it is never too late for us to begin the process of discovering the masterpiece within.

FEBRUARY 1992

The responsibility to discover the masterpiece within lies solely in our own hands. We must come to a crossroads in our lives, where we either make the choice to aggressively pursue the path of discovery or choose to settle for second best or far worse. For some, the choice may be made during a crisis, while for others, the light may go on in the stillness of their hearts with little or no fanfare. As fate would have it, in February of 1992, in two separate countries, the authors both made the pivotal decision to take responsibility for their past, present, and future life choices. No longer would we allow toxic people, toxic thoughts, or outside circumstances the power to influence us or steer us off the path of pursuing our dreams. We reclaimed the belief that there was a masterpiece to be found within us and stepped wholeheartedly back on the path.

February 1992: Claudia's Story

Some of my earliest memories as a child have to do with the excitement of going with my family to see movies at our local theater. One of my favorite films has always been *The Wizard of Oz*. I was eight years old the first time I saw the film at a classic film screening, and I will never forget the moment Dorothy, in sepia tones, opened her front door to the vibrant, breathtaking color in the land of Oz. In the days following, I remember deciding that if grand adventures could happen for Dorothy, maybe they could happen for me as well. I dreamed of traveling to far away lands, and I set my plan in motion. Curious as to how others had achieved success, I, as a third grader, began to devour all the available biographies in our school library. Honest Abe Lincoln, who walked six miles to return five cents; Helen Keller, who refused to be a victim to her blindness and deafness; as well as J.C. Penney, who started with only a cart selling his wares were a few of my preferred inspirational life stories. The thought occurred to me that if these people started from humble beginnings and achieved success in their lives, maybe I could as well. School became an honor for me to attend, because I believed the more knowledge I gained, the further it would take me. I diligently mapped out the progression of my life in the entertainment arts as a model, country music artist, and actor.

My life sequence was right on schedule. After graduating from college, I signed with the Kim Dawson Agency in Dallas and then Karin Models in Paris. My work took me to breathtaking destinations around the globe, and I could not have been happier to be on my own grand adventure. I began dating a musician friend I had known for many years, and believing we shared an unbreakable love for one another, we were married the following year. We immediately moved to Nashville, Tennessee, to pursue our mutual dreams in music. I was living my dream! So I thought.

In February 1992, my life took an unexpected turn when I had to admit to myself that my presumed fairy-tale marriage was definitely not a fairy tale after all. I have always taken pride in being the type of person who could see hope in every situation, but even the marriage counselor we went to see believed there was no hope for the survival of our relationship. This period of time was devastatingly painful, and for the first time in my life, I experienced hopelessness and faced self-doubt, low self-esteem, and a deep inner sadness. I struggled with painting on a happy face for my modeling jobs. I knew I had to address my loss of joy or else my career would take a beating. I had never before imagined myself as the kind of person who needed therapy, because I came from such a loving family environment, but I knew I had to do something to address my escalating depression, or else I would find myself in a perpetual spiral of despair. I was determined to find happiness again and to not allow any of my marital trauma to negatively affect my own self-worth, my career dreams, or any future relationships.

I began taking walks at Radnor Lake in Nashville, which has always served as a very peaceful place for me to go. I filled journals to release my inner sadness, anger, and disappointment; made lists of what brought me joy; read as many inspirational books as I had time for; and joined a weekly therapy group. I finally became comfortable in my body again, while discovering strength, balance, confidence, and a renewed sense of hope. I began realizing we all have potential for peace and happiness when we take responsibility for our lives. I practiced looking at every life experience as an opportunity for growth and accepted that had I not experienced my divorce, I may not have discovered such life-changing personal growth. My ex-husband and I made the mature decision to release hurt feelings and to establish a lifelong friendship.

Through my journey, I was able to reignite my dreams in the entertainment arts, and in 1999, my first CD was released on Warner/Reprise Records. I also developed a very healthy, loving relationship with an amazing man, Rodney Crowell, who became my husband six years after we met.

February 1992: Guy's Story

I am a dreamer! I have always believed in the power of dreams. Over a period of years, I slowly learned that in order to experience meaning and purpose in life, we must intentionally set our hearts in the direction of our dreams. As I became more serious about pursuing my dreams, I began to realize my expectations may not turn out to be what I had originally envisioned. Yet, the good news was, as I remained genuinely committed to following my dreams, my personal growth continued to improve, and in turn I was becoming a positive influence in others' lives.

I had not always gone after my dreams with the passion and commitment necessary to see them through. I was in my early thirties when I began to feel like I needed to seize my dreams and stop waiting for others or circumstances to make them a reality. Throughout my life certain movies, stories, and songs have inspired my thoughts and outlook on life. A favorite scene or line often becomes a part of my personal lexicon. The convergence of seeing a highly successful film in 1989 and listening to a radio talk show in 1992, served as a huge motivation for me. *Field of Dreams*, starring actor Kevin Costner as Ray Kinsella, is about a man who feels life is passing him by and his dreams are slowly flickering out. In the film Ray frustratingly conveys to his wife Annie, (Amy Madigan) "I'm thirty-six years old and scared to death I'm turning into my father. I never forgave him for being old. He must have had dreams, but he never did anything about them. Not doing one spontaneous thing. I'm afraid that might be me." As a baseball fan, a dreamer, and a man who grew up in Saskatchewan, the Canadian equivalent of Iowa, I identified with Costner's character.

The pivotal line from the film, "If you build it he will come," became a challenge for me to become more aggressive in taking control of my life regardless of inner apprehensions or worrying what others would think of me. I knew in my heart I needed to become more of an initiator of my dreams no matter where the path took me. For the next two and a half years the inspiration of this film combined with my own personal studies kept me on the path of building my life around my dreams.

In February of 1992, the decision to pursue my dreams came to a head for me while on a trip to Edmonton, Alberta where I had been invited to be a guest lecturer at a theological college.

Ironically Edmonton is the birthplace of W.P. Kinsella, the author of the book based on *Field Of Dreams*. On this particular occasion, I was asked to lecture on a subject very dear to me; taking our passions, gifts, and talents and using them in the world around us to make a difference. Part of the lecture was based on the message, "If you build it he will come." The concept was that if we listen to the inner voice of our soul, God will be there for us, and He will help us achieve our dreams. I was looking forward to the challenge of presenting the material and seeing the audience's reaction. Little did I realize I was about to experience one of life's rare "aha" moments that would propel me further along the path to aggressively follow my dreams. I have always aimed to practice what I teach, but I was about to be challenged to the core.

The journey to Edmonton was a three hour trek, so I tuned into one of Western Canada's most popular radio sports talk shows. The topic for the evening was, "What separates the great athlete from the merely good or average?" The conclusion of the show was unanimous. The dominate sports stars like Wayne Gretzky, Michael Jordan, Steffi Graf, Joe Montana, and Mario Lemieux were viewed as "initiators." These performers took it upon themselves to set the tone and outcomes of their contests. Whenever any of these athletes took responsibility, their choices caused a chain reaction throughout their teams elevating the performance level of their teammates. Whether it was the Oilers, Bulls, Wimbledon Tennis, 49ers, or the Penguins, these dominant athletes were aggressive participants. They were not passive performers waiting for the game to unfold.

Listening to this talk show on a long drive in the middle of a frigid Canadian winter inspired me to become more of an initiator in life. The radio show that night inspired me to continue to discover and develop the masterpiece within me. I was no longer content to simply teach the theory or bounce around between being a participant in life to being a non-participant. I desired to be a practioner of life at a completely deeper level with the drive and consistency of a Gretzky or a Graf.

Fast forward twenty-one years to August 2013 and a bucket list item. I found myself in Dyersville, Iowa, the home of the *Field of Dream* baseball field used in the film, for a little fresh inspiration to keep following my dreams. I had just wrapped up writing a one year book project with a well known NHL player who was not sure if he wanted the book released during the timeline we had first agreed upon. Out of respect for his wishes, my agent and I, made it known to him we would hold off in pursuing interested publishers.

The *Field of Dreams* was better than anticipated. I walked around the field in my bare feet to soak up the ghosts of White Sox past. I ran the bases just because I had to and then walked into the cornfield to pick a few corn cobs to dry and serve as a constant metaphor, "To go the distance," as the voice encouraged Ray Kinsella in following his dream. It was the perfect tonic for my soul to keep pursuing the dreams in my heart and to strive to make a difference with my life despite hardships, obstacles or even crushed dreams. A lot of life had happened since February 1992, some bitter but mostly sweet. But enough bitter times to test my capacity to dream.

Then the inspirational burst came. One of the locals, Frank Dardis, who played a White Sox ghost in the film, appeared in a full cotton early 1900's uniform to answer questions. I was amazed when Frank told me ever since the film was released the *Field of Dreams* averaged sixty-five thousand visitors per year. He continued, "This is a bucket list place and I see people walk out of here inspired. " I asked Frank if he wanted to play catch. He graciously said, "I'd love to, but if we do, we have to play catch in the exact spot where Ray played catch with his dad at the end of the movie." For fifteen minutes we tossed the ball and chatted off and on. Frank played the part perfectly. I felt like I was playing catch with my dad as a little kid in Saskatchewan and my soul was being reinvigorated with youthful passion. I knew I could do anything as long as I followed my heart.

Our paths crossed through Claudia's music and we soon realized we shared a common vision to write a book that would challenge and inspire others to achieve their dreams and to make a difference with their lives. We believed our diverse backgrounds, along with our experiences, could create a unique combination of life knowledge. One who worked primarily on a stage- the other from a podium or pulpit; a country music artist - an ordained minister; an actor - a sports writer; a professional model - a social worker; a photographer - a competitive curler; a woman - a man; an American - a Canadian; Yin and Yang! We set plans in motion to begin co-writing *The Masterpiece Within* and speaking together on the material at workshops and seminars.

A LIVING MASTERPIECE

Michelangelo's own personal life story serves as an educational view into the passion behind one person's quest to make the most of his life. Michelangelo was born in the small village of Caprese, Italy in 1475. Shortly following his birth, his mother fell very ill leaving her unable to care for Michelangelo. He was cared for by a wet nurse in the nearby stone cutting village of Settignano where he lived off and on for the next decade, as a result of his mothers failing health and eventual death. As a boy of six, Michelangelo was already aware art was his passion so living in a creative stone cutting environment proved to be the ideal setting to encourage his artistic instincts. When he was ten years old, his father remarried bringing Michelangelo back home to live with his family in Florence. Michelangelo would spend hours and hours walking around the city sketching whatever caught his interest.

He quickly became friends with a neighbor boy named, Francesco, who studied as an artist's apprentice. Francesco, impressed with Michelangelo's talent, brought home drawings for his friend to study and copy so he could bring them back to the master painter, Domenico Ghirlandaio. When Michelangelo turned thirteen, he asked his father for permission to become Ghirlandaio's apprentice. This enraged his father who considered a career in the arts a waste of time because it brought neither honor nor monetary gain to the family. He believed a career in literature awaited all five of his sons. His father even resorted to beating Michelangelo numerous times in desperation to dissuade him from a life in the arts, but he would not budge.

Due to the persistent urgings of Ghirlandaio, Michelangelo's father became convinced of his son's incredible gift and finally granted him permission to study with the master painter. Michelangelo quickly became the top student of his class which allowed him to receive pay for his commissions. He studied fresco painting until the Florentine leader, Lorenzo de' Medici, hired him to create statues for his elaborate gardens. Lorenzo was so impressed with Michelangelo's talent that he moved the artist into his home to be educated along with his children and to live as his own son. While living in the palace, Michelangelo was able to study poetry, philosophy, science, and art. He often conversed with the most famous and brilliant men of his time who frequently visited the Medici family. His reputation as a brilliant artist and master sculptor grew rapidly throughout the region.

Michelangelo's life achievements and passion for living can serve as an inspiration to us all. His curiosity for life grew continually with age. He never lost sight of the fact that there was always something new he could learn whether it be in the areas of art, spirituality, philosophy or life in general. He maintained the same persistent determination and intensity right up until six days before his death, a few weeks shy of his ninetieth birthday. During his lifetime Michelangelo reached such a high level of monetary wealth and respect he could have rested on his laurels, but instead his passion remained consistent in his pursuit to develop the masterpiece within. Hours before his death he stated, "Dying just as I am beginning to learn the alphabet of my profession." Today, over five hundred years after his birth, he is still recognized as one of the most gifted artists of all time and the *David* is acknowledged as being one of the greatest and most inspirational works of art ever created.

It is our belief that we all have the ability to not only become living works of art but living masterpieces through consistent hard work, determination, intense hopefullness, and living a life of integrity. The responsibility to take the first step lies solely in our own hands. We must be courageous enough to take this initial step and bear in mind the ancient Chinese proverb, "The journey of a thousand miles begins with one step."

CHAPTER 2

MASTERPIECE TOOLS

In the long run we shape our lives and we shape ourselves. The process never ends
until we die. And the choices we make are ultimately our own responsibility.

Eleanor Roosevelt

Unlike the numerous artists who had attempted and failed to create a symbolic statue for the city of Florence, Michelangelo was able to take on the task and succeed because he had diligently perfected his craft to such an impressive depth. This level of confidence and commitment gave Michelangelo the perseverance to create what many believe to be the greatest sculpture in history. What is it that fuels artists like Michelangelo or humanitarians like Mother Teresa to live up to their potential? We found in our research of those who have chosen the path to become a living masterpiece there are certain attitudes possessed by these individuals. These attitudes or "masterpiece tools" as we prefer to call them when embraced will help to manifest positive results. Our lives begin to flourish, our personal growth accelerates, we experience more internal joy, we become an inspiration to those around us and we gain the motivation to remain on the masterpiece path throughout our lives.

Masterpiece Tool #1: ACKNOWLEDGING THE MASTERPIECE WITHIN

In order to discover the masterpiece within, we must first ask ourselves, "Do I truly believe a masterpiece exists within me?" This kind of question can be tough to face and to admit the truth especially if we have not devoted much work on our inner self. If we are not convinced there is a masterpiece within, the turnaround may be as simple as making the choice to retrain our belief system toward a more positive attitude. A faulty belief system can be our greatest enemy because the damaging effects can do more harm than almost anything else in our lives. This type of belief can leave us paralyzed and numb toward a vision for personal worth or growth potential. A positive belief system, however, can serve as our greatest ally. The beneficial effects will take us in the direction of our dreams and will serve as fuel to get us past life obstacles. Hearing words of positive reinforcement from others is always helpful, but words alone will not necessarily change our beliefs. We must work diligently on our own to create the belief within ourselves. Sometimes acting "as if" we believe in ourselves and our abilities is the most useful method to kick start the belief.

When director Steven Spielberg was asked how much belief he had in his abilities when he started in the film business, he answered, "Zero... absolutely zero belief, but I just pretended I did anyway and because others saw that I believed in myself so much they believed in me too." When we believe our presence on earth truly matters, our life possibilities become limitless.

The classic film, *The Wizard of Oz*, is another example of how our belief system affects our lives. The film's main character, Dorothy played by Judy Garland, is on a quest to find her way back home to Kansas. While on her journey in the land of Oz, Dorothy faces various adventures and challenges. She is able to face and overcome these obstacles with the help of a support team she gathered along the yellow brick road. Members of the support team include a scarecrow without a brain, a tin man without a heart, and a lion without courage. As the film draws to a close, all three of these characters are able to find what they are searching for, but Dorothy remains stranded in Oz. She once again calls on Glinda the Good Witch of the North, played by Billie Burk, who has helped her throughout her journey. Dorothy asks Glinda, "Will you help? Can you help me?" Glinda replies, "You don't need to be helped any longer. You always had the power to go back to Kansas." The scarecrow asks why she had not given Dorothy this information from the beginning. Glinda replies, "Because she wouldn't have believed me; she had to learn it for herself."

Dorothy then begins to understand why her long and tiresome journey was necessary in order to find her way home. The life lessons she learned along the way opened her eyes to accept, acknowledge, and believe that she could make it home to Kansas on her own. Glinda asks her to click her heels together three times and to repeat, "There's no place like home, there's no place like home…" She then awoke in her own bed surrounded by her family and friends.

Dorothy's strong desire to find her way home gave her the determination to bravely face the unknown. She wisely gathered a loyal support team with similar desires and together they overcame every obstacle they encountered. All four characters agreed to go on the journey and in doing so learned the life lessons necessary to create a strong belief in themselves, and to acknowledge the masterpiece was within them all along. When we choose to believe our lives are meaningless and useless, a negative outcome is guaranteed. When we choose to embark on our journey with a positive belief system, we too open the door to infinite possibilities.

Masterpiece Tool #2: BUILDING A NOBLE FOUNDATION

Building a noble foundation begins with the development of three essential virtues: character, passion, and discipline. Character builds resilience, passion fills us with boundless energy, and discipline brings joy from experiencing positive results. As these virtues mature over time our masterpiece potential becomes immeasurable. If we neglect any one of these three virtues we become stagnate and disillusioned. When all three work in unison we begin to live productive and meaningful lives.

Character can be defined as the combination of our thoughts, habits or beliefs governed by either a noble value system or an ignoble value system. Someone with character consistently strives to live a life of integrity and stands strong to honorable convictions. The depth of our character is often developed away from the spotlight and acclaim where few if any are aware of our actions. We can examine the times when we are tempted to commit acts such as lying, cheating or stealing. We may try and convince ourselves a little dishonesty here and there will not hurt anything but there is no such thing as a little lying, a little cheating or a little stealing because we know the truth. How we choose to live in the "little" areas of life will eventually go on to affect the "major" areas as well.

Our character is always in training or being tested and we can either fail to our detriment or pass with flying colors. These times are golden opportunities to build character whether anyone else is watching or not. Every choice we make in life establishes a pattern or habit of behavior, which builds either a weak or strong foundation. Honorable behavior begets honorable returns and dishonorable behavior begets dishonorable returns. Character depth is best revealed in moments of crisis or adversity. The deeper our character is developed, the larger our reservoir of strength becomes to make wise and honorable choices in times of trial as well as times of praise.

Passion is the driving force, the joy, the excitement, the zeal for living that helps us remain motivated no matter what obstacles come our way. Passion comes from the heart and is based on the purity or childlike innocence of love, where self-imposed limits or boundaries have not yet been established. "When man acts from great passion," as Benjamin Disreali reminds us, "He does great things." Without passion we lack the fuel to maintain a noble foundation and the desire to discover the masterpiece within. Maintaining a high level of passion takes continuous effort throughout our lives due to its natural ebb and flow. At times, we can even feel a total loss of passion due to life upsets or negative circumstances. During these moments, we must pull ourselves back into reality and remind ourselves we always have the power of choice, and to surround ourselves with people who truly understand and believe in us. Both can serve to rekindle our passion.

Misplaced passion is a negative form of passion, which is subtle and can be extremely damaging. Parents can be completely passionate about their parenting, but to such an extreme they become a detriment not only to their children's lives, but to their own lives as well. They attempt to live vicariously through their children, placing undue pressure on them to fulfill their own expectations and happiness. This approach can strip a child of having the opportunity to voice their own opinions or express their own passions. Unless this cycle is broken, neither the children nor the parents will ever get to experience healthy passion. We must focus on parenting our own passion and give others the freedom to form their own opinions and to explore their own passions.

Discipline is consciously accepting the dedication and hard work required to achieve a desired end result. Discipline provides us with vital structure and persistence to remain focused and on the path, regardless of the work involved. There are two types of discipline, which we can attain:

external and internal discipline. External discipline focuses on our outward appearances which provides us with social acceptance. This can be a healthy discipline to cultivate to a certain degree, but not at the expense of compromising internal discipline. Internal discipline focuses on cultivating a constant awareness and accountability to do whatever it takes to live up to our fullest potential. Developing both disciplines is beneficial to our lives, but we will be unable to build a noble foundation without making the commitment to foster internal discipline.

Romantic relationships are a good example of the use of internal and external discipline. New love inspires the desire to express and maintain both disciplines in order to keep the relationship moving forward. At this stage, the couple is usually willing to do whatever it takes to keep the relationship fresh and alive. As the relationship enters into marriage, the discipline first expressed, which kept the relationship exciting, often begins to wane. Unless the initial disciplines of communication, care for our outward appearance, compromise, and kindness are restored, the couple is in danger of a dying romance. In the same sense we must learn to maintain discipline in order to develop the masterpiece within. When discipline is consistently implemented into our lives, confidence increases, desired goals become achievable, self-control is strengthened, and setbacks are kept in proper perspective.

When we make the effort to build a noble foundation, an overall positive life effect quickly begins to materialize. Those around us will begin to notice the difference and question what changes we have made. When all three virtues of character, passion, and discipline collectively mature, we can feel we are experiencing the fountain of youth. Our energy increases and the masterpiece within begins to appear possible regardless of the work and effort required.

Masterpiece Tool #3: COURAGE TO REMAIN ON THE PATH

Fear is the biggest ongoing challenge throughout our lives and can be especially menacing while on the journey to discovering the masterpiece within. If we allow this grimacing monster control over our lives, we will remain emotionally incapacitated and unable to achieve much of anything. Courage is the antidote for allowing fear to control how we live. As Mark Twain wrote, "Courage is resistance to fear, mastery of fear, not the absence of fear." We all experience feelings of inadequacy especially when we take risks; no one likes to be ridiculed, embarrassed or appear to be a failure. It is important to remind ourselves failure is rarely as devastating as it initially appears. Even when we do experience failure, we usually gain important life lessons, which aids us along the path of discovering the masterpiece within. Choosing to take steps of courage builds our confidence and will eventually put fear in proper prospective.

In order to function in society, we often develop masks to cover our fears as a coping mechanism. When we wear these fear masks, we camouflage our inner fears and insecurities by creating a facade of strength. Although this tough exterior may yield positive initial results, the exhausting false front is difficult to maintain because it continuously wears down our self-worth. We may believe we are hiding our true feelings by wearing these fear masks, but frequently they are transparent to our close friends, family, and colleagues. As Francois VI, Duc de La Rochefoucauld stated, "We are so accustomed to wearing a disguise before others that eventually we are unable to recognize ourselves."

We must be willing to remove this self-imposed armor and risk exposing our core fears in order to fully develop our masterpiece within. Removing our fear masks brings a new sense of clarity, emotional freedom, and a strong conviction to reject "second best" for our lives. We are more willing to participate in life rather than being content to sit in the wings and observe others in the arena of life. Most importantly, we begin to clearly see the fallacy behind wearing fear masks, which provide a pseudo sense of protection from life's hurts and disappointments. We find ourselves finally able to risk exposure of our true selves and the freedom to actively discover the masterpiece within.

Common Fear Masks

1. Humor Mask

When someone wears the humor mask, almost every situation in life is joked about or laughed off. A good sense of humor can be a great personal asset, but when we use humor to disguise our insecurities it can be a very destructive mindset. A dark sarcastic sense of humor can be the easiest humor mask to recognize. This person makes everyone around them feel defensive and uncomfortable. Someone who uses self-effacing humor or who is genuinely entertaining can be harder to spot. They tend to make everyone comfortable and are a joy to be around. Oftentimes, we later find out these people are not as happy and fulfilled as we assume they are. However, a healthy balanced sense of humor can be of tremendous assistance along the path to discovering the masterpiece within. Healthy humor teaches us not to take life too seriously during challenging times.

2. Victim Mask

This mask is identified as, the "poor me" belief system. When someone plays the role of victim they have usually mastered the art of blame-shifting. The victim blames other people or outside circumstances for every negative life hardship they encounter. They continually make excuses to convince themselves and others around them they are incapable of improving situations in their lives. Victims may even insist upon other people making choices for them so they do not have to take responsibility for the outcome themselves. They live in a paralyzing whirlwind of negativity believing nothing good can happen for their lives. Once victims are able to learn the importance of taking responsibility for their choices, they become capable of pulling themselves out of this dark abyss. Making this decision will empower them to control their own life paths rather than living a life of constant blame-shifting. Life adversities can be extremely difficult to deal with at times, but without addressing them head on, we decrease our chances of ever unearthing the masterpiece within.

3. Intellectual Mask

We all feel insecure on an intellectual level at various times in our lives, but someone who wears the intellectual mask frequently tries to overcompensate for their insecurities. These people can come across in polar opposite extremes; "the know it all" type or the "I know nothing" type. The "know it all" type feels there is nothing new they can learn, because they know everything about everything already. They tend to come across as always trying too hard and although they may feel they appear to be the most knowledgeable person in a group, they are most often seen as arrogant bores. Knowledge displayed in a "know it all" manner is almost always a turn off. The

"I know nothing" type rarely talks at all in groups of people. They tend to appear uninterested in becoming a part of just about any type of discussion, but deep down they actually yearn to contribute to the conversation. When they rarely do contribute, the subject matter is usually very light in nature. Whichever type of personality is displayed, they are both deeply insecure, and afraid of presenting themselves as uneducated and ignorant. Everyone longs for approval, but by wearing either intellectual mask these people if truth be told are losing respect and approval. When we make the commitment to discover the masterpiece within and remove either of these masks, we are able to remain teachable and to see life as a lifelong learning endeavor.

4. Procrastination Mask

Procrastinators stall and wait for the perfect conditions before pursuing their goals and dreams. They make excuse after excuse to justify why they have lacked the motivation to take any action. This inaction attempts to camouflage a paralyzing fear of failure, possible embarrassment in front of others and insecurities regarding their talents. The procrastinator has not yet learned the importance of taking risks in order to forge forward. Risking the first step is often the hardest one to take. Once they see for themselves that failure is not the end of the world, they can begin to recognize how failure in one area may open a door of opportunity in another. Patience with ourselves can be a productive and necessary ingredient in order to discover the masterpiece within, but patience should not be confused with infinite stalling.

5. Financial Mask

When the financial mask is worn these people are in a constant inner battle to prove their value to the rest of the world. They cling to the belief that large sums of money will take them to a higher level of importance. This mask comes in many forms and extremes. The more overt mask comes in the form of flaunting one's financial success by always having to be the richest and biggest spender of anyone in the room. They tend to feel money buys them everything including intelligence, emotional stability, and friendship. On the other end of the spectrum are the kind of people who believe until their financial ship comes in, their lives have no real merit. When people live under this illusion, they envy those who have money and either settle for less because they do not believe in their abilities, or they eventually gain financial security and simply upgrade their masks. Money is a wonderful asset to have, but when our ego rules our primary choices the outcome can be extremely destructive on personal, social, and professional levels. When working to discover the masterpiece within, we become keenly aware that no amount of money can ever buy genuine happiness and fulfillment.

6. Romance Mask

Those who wear the romantic mask deeply crave love and acceptance, but go about the pursuit in a misguided fashion. There are three different levels in which this mask can be played out. The first level mask avoids relationships at all costs; the second level mask is willing to get into a relationship, but has minimal emotional or physical contact; the third level mask is never without a relationship because they move from one physical relationship into another without ever exposing themselves emotionally. There is a deep seated fear of genuine intimacy at all three mask levels. They believe by staying closed off from others they reduce their chances of being rejected. Since we are relational beings, we must seek out an emotional connection in some way. Those who wear romance masks often find their emotional connection through characters in romance novels, television shows, films or through the lives of celebrities, co-workers, friends, or family members. This method of thinking creates an artificial emotional involvement without having to expose a true inner self and the possible risk of rejection. Until this mask is replaced with a healthier self-image, true intimacy and soul satisfying relationships will be next to impossible to attain.

7. Vanity Mask

The overemphasis on physical and outward appearances can become a major hindrance for those who desire inner wholeness. Those who wear a vanity mask focus all their attention on how they present themselves to themselves and to others. They believe all their personal value is based upon one or more of the following: the kind of vehicle they drive, how trendy or expensive their clothing is, who they socialize with, where they are seen, or in what style of home they live. These people are willing to go into great debt or allow their close relationships to suffer, if necessary, in order to maintain a facade of "having it all." Because this mask is based on the material or temporal, genuine life meaning and emotional fulfillment tends to be elusive. When working the necessary steps to unearth our masterpiece within we begin to understand the value of life balance. The emphasis on outward appearances begins to dissipate freeing us to pursue overall personal growth.

8. Loner Mask

Through her travels and ministry, Mother Teresa of Calcutta came to the conclusion that loneliness is the most rampant disease among the human race. The people who wear the loner mask can easily be the most overlooked and forgotten. They do enjoy the benefits of being alone on occasion while resting, recharging, and relaxing, but on a deeper level they long for a close personal companion. These people may appear to be completely content on their own, but in reality they are masking their pain. There are many reasons why someone would choose to wear the loner mask. In some cases, it may be extreme shyness or insecurity in developing new or close relationships. For others, disappointments and deep wounds from prior relationships have made them leery of ever trusting anyone with their hearts. Sociologists have discovered people are choosing to marry at a later age in life. This trend continues to escalate every year. Heavy work schedules leave us with barely enough personal time let alone significant time for socializing. Unless the ideal partner comes along in the workplace, the chance of developing a romantic relationship can be extremely slim. In order to remove the loner mask a person must be open to create new avenues for meeting people and must learn to take baby steps toward developing strong social and personal connections.

9. Lazy Mask

There are many facets regarding laziness that can deem these individuals as virtually lifeless. A distain of hard work, lack of direction or goals, low personal standards, lack of motivation, and lack of energy. People wearing these masks tend to wait for opportunities to fall in their laps rather than searching for or creating something of value. Even when golden opportunities come their way, they tend to let them pass by. Nothing seems to inspire them and settling for second or third best will do just fine. Those who wear this mask may work hard to keep up the front that as long as they are fed, clothed, have a roof over their heads, a smart phone or television, and a few friends with whom to hang out occasionally, their lives are pretty good. Indeed it may appear to be "the good life" but these people are rarely if ever genuinely fulfilled. What they are masking is a deep seeded fear of success, fear of responsibility or fear of failure. Because success means hard work, responsibility means less "fun" time, and failure means the possibility of even lower self-worth. The only way to get out of this self-destructive rut is to accept life challenges and to come to the understanding that personal growth does not come with a magic wand, but through genuine hard work and discipline.

10. Status Quo Mask

Michelangelo prayed, "Lord grant that I may always desire more than I can accomplish." For the masterpiece within to be revealed we must strive for growth. The status quo mask resists change or growth of almost any type because these people have found a presumed comfort level which grants them a satisfying amount of influence, power, and status. When change approaches on the horizon, their dark sides begin to appear. They become very angry, controlling, and manipulative because their source of ego stroking is threatened. To remain in this mask is to stifle any internal growth because of the refusal to be stretched beyond current comfort zones. When the status quo mask is removed the desire for personal growth increases, new doors begin to open and change is always a welcomed opportunity.

Wearing fear masks gives us a temporary pseudo-sense of self-worth and pride, which misleads us into thinking we are making personal progress. Unless we are willing to remove these masks and risk exposing our inner selves, we will never be able to truly acknowledge or reveal our natural inner beauty. Michelangelo, in his depiction of the *David*, intentionally sculpted the statue in the nude. His reasoning behind the decision was to reinforce the biblical story of the battle between David and Goliath. The shepherd, David, had gained a reputation for courageously facing lions and bears armed with only a slingshot and a stone. He was approached to go into battle with the giant Goliath, whom no one was previously able to defeat. The king dressed David in his finest armor to prepare him for battle, but wearing this cumbersome armor made David fearful despite his protected appearance. As he faced Goliath, he stripped away the unfamiliar armor, and to everyone's amazement, he regained his courage. David was able to defeat Goliath using his handmade slingshot and a single stone. From an outside prospective, it would seem that any form of armor would create a sense of courage, but in reality this "masked" courage is temporary at best. Continually risking steps of courage will progressively guide us toward mastering our fears and allow us a clearer path to becoming a living work of art.

Masterpiece Tool #4: UNDERSTANDING THE LIFELONG PROCESS

How often do we hear about an overnight success taking some twenty years or more to occur? Anything of value in life takes time, patience, practice, sacrifice, hard work, and commitment. We may imagine that once we get to a certain level of success the hard work is over. However, we quickly find there is always a new mountain to climb. The road to discovering the masterpiece within is rarely a clearly paved path. We will inevitably come across unexpected roadblocks, detours, and obstacles, which seem to throw us off the path for periods of time. Instead of getting discouraged we can turn roadblocks into opportunities, detours into exciting adventures and see obstacles as a challenge to remain committed to the process. As long as we find our way back onto the path, these presumed stumbling blocks can serve as a huge learning and growing experience.

It was the winter of 1998 and I (Claudia) was in my hotel room in Lake Tahoe only two hours away from performing in front of a few thousand people. These audience members worked at radio stations all across the country and had been flown in by my record company to watch me perform. They carried with them the power to make or break my career as a newly signed country music recording artist. From my earliest memories music has always been my first love and all my hard work and determination was finally paying off. I was signed with Warner/ Reprise records, the label created for Frank Sinatra and it was the most exciting time of my life. My dreams were finally coming true! Why then was I paralyzed with fear? I had performed countless times previous to this night. Like most performers I have come to understand how the fear of failure is hard to release but this fear was like none I had ever felt before. Why after all these years and of all times did fear of this magnitude have to appear during one of the happiest moments of my life?

I turned on the television trying to divert my attention and found one of the great singers of all time, Mr. Tony Bennett himself, as a guest on *Larry King Live.* I listened to the interview, hanging on to every word, trying to get some form of relief. Larry asked Tony, "After all these years do you ever get nervous before a performance?" Tony replied, "Yes, every time I am about to go on stage I get nervous. If I didn't that would mean it wasn't important to me. The day I don't get nervous is the day I know I need to quit." Well, that did it! I knew how much this night meant to me and decided to use my fear as motivation to give the best performance of my life. After so many years of hard work, highs, lows, sadness, and joy, tonight was my opportunity to shine and I had found the inspiration I needed to make the most of the it. The audience responded very favorably. My first single was released and began climbing the charts. Many times since that night I've been able to share Tony Bennett's words of encouragement with other performers and like magic his wisdom works everytime.

We have the power within us to change the direction of our paths at any time. Taking control of our life circumstances and not allowing "wing clippers," as our friend and director, Trey Fanjoy, calls them to rob us of our hopes, dreams, and our self-worth is a good starting point. Wing clippers are jealous and insecure people who are driven to damage or destroy our inner beauty and the motivational wings which carry us toward discovering our masterpiece within. Consistently utilizing the masterpiece tools gives us the confidence and strength to remain firm in our vision even when fear strikes or when wing clippers come our way.

One of the most motivational experiences we can have in life is to spend time talking with or studying older individuals who have continued to live up to their potential. Because they diligently work to develop their masterpiece within, they have found peace, self-love, generosity, joy, and wisdom. On the other hand, one of the most disheartening and disturbing experiences we can have is to spend time with someone facing their twilight years who has done little to find their masterpiece within. This person in many instances lives in constant regret, despair, cynicism, anger, and sadness. Living an unexamined life may first appear to be the easier road to take, but in the long run we will always find this road to be the harder and more painful chosen path.

Every moment life provides us, we have the choice to grow stronger or weaker. Choosing to stand and face life's adversities is similar to a forest withstanding the tiresome wind, rain, and cool evenings preceding the fall season. Without the right climate conditions, autumn's colorful leaves, which paint one of nature's most beautiful masterpieces, would not occur. Our lives can also become vibrant masterpieces due to the strength we gain from the rainy seasons of life. It's not the absence of obstacles we need to strive for, but instead the perseverance and skills to overcome them. Every person born on this planet, who chooses to develop the masterpiece within, has the potential to create a life just as vibrant as a tree full of colorful fall leaves and just as breathtaking and inspirational as Michelangelo's statue of the *David*.

> *If one advances confidently in the direction of his dreams,*
> *and endeavors to live the life which he has imagined, he will*
> *meet with success unexpected in common hours.*

Henry David Thoreau

CHAPTER 3

WORKBOOK CHALLENGES I

Throughout *The Masterpiece Within* we include nine chapters titled, *Workbook Challenges.* These chapters take readers on a quest to discover themselves on a deeper level. Each chapter is divided into three distinct parts; *Get to Know Me, Practical Power Tools,* and *Brain Medicine.* The purpose of these exercises is to inspire personal examination, to better comprehend the material, and to accelerate personal growth. We have made each of them easy to complete, interesting, fun, and time manageable. Simply reading through the book will give valuable life knowledge, but in order to achieve the maximum benefits from the material we highly recommend completing the workbook challenges.

Get to Know Me contains a list of questions designed to serve as a self-discovery and awareness tool which gives the reader the opportunity to gain valuable personal knowledge. The term "get to know me" originated nearly three decades ago during a Christmas gathering. My (Claudia) family began to realize, although we had always been very close, that having six of us spread among four states was starting to take its toll on how well we still knew each other. Together we created the *Get To Know Me* game, which consisted of ten questions we all had to answer about ourselves. On a small slip of paper we placed our name, the number of the question and our answer to the question. The paper was folded and placed in a bowl. After each person had answered all ten questions and placed the folded papers into the bowl, the first person would draw an answer while the person to their left tried to guess whose answer it was and to what question. If an incorrect person was guessed, the answer would be refolded and placed back in the bowl. If answered correctly, a point would be given. The person with the most points at the end of the game would get to choose a family activity for the following day. We found through playing the game, we not only developed a deeper understanding of our family members, but ourselves as well. And the game naturally generated further discussions on a variety of topics. We continue to play this game often as it has become a favorite among extended family members and friends as well.

Practical Power Tools (or PPT'S as we like to call them) contains various projects, tasks, and assignments designed to place the reader on the path to discover and develop the masterpiece within. In the book, *Life Lessons*, tennis great Martina Navratilova credits Katharine Hepburn with teaching her the life lesson she most values. She once told Martina,"It's not what you do in life, it's what you finish! But many people don't even start, because they are afraid of failure. To me the only failure is when you don't even try. So set your path, be brave, do your best and smile because you are doing all of the above." Finding the courage to initially get on the path and taking time for ourselves by utilizing these PPT's will help fuel the desire to remain on the path to becoming a living work of art.

Brain Medicine consists of positive affirmations or phrases designed to bolster our inner and outer self-talk in order to help manifest our goals and visions for our lives. Most successful people give credit to affirmations as being a major contributor to their success. Actor-comedian Jim Carrey began using positive thinking, speaking, and visualizations long before his career took off. He motivated himself by repeating phrases such as, "I am one of the top five actors. Every director wants to work with me." He also signed a check to himself which read, "For acting services rendered, $10,000,000." He credits using these practices as a major part of his continued success. In the prime of his career, Carrey was paid $25,000,000 for his work in the film, *Bruce Almighty.*

Olympic athletes and sports figures for years and years have used affirmations to encourage their performances. As Legendary golfer Jack Nicklaus says, "There is no room in my mind for negative thoughts." *Chicken Soup For The Soul* book series creator, Jack Canfield says in his book, *Key to Living the Law of Attraction*, "Like attracts like. If you are feeling excited, enthusiastic, passionate, happy, joyful, appreciative, or abundant, then you are sending out positive energy. On the other hand, if you are feeling bored, anxious, stressed out, angry, resentful or sad, you are sending out negative energy."

Affirmations can be seen as "medicine for the brain" as a means to help further facilitate our journey to discover the masterpiece within. There are many schools of thought as to the exact amount of steps to take in practicing affirmations. We have chosen to use the following four steps.

Step #1: Establish what is wanted in writing
Step #2: Recite the want aloud
Step #3: Visualize the want as a reality
Step #4: Apply the work to achieve the want

Each section contains five affirmations based on the material in the previous chapters. We then provide five blank spaces for the reader to write additional affirmations.

WORKBOOK CHALLENGES I

GET TO KNOW ME

1. Do I believe there is a masterpiece within me?
   Yes _____   No _____   Somewhat _____

2. Have I built a noble foundation for my life?
   Yes _____   No _____   Somewhat _____

3. Do I have the courage to remain on the path to discovering the masterpiece within?
   Yes _____   No _____   Somewhat _____

4. Do I accept the path to discovering the masterpiece within me is a lifelong process?
   Yes _____   No _____   Somewhat _____

5. Which of the four masterpiece tools do I need to strengthen?
   Building a noble foundation _____   Acknowledging the masterpiece within _____
   Courage to remain on the path _____   Understanding the lifelong process _____

6. Which fear mask(s) do I tend to wear?
   Humor _____   Victim _____   Intellectual _____   Procrastination _____   Financial _____
   Romance _____   Vanity _____   Loner _____   Lazy _____   Status Quo _____
   Something else, and if so, what kind of mask do I wear? _____

PRACTICAL POWER TOOLS

1. Create an autobiography box to get to know yourself on a deeper level. Look through as many pictures of yourself you can find along with letters, cards, quotes from school yearbooks, etc. Compile your own personal life story box to represent who you are as an individual. You can use a shoe box or whatever kind of box that feels right. Decorate the box if you wish to represent your own personal style. Consult family and friends asking

them what you were like when you were younger and what you dreamed of becoming when you were older.

2. Take a realistic look at yourself. Stand in front of a mirror and really study yourself as a human being. Answer this question, "Do I like who I see?" Do not focus on what you see because this exercise is not meant to be physically judgmental or designed to create a defensive response, but instead is intended to consciously reinforce our self-love and self-respect. Strip away the excess such as make-up, jewelry, fear masks, titles, and even clothes if you are brave enough. Ask yourself, "What are my insecurities, fears, and weaknesses that may be holding me back in life? What do I love about myself? Am I able to see the masterpiece within? What changes do I need to make to fully develop the masterpiece within?" Be completely honest with yourself.

3. Create a file, scrapbook, notebook or list of inspirational resources. This list can range from books, magazine or newspaper articles, films, quotes, life stories, or whatever you find inspiring. The library and Internet is a good inexpensive resource. Observe and consult friends, family, or colleagues whom you admire who have made wise choices.

4. Life Mapping. List below what you wish to accomplish in both your career and personal life. Planning well into the future is recommended. For the years you have already completed list your achievements during that particular time span.

Personal: Ages 15-19: _____
Career: Ages 15-19: _____

Personal: Ages 20-29: _____
Career: Ages 20-29: _____

Personal: Ages 30-39: _____
Career: Ages 30-39: _____

Personal: Ages 40-49: _____
Career: Ages 40-49: _____

Personal: Ages 50-59: _____

Career: Ages 50-59: _____

Personal: Ages 60-69: _____

Career: Ages 60-69: _____

Personal: Ages 70-79: _____

Career: Ages 70-79: _____

Personal: Age 80 plus: _____

Career: Ages 80 plus: _____

5. Develop a plan to discover the masterpiece within. Consider how you can prioritize your life in order to bring this plan into fruition. Set time line goals or keep an accountability log if you wish to chart your progress. Create a vision of the process and the final results, imagining what your life will look like as you work on the masterpiece within.

BRAIN MEDICINE

PERSONAL BRAIN MEDICINE

1. I acknowledge the masterpiece within me
2. I have the courage to discover the masterpiece within
3. I release my fear masks
4. I honor, respect, and love myself
5. I am a living work of art

1. _____
2. _____
3. _____
4. _____
5. _____

No human masterpiece has ever been created without great labor.

Andre Gide, French author, Nobel Prize in Literature, 1947

LIFE SKILL #1

CHOOSING WISELY

The soul is dyed the color of its thoughts. Think only on those things that are in line with your principles and can bear the full light of day. The content of your character is your choice. Day by day, what you choose, what you think, and what you do is who you become. Your integrity is your destiny...it is the light that guides your way.

Heraclitus, Greek Poet and Philosopher

CHAPTER 4

THE GIFT OF CHOICE

*We cannot lead a choiceless life. Every day, every moment, every second,
there is a choice. If it were not so, we would not be individuals.*

Ernest Holmes

Decision making on a daily basis is a task that has the potential to branch off into an infinite number of paths, leading our lives as well as influencing the lives of others in various directions. If we were given the ability to measure the numerous choices we make in a day, a month, a year, or even a lifetime we would be astounded. When we recognize we are all given the gift of choice we begin to build a foundation for taking control of our lives. Our hope is reignited, our options become limitless, and our dreams become attainable. Our self-confidence begins to grow and our purpose for living begins to feel more energized and alive. A growing sense of inner peace begins to manifest deep within because we always have the comfort of knowing a light exists at the end of any dark tunnel.

A man whom many would consider to be a person who lived without the gift of choice is Dr. Viktor Frankl, the acclaimed Austrian psychologist and author. During WWII, Frankl was imprisoned for three years in the concentration camps of Auschwitz and Dachau. He endured some of the most horrifying situations ever imaginable. He could have easily settled into a victim mentality, but instead made the conscious choice to live above his abhorrent living conditions. When the war ended and Frankl was released from Auschwitz, he documented his observations of human suffering and evil. He found all concentration camp survivors came out scarred internally for life, but he surprisingly discovered many holocaust survivors came away from their experiences stronger and more resilient. The key factor for those who were able to keep a sliver of hope alive was their belief in the gift of choice. The prison camps taught Frankl that no one, regardless of how cruel they may be, can take away without our permission our ability to choose where we allow our minds to take us. Political regimes may try to destroy our personal freedoms, but they can never steal away our values, beliefs, or convictions unless we choose to surrender them. Frankl stated:

"Everything can be taken from a man but one thing; the last of human freedoms- to choose one's attitude in any given set of circumstances, to choose one's own way. And there were always choices to make. Everyday, every hour offered the opportunity to make a decision, a decision which determined whether you would or would not submit to those powers which threatened to rob you of your very self and your inner freedom."

We must first respect the gift of choice to experience the freedom the gift can provide. The ability to choose represents the freedom to truly express who we are as individuals. No two people are alike. We are all capable of unique contributions to this world. As we continue to take responsibility for our choices, our self-imposed restrictions are lifted, our creativity is enhanced, and our attitude shifts to a more positive life approach. We develop a more realistic sense of self, which can help us manage more effectively the inner monologue of doubt and fear with which we are all prone to wrestle. Our strengths and our talents become more apparent to us and we are better able to address self-imposed weaknesses, insecurities, faults, and limitations.

We could be apathetic or reject taking responsibility for our choices, but that in turn would limit our potential and take away our freedom to direct our own paths. The consequences of not using our gifts or living under the assumption we have zero choices will eventually bring us to a place of hopelessness, discouragement, shame, resentment, loss of self-respect, numbness, and cynicism. We may not be able to completely eliminate insecurities and fears from our lives, but we can become better equipped to minimize their potential damage when we choose to embrace the gift of choice. Taking control of our choices allows us the opportunity, even in the greatest of adversities, to stay empowered rather than feeling beaten down and defeated. We become warriors! Our endorphins are triggered and we develop a sense of joy, self-love, and self-respect.

William Shakespeare is quoted as saying, "The choices we make dictate the lives we lead." We must step back every now and then to consider the quality of our choices and the path which our choices are taking us. It is also important to be brave enough with ourselves to take a good honest overall look at how our choices have affected and are affecting our lives. Self-evaluation can be a powerful tool that helps ignite our hopes and possibilities for our future, and very often opens the door to a deeper level of personal growth. Asking ourselves a few simple questions will help us gain new and valuable personal knowledge, and inspire us to grow even further. Do I feel I have the gift of choice? Am I proud of most of the choices I have made in my life thus far? Do I feel stuck and out of control of my own destiny? Am I living in a vicious cycle and unable to get out of the whirlwind of stress? Is it easier for me to live as a victim than to deal with issues that need to be addressed? The gift of choice is the most essential tool we possess in taking control of our lives. Without engaging the power to choose we may never know the possibilities or life breakthroughs awaiting us right around the corner.

CHOOSING TO BE A WARRIOR

Life naturally throws obstacles along our paths. Sometimes we are able to face them and come out victorious, but other times we come out wounded, shamed, exhausted, hurt, or rejected. These obstacles can come in the form of environmental restrictions, life circumstances, relationship setbacks, unfulfilled personal expectations or personal choices that do not pan out. When multiple stressful events begin to compound on top of each other, being dragged down into the mind-set of a victim becomes the easier choice. Once we get caught up in this belief, choosing to stay in a destructive downward spiral may seem easier than pulling ourselves up and out of it. In the most extreme cases, we begin to exhibit traits similar to post-traumatic stress disorder, because we may be experiencing emotional numbness, denial, lack of sleep, flashbacks of hurtful experiences, or a dread of living. Research has shown an actual physical and chemical change commonly occurs in the brain during periods of extreme stress. If we remain in this state of unmanaged stress, our bodies begin to wear down mentally, physically, spiritually, and emotionally. When kept unchecked, living in this state will destroy our hopes of following our dreams and living at our full potential.

Since we are relational beings, one of the most common obstacles we tend to face are people who negatively affect our lives. We must learn to set healthy boundaries with these people. Confronting the situation may be easier said than done. These individuals can catch us off guard and come across as a bit shocking, especially when incidents take place in social situations. Responding in a mature manner can seem virtually impossible. So often genius responses come flooding in during the moments following the negative confrontation. If there is an emotional connection or a history with the relationship, keeping healthy boundaries in place can prove to be an even more difficult task.

Workplace bullying, according to Psychologist Michael Harrison, PhD costs companies one hundred and eighty billion per year in lost time and productivity. The first step out of the victim role is taking responsibility for ourselves and not responding defensively, regardless of how deep the wound. When we hold ourselves accountable to setting strong boundaries, we are better able to stay in our power even at our most vulnerable moments.

I (Claudia), have always been naturally shy and tended to shut down in confrontational situations. I endured years of frustration and heartache before I was able to discover two highly effective boundary setting techniques. Dr. Maya Angelou, best selling author and Renaissance woman, taught to simply state the word "stop" when someone attempts to cross our personal boundaries. Repeating the word "stop" until they back away. When I first used the "stop" technique, I was amazed at how one word could safely and effectively defuse an uncomfortable situation. The person I encountered backed away without becoming defensive because I did not engage an argument. I simply put a stop to their destructive words. Another technique I found to be extremely effective, is to not engage the person in any form when they are coming at me in a harmful manner. I remind myself to visualize the violator as a train coming down a railroad track at full speed ahead. When this happens, we are faced with two options in dealing with this kind of destructive person. We can either go out on the tracks and wait for them to hit us head on and drag us down the tracks with them, or we can put a boundary between the two of us, refusing to engage the person at all and just sit patiently on the sidelines until they pass. Creating a mental image of flashing caution lights and a crossbar coming down as a protection whenever these type of individuals come around, can serve as a reminder to set strong healthy boundaries.

Never make someone a priority when all you are to them is an option.

Dr. Maya Angelou

Embracing the reality that we have a choice to live as either a victim, or a warrior gives us the power to control our own destiny. Only we can make the decision of which direction to take for our lives. If we choose to remain in a victim role, we lose sight of all the possibilities and options at our disposal because we operate in panic mode under the assumption that we have no choices whatsoever. Also as a victim, we put up a defensive wall refusing to take responsibility for our own lives, attitudes, and happiness. As a warrior, we understand the value of the gift of choice and seek to continually take responsibility for our lives regardless of obstacles, adversities, or outside circumstances. Warriors may or may not know the length of the journey, but they prepare themselves for whatever it takes to remain in their power and on the path to discovering the masterpiece within. The following list shows contrasting traits between a warrior and a victim.

WARRIOR TRAITS	VICTIM TRAITS
Takes responsibility	Blame shifts
Willing to learn	Closed to new knowledge
Sees life as an adventure	Sees life as a struggle
Positive outlook	Negative outlook
Participant in life	Spectator of others' lives
Based in love	Based in fear
Sets healthy boundaries	Sets few boundaries if any at all
Forgives	Hold grudges
Clear vision for the future	No hope for the future
Embraces the gift of choice	Denies the gift of choice
Faces obstacles head on	Refuses to face obstacles
Takes control of their lives	Allows others to control their lives

Through living the human experience, we all struggle at times trying to prevail as warriors instead of victims. In order to mature mentally, emotionally, and spiritually it is imperative we learn to nurture a warrior lifestyle. We must guard against fooling ourselves into thinking that continuing or reverting back into a victim state of mind is safe and comfortable. The reality is the longer we remain a victim, becoming a living masterpiece is harder and harder to achieve. When we allow the warrior spirit to flourish, our lives become empowered with hope, strength, and courage, and our integrity remains intact.

Throughout history those who are considered warriors have gained respect and inspired not only their allies but in many cases their enemies as well. Their names become those of legend because they are seen as heroic, magical, and inspirational leaders. Studying the lives of these warriors, whether from modern day or from historic tales, can provide the motivation to overcome adversity in our own lives. We are then able to view our own heartbreaking obstacles as opportunities, and defeating life setbacks or tragedies as a chance for personal growth. When we choose a warrior mindset, we choose to accept nothing but the best for our lives and in turn, we inspire and impact the lives around us in a positive manner.

Alcoholics Anonymous, or "AA," is one of the most well known organizations in the world, but many people do not know the story behind the program and how it began. William "Bill" Griffith Wilson was born on November 26th, 1895, in East Dorset, Vermont. The son of a hard-drinking father, Bill continued in his father's footsteps with his own addictive behavior by taking his first drink at the age of twenty-two, while serving as a soldier in World War 1. After the war, Bill began drinking during the day to celebrate his Wall Street victories as a successful businessman. He was also a man who suffered many depressions and would drink well into the night to alleviate his pain, which included the heartache of devastating financial losses in the stock market crash of 1929. Although he did regain his financial footing for a short period of time, he quickly deteriorated and went from a leader to an unemployable drunk over the ensuing five years. Beginning in 1933, Bill would be hospitalized for alcoholism on four separate occasions. His drinking escalated to the stage where alcohol became Bill's substitute for food. He was literally wasting away in body, mind, and spirit. But in November of 1934, inspired by a friend who had stopped drinking, Bill made the pivotal choice never to drink alcohol again.

Five months later, due to a business deal gone bad, he was tempted yet again to drown his sorrows in a bottle of gin. Upon entering a hotel bar, he noticed a man who was already intoxicated. The thought occurred to him that if he made the choice to help this man, just as his friend had five months earlier instead of drinking, he would in effect be saving himself. The magnitude of this choice is still being felt today. Bill, along with Dr. Robert "Bob" Smith, started the first Alcoholics Anonymous meeting in 1935, which lead to the formation of the 12 Step Program. The first printing of the best selling book, *Alcoholics Anonymous,* took place in 1939.

Bill's wife, Lois, who endured heartache after heartache due to her husband's alcoholism, would go on to create Al-Anon to help families of alcoholics. The 12 Step process also gave birth to other successful programs for eating disorders, gambling, sex addiction, and narcotic abuse. The Alcoholics Anonymous Program has positively affected millions around the world for over seventy-five years and will continue for many years to come. In a special collectors edition of *Time* magazine, Bill Wilson was named as one of the, "Top 100 Heroes and Icons of the 20th Century." In the article renowned English writer, Aldous Huxley, is quoted as saying, "Bill Wilson is the greatest social architect of our century."

Because Bill faced his obstacles and engaged his gift of choice, his life was greatly altered. He was able to live an enriched life of joy and hope rather than one of constant despair. By altering the direction of his destructive choices he was able to change the life course of millions of total strangers. The domino effect of Bill's choices has affected not only the lives of millions of addicts, but the lives of their family members, their friends, their friend's friends, and so on.

Claudia and I (Guy) have personally witnessed the profound effects of the AA program with friends and family members, as well as in my profession for nearly three decades as a counselor and as a minister. While attending the University of Regina in Saskatchewan, Canada, my social work practicum focus was in the area of addictions. The first phase of my training was not only to observe, but to participate as well, in a four week AA treatment facility program. The second phase of my training, required me to work alongside an addictions counselor for the remaining eight weeks. As a counselor for over the past thirty years, the AA philosophy and principles have probably made the biggest impact in counseling clients whether or not they were dealing with addiction issues.

Respecting the gift of choice and becoming more conscious in making wise choices gives us the courage to face obstacles head on, to take responsibility for ourselves, and to continue the path to discovering the masterpiece within. When activating the gift of choice, our life possibilities come alive and small victories begin to materialize. We find we no longer feel comfortable in a victim state. Our endorphins are triggered which strengthens the desire to live as a warrior.

CHAPTER 5

THE POWER OF CHOICE

Always choose the right thing, for brief is your choice.
It is like a moment, but it is also eternity.

Anonymous

What if...*Mother Teresa* had chosen her family's wealth over a lifetime of serving humanity? What if...*Ludwig Von Beethoven's* mother had chosen to abort her son as the doctor recommended in view of her syphilis?

What if...*Anne Sullivan* had never taught *Helen Keller* how to overcome her physical disabilities?

What if...*Jesus of Nazareth* had chosen to remain a carpenter rather than spreading the message of unconditional love?

What if...*Mohandas Gandhi* had chosen to compromise his convictions by becoming a follower instead of a leader in establishing his country of India?

What if...*Michael Jordan* had given up on his sports dreams after he had been cut from his high school basketball team?

What if...*Nelson Mandela* had chosen to give into mainstream South African politics instead of fighting to end Apartheid?

What if...*Johannes Gutenberg* had not invented the printing press accelerating the explosion of knowledge around the world?

What if...*Alexander Fleming* had not discovered penicillin known to be one of the most important life saving drugs of all time?

What if...*Lech Walesa*, had remained a quiet worker in the shipyards of Gdnask, Poland instead of founding the Solidarity movement, which lead to the downfall of communism?

Historical choices contain a wealth of information and wisdom from which we can draw. When we examine the long term effects of past choices, we are able to educate ourselves on the importance of choosing wisely. From the beginning of time, man has been faced with myriad choices, and with the influx of technology and an ever increasing population, we will progressively face more and more choices throughout our lifetimes. We may ask the question, "How can our lives and choices go on to affect millions?" Every single person born on planet Earth makes an impact, just by being here. It is up to each of us to decide what that impact or statement will be.

What if...*Genghis Khan* had not chosen to barbarically slaughter the people of Asia?
What if...*Man's greed* had been kept in check? Would famine, war or disease even be an issue?
What if...*Hardcore drugs* such as *Heroin or Methamphetamines* had never been introduced into society?
What if...*Hitler* had chosen love over hate for the Jewish race?
What if...*Terrorists* had never chosen to attack the World Trade Center and the Pentagon?
What if...*Slavery* had never been allowed and every human had always been treated as an equal?
What if...*Idi Amin* had not been allowed an eight year reign of terror on Uganda?
What if...*Environmental destruction* of planet earth had never been allowed to occur?
What if... *Joseph Stalin* had not chosen to abuse his power as leader of the Soviet Union?
What if...the *Columbine High School shootings* had been prevented before they occurred?

We can never underestimate the power of one choice. A choice made from a heart of fear, greed, uncontrolled power, anger, bitterness or resentment can bring immeasurable damage to mankind. On the opposite end of the spectrum, a choice made from a heart of love can positively influence society for all eternity.

FILTERING OUR CHOICES

We, as authors, are perpetual students of human behavior, history, and social trends. In supplementing this book beyond our life experiences, educational, vocational, and counseling backgrounds, we conducted a study of over one thousand individuals from all over North America. We addressed numerous issues such as how often the respondents felt they made wise choices; if they were actively living in their bliss, life purpose or passion; if they believed they made a difference in their corner of the world; and how well they were taking care of their body, mind, spirit, and emotions. In analyzing the results, we discovered that regardless of age, ninety-five percent of those surveyed believed all areas of their lives would greatly improve if they could learn better skills for making wise choices.

Always keep in mind, making wise choices is not about making perfect choices all the time. Expecting perfection from ourselves places undo pressure and leads to many negative self-concepts. Choosing wisely is weighing our choices deliberately and intentionally before a final decision is made. Disciplining ourselves to choose consciously versus unconsciously creates a strong foundation, which increases our ability to consistently make wise choices. When we commit to a conscious lifestyle, our opportunities to live out our dreams and to discover the masterpiece within are greatly enhanced.

Examining the training techniques of Olympic athletes is a good illustration of conscious choice. When these athletes begin to train for competition, they use trial and error to determine what techniques work best to enhance their athletic performances. They incorporate these chosen techniques into their training programs and practice them in a deliberate manner until they become second nature. When it comes time for an Olympic or World Championship competition, these athletes are primed and ready to perform their events. Once having competed, they may find they need to adjust their choices for better results. We can use this lesson in our own lives. Many times we can believe we have made a wise choice, but once we commit to the path, we may find that, for whatever reason, we need to make slight adjustments. As long as we are willing to remain flexible and teachable, all is not lost. We simply need to learn from our previous choices and consciously move on with a better choice. Learning to filter our choices through a reliable system of evaluation is the key to an even deeper level of consciousness. By filtering our choices, we not only increase our ability to make wise choices, but we also learn how to approach life from a healthy loving place rather than from a place of fear. We have created five filters, which can help determine the best path to take with our choices when facing important life decisions. When incorporating these filters into our lives, we gain a greater sense of peace and power in our decision making, because we are choosing consciously rather than unconsciously.

CHOICE FILTERS

Choice Filter #1: A NOBLE VALUE SYSTEM

Our value systems begin to develop in early childhood. As we grow and mature into adults, we establish our own set of values. A strong or noble value system is founded on a high standard of personal integrity and is based in love. The greatest sages, humanitarians, and philosophers throughout history such as Einstein, Schweitzer, Mother Teresa, Jung, Frankl, Gandhi, and Mandela all believed love to be the most noble virtue in the universe. Elizabeth Kubler-Ross, who made a name for herself with her lifelong research on near death experiences, found that almost everyone she interviewed came back from these experiences with a sense of peace and a common message: "It's all about love. We are to love ourselves and others unconditionally with the purity and innocence of a child free of restrictions, judgment, and fear." We all have the natural desire for love and acceptance, but how we go about pursuing love will determine the depth and wisdom of our choices. A weak or ignoble value system is based in fear and is driven by low standards of living, low expectations of personal potential, and misguided priorities. When we live by an ignoble value system, we are willing to accept less than we deserve and low self-esteem is very often the end result. Filtering our choices will reveal whether the choice is motivated by a noble value system or an ignoble value system.

Marilyn Monroe is considered to be one of the world's most loved and admired celebrities of all time. As a young girl of nine years old, she was placed in an orphanage after her mother was committed to a mental institute. At the age of eleven, she began to be shuffled from foster home to foster home. Marilyn constantly struggled with the desire for love and approval. As a child, her foster families would often send her to the movies to get her out of the house. She would spend the entire day and evening alone, but instead of being frightened, she found she loved it. Marilyn began to believe if she became famous and if she could create a family of her own, she would finally find the love she so severely lacked.

Marilyn, at the age of eighteen, took a job on the assembly line at the Radio Munitions factory in Burbank, California. A photographer, David Conover, came to the factory to take photos of women contributing to the war effort. He found Marilyn to be a photographer's dream. Her photos appeared in *Yank* magazine, which lead to numerous modeling jobs as well as an eventual studio contract with Twentieth Century Fox. She swiftly became one of America's popular pin-up girls and one of Hollywood's most sought after actresses. Despite the worldwide fame she achieved over the subsequent two decades, Marilyn experienced endless heartache over three failed marriages and numerous miscarriages. The path that she believed would take her to a lifetime of peace and joy was actually leading her to a life of extreme loneliness.

In July 1962, Marilyn granted *Life* magazine writer, Richard Meryman, a very candid interview. The article came out in the August 3, 1962 issue. A week later, Marilyn was dead at the age of thirty-six. In the article she stated: "*Fame to me certainly is only a temporary and a partial happiness. Fame is not really for a daily diet, that's not what fulfills you. It warms you a bit, but the warming is temporary. It's like caviar, you know--it's good to have caviar, but not when you have to have it every meal and every day.*"

Marilyn believed she had set up a path that would lead to happiness for herself, but in actuality her belief system led to a life filled with disappointment, frustration, and loneliness. Gaining career success and fame certainly gave her financial freedom and sporadic moments of joy, but genuine fulfillment and meaning in life always seemed to escape her. Marilyn's choices were filtered through a fear based value system. One of the primary motives she was driven by was finding fame, because she believed fame would grant her unconditional love. Making choices from a place of fear may have positive initial results, but the long term effects are not always positive or soul satisfying.

Marilyn's reflections in the *Life* magazine article were very profound in that she seemed to finally understand the deeper meaning of life. She had recently reunited with her ex-husband, Joe DiMaggio, after discovering they had both been alone the previous Christmas. Following this discovery, they agreed to always reach out for each other so neither one of them would feel isolated and alone ever again. It is hard to fathom that two of America's most loved and respected celebrities of all time would have spent a major holiday totally alone. Once known as America's sweethearts, Joe and Marilyn were rumored to be planning an August 8, 1962 wedding ceremony. Her untimely passing may have robbed her of the joy she was about to finally attain. Deeply saddened by Marilyn's death, Joe had roses delivered to her grave three times a week for twenty years.

Pursuing a life of love and true happiness without developing a noble value system will eventually lead to a brick wall of loneliness and a lack of inner fulfillment. An ignoble value system confuses the means with the end by using money, power, fame, status, pleasure, or knowledge as a catalyst to find unconditional love. When incorporating the desire for these elements into a healthy balanced life based on a noble value system, they are not necessarily negative in content, but they can serve as allies to achieve our desired goals. We have identified six philosophies that can lead to a brick wall or dead end road.

Six Brick Wall Philosophies

A. Economics: Financial security is a common sense goal, but to base our entire life's happiness upon monetary gain leaves us frustrated and empty.

B. Narcissism: This is a "pleasure first" way of living without regard to how the outcome will affect others. Healthy self-love is natural and necessary to unearth the masterpiece within, but complete selfishness leads to a dead end road.

C. Religion: Religion has the potential to degenerate into an empty, rules oriented faith system that puts cultural traditions and non-essential issues ahead of loving relationships and serving one's fellow man. Strictly adhering to religion as a rules based philosophy without regard for one's neighbor will lead to self-righteousness, intolerance, and hypocrisy.

D. Quick Fix: Almost everyone would love to win the lottery or skip a few necessary steps vocationally speaking, yet we all know life's greatest lessons are learned through hard work and persevering through adversities.

E. Science: New and exciting advances in technology can serve as a form of mental stimulation, but focusing on tangible scientific theories alone for answers to our deepest needs without inner soul development creates a very dark universal picture.

F. Status or Titles: Attaining positions of power or status can be viewed as validation of a job well done, but if the primary focus is on self-oriented perks and praise versus overall human development, we are left feeling isolated and hollow when we are away from the adoration of the crowd.

Many times following one of these brick wall philosophies is not even a conscious self-realization. It is important to take the time to thoroughly examine whether we live by a noble or ignoble value system. When we practice an ignoble value system, money equals a false sense of security, pleasure equals harm to self or others, religion equals self-righteousness, knowledge equals arrogance, and status equals a fleeting moment leading to loneliness. When practicing a noble value system, these six philosophies are not harmful in themselves because the acquisition of money leads to generosity; pleasure leads to joy and creativity; spirituality brings peace, hope, and a service perspective; a quick fix brings gratefulness and the inspiration to give in return; science leads to new discoveries, open mindedness, and hope for the future; and status opens doors to positively contribute to society.

Choice Filter #2: OUR INNER VOICE

Our inner voice is our internal guidance system, which can be referred to as intuition, instinct, impression, gut feeling, our connection to God, or our conscience. We are never alone when faced with filtering our choices because we have a constant companion, a respected teacher, and a wise sage to chaperone us throughout life. An inner voice is granted to all of us at birth, but similar to any healthy relationship we must nurture and develop it throughout our lifetime in order to receive the full benefits. We can choose to embrace this gift or allow various self-imposed distractions to drown it out. When we listen to our inner voice, we tap into a deep well of wisdom keeping us from harm's way. Choosing not to listen to this internal guidance system sets us up for a life of unnecessary struggle and frustration. Our inner voice is one of wisdom and love waiting to be of service to us throughout our lives.

Three months into my college years, I (Claudia) began to take notice of my inner voice. My sister, Teresa, who attended college in Utah, had planned to fly to Dallas to drive with me and a college friend to Ohio for our Christmas break. About three weeks before our drive, I began getting a strong impression we should be very careful about driving the eleven hundred-mile trip. As the days passed, it was as if I could hear a voice inside saying, "Be very careful; there is going to be an accident." The voice became relentless. Day after day this voice not only stayed, but it seemed to grow even louder. I shared my fears with my family, but I was not comfortable enough yet with my new friend to tell her I feared we would have an accident in her car.

When Teresa arrived, she lovingly reassured me everything would be alright and kindly agreed to stay awake with me the entire journey. The next morning, before we got into my friend's car, my sister and I said a long prayer to keep us safe. Because the message was not saying, "Don't get in the car" only to be careful, I decided to stick to our travel plans. As we drove out of Dallas, my college friend announced that we were picking up a guy she had met a few weeks earlier who would be coming along on the trip to share expenses. Immediately after he got into the car and started driving, I realized by his behavior he had to have taken some form of downer drug, so I insisted he pull over immediately and not be allowed to drive at all. I grew really upset with my friend that she had not told us about her plans to pick up a virtual stranger. Teresa wondered if he was the cause of my accident fears, and as long as we did not let him drive we would be okay. No such luck. The voice was still blazing like a bugle exclaiming, "Be careful there is going to be an accident." I also decided to reveal my fears to my friend and told her because of them I thought we should be extra careful. I could tell she was not interested.

While we were stopped in Memphis for gas, our male driving partner, who kept trying to convince us he was okay to drive, finally passed out after taking what he called "aspirin." I later discovered the pills were Quaaludes. At 7:00 a.m., we pulled into my parents' driveway, and the minute I got out of the car, I ran straight to my mothers' arms and started bawling like a baby. I was exhausted and so was Teresa from her nursemaiding.

Christmas with my family proved to be very loving and restful. I felt ready to go back to college having been relieved of my inner voice's warning. Two days before we were to make the return trip, I received a phone call from my college friend saying she would not be able to make the trip back to Texas so we would have to find our own transportation. She let me know she was sorry she had not called sooner and began to explain why. About a mile away from my parents' home, my friend apparently hit a patch of black ice and lost control of her car. It rolled many times and landed in a ravine totaling the car and breaking numerous bones in her body. Her male friend had been hospitalized for two weeks as well. It was at that moment I knew, I would listen very carefully to my inner voice for the rest of my life.

Sometimes our inner voice can come in as loud and clear as a bugle, or as quietly as a whisper. Our inner voice is always there waiting to serve as our own personal "sage" as long as we are open to listening to its guidance. We can use the initials "I.V." to serve as an analogy and helpful reminder to use our inner voice. Much like a hospital uses an I.V. to help sustain a patient's vital fluids and electrolytes, our inner voice is there to serve as a lifeline to healthy decision making. Another helpful way to use the inner voice is to imagine its language as that of a traffic light. When seeking answers we can visualize the response in three ways: as a red light, "Stop, do not proceed!" or as a yellow light, "Proceed through, but use caution," or as a green light, "Proceed without reservation." When using our inner voice to help filter our choices, we create a constant spirit of hope to overcome our fears. This ally is not motivated by anger, fear, hatred, or selfishness, but solely by wisdom and love. Training ourselves to follow our inner voice, gives us an inner strength and joy to persevere through the inevitable tough times and adversities of life. The more we tune into our inner voice and consciously choose to filter our choices, the wiser our life choices will become on a regular basis.

Choice Filter #3: OUR SELF-TALK

Self-talk is a combination of our inner monologue and outer dialogue. Our inner monologue is our thought process, which continually flows through our minds. These thoughts influence what we say about ourselves to ourselves personally. Outer dialogue is what we convey about ourselves to others, whether with our voice or our body language. When using the self-talk filter for decision making, it is imperative we ask ourselves how this choice will affect our inner monologue and outer dialogue over the long run. Often we are not even aware how much our self-talk factors into our day to day living. Giving into unhealthy negative self-talk can hinder us from making wise choices and living up to our full potential. We must learn to monitor this endless dialogue as often as possible with thoughts and words that are positive, balanced, and valid. Our inner monologue can play out in positive, realistic statements such as, "I know I am more than qualified to be hired for this job." Or in negative, unrealistic statements such as, "Even if I am qualified they will never hire me for this job, because I will come across as an unprofessional loser."

When our inner monologue is constantly critical or self-abusive, we create a negative inner dialogue and self-image, which hinders us from becoming living masterpieces. We must remember the main way people form opinions of us is by what information we choose to give them. If we choose to convey a negative message to others, it is as if we are rooting them on to have a negative impression of us. If, instead, we choose to convey a positive message, it is as if we are encouraging them to feel good in our presence and to be inspired to see us again. Now which type of person would we rather be around?

The New England Patriots are a classic example of the importance of developing a positive inner monologue and a positive outer dialogue on a collective level. Prior to their 2002 Super Bowl match-up versus the St. Louis Rams, the odds-makers listed the Patriots as the longest shot in NFL history to win the championship title. Coming off an underachieving last place season, the Patriots were also mourning the loss of an assistant coach who died of a heart attack in training camp. They started the new season with a one-and-three record. They then lost their starting quarterback with a career threatening injury, which left the team with a second year quarterback, Tom Brady. He had thrown only two passes in his brief NFL career. The prognosis was bleak. The team could have thrown in the towel and casually played out the season, but thankfully the team was loaded with veteran savvy players and a wise coaching staff. These core veterans were players who believed in the concept of "team," who took responsibility for their assignments, and who kept their mistakes to a minimum.

Even though the Patriots went on an unbelievable winning streak, they continued to remain underdogs all season long, and well into the playoffs. As a result, their overall team confidence and self-talk began to grow. They believed in their overall potential in spite of the negative perceptions held by the outside world. *The Sporting News* summed up the Patriots season this way, "It was an extraordinary demonstration of the power of 'team,' because there is no way the Patriots should be this good. They just believe they are, and for them, that's been enough." The Patriots relished the challenge of playing their hearts out despite this underdog perception. They honestly believed in their system and abilities to compete with the best is spite of the fact that most NFL fans could not name two or three Patriot players prior to their championship win. The New England Patriots could have listened to their negative press clippings and integrated them into their belief system, but despite odds and opinions, they chose to keep their self-talk positive. In light of their 2002 season, it is almost hard to believe the Patriots went on to win three of the next four Super Bowls.

Becoming more cognizant of how our choices affect our inner monologue and outer dialogue is one of the most beneficial checks and balances we can use in filtering our choices. When we make wise conscious choices, our self-talk tends to be positive and self-affirming increasing our confidence, self-esteem, and chances of making wise choices well into the future. When we make unwise choices, our self-talk becomes extremely negative and critical. The chances of making wise choices greatly decreases, thus creating a difficult cycle to break. It is helpful to remember the wise proverb, "To talk without thinking is like shooting without aiming."

Choice Filter #4: OUR RELATIONSHIPS

To love and to be loved, is the greatest of all human needs and experiences. Relationships hold the key to living a fulfilling and meaningful life. When we take the time to develop a strong, healthy relationship with ourselves, we create a solid foundation of self-love and self-respect. We are then free to genuinely love others. In order to cultivate and maintain a strong relationship with ourselves and with others, it is vital to create a habit of filtering our choices through the lens of relationships. We can ask ourselves, "How will this choice affect my relationship with myself or with others? Will this choice be beneficial or harmful? Will it enhance or dampen my overall growth? Will my self-talk be positive and uplifting?" By asking these questions we create a fertile foundation for wise choices to prosper.

In reviewing the results of our *Masterpiece Within* poll, we discovered one very common thread: unwise choices were often made due to pressure from outside sources such as coercive peers, unhealthy family relationships, or stressful workplaces. Far too often we allow ourselves to feel pressured into making choices which we do not necessarily agree with. These actions may serve as a temporary solution, but in the long run these choices can leave us feeling resentment, shame, and regret. The best way to prevent these occurrences, which leave us feeling boxed into a corner, is to take the time to step away from the situation, regain our sense of personal power, filter our choices, and then return to the situation armed and ready to face the conflict from a place of integrity. By establishing these guidelines for ourselves, we alleviate negative outside influences and are better prepared to wisely respond to tense situations in the future. We begin to stand strong in our convictions and learn the importance of holding ourselves accountable for our choices, rather than blaming others for their influence.

In the highly successful film *Cast Away,* Chuck Roland, played by Tom Hanks, is a FedEx employee who is ruled by the clock. His life takes a drastic turn when he chooses to accept a last minute business trip to Australia on Christmas Eve, instead of staying with his girlfriend, Kelly, played by Helen Hunt. Eleven hours into his flight, his plane crashes into the South Pacific and he finds himself the lone survivor of the six men on board. Stranded on a deserted island, he soon finds everything he thought was important to him such as his pager, his watch, and his cell phone are worthless and waterlogged. As the first few days pass by, FedEx packages from the downed plane begin to wash ashore, but Chuck being the consummate professional does not open any of the boxes in hopes of being rescued and safely delivering them to their rightful owners. He soon begins to realize there is only a remote chance of survival and rescue unless he takes matters into his own hands.

Chuck makes the pivotal decision to open all but one package in hopes of finding materials to create a makeshift boat or anything else to help with his survival on the island. He finds various items such as a Wilson volleyball, a pair of figure skates, which he turns into an axe, the netting of a dress, which helps with his fishing, and a video tape, which he uses as rope.

Without the convenience of matches, he painstakingly attempts primitive methods to create fire for a rescue signal and for cooking his fish. In one of his futile attempts a stick snaps, deeply piercing the palm of his hand. He grabs the volleyball and throws it across the sand out of pain and frustration. Once he calms down, he realizes the blood print on the volleyball looks very similar to a human face. Chuck places his new found friend on a tree stump next to him and after continuing his effort to create a fire, jokingly asks Wilson, "You wouldn't happen to have a match would you?" And in one significant moment Chuck manages to create two of the five essential elements he had yet to achieve for survival and sanity. He adds fire and companionship to previously discovered shelter, fresh water, coconuts, and fish. This is a key moment for Chuck, because he now has all the elements needed for survival, all created from his own resources. Having his new companion, Wilson, and a photo of Kelly he is able to remain inspired to stay alive while developing a deeper understanding of himself.

Over the next four years, Wilson serves as a constant reminder of the importance of relationships. Chuck becomes even more driven to get off the island and to return to Kelly. When two sides of a port-a-potty wash ashore, he studies the material to figure out how he can best use them. He realizes he may finally have the missing pieces to create a makeshift sail for a raft to take him over the ocean's waves, and out to sea for a possible rescue. He carefully plans his journey and awaits the ideal weather conditions. When the perfect day arrives, Chuck and Wilson successfully make it past the island's strong waves, and they set sail on the open ocean hoping for a miracle. One evening, while Chuck is asleep after weathering an intense storm, Wilson gets blown off the raft. When Chuck discovers Wilson is missing, he jumps into the ocean and attempts to rescue his longtime companion. When the raft floats in the opposite direction, he faces losing his only hope of being rescued. He has no choice but to let his friend go. We, as an audience, are moved by the extreme agony Chuck goes through when he loses Wilson and he is once again completely alone. It is a critical moment in the film, and Chuck clearly shows us how relationships are the most cherished value in the human psyche. He continually cries out, "I'm sorry, I'm so sorry."

Crisis situations often prove to be the main catalysts for growth. They force us to reevaluate our choices, priorities, and the way we lead our lives when we may have been too busy to take notice in the past. Chuck's experience proved to be life changing for him because he had the time to look at how his choices were affecting his relationship with himself and with others.

Because of his growth, his future relationships will be stronger and more fulfilling. When we neglect to filter our choices through our relationships, they eventually suffer the consequences and we are left feeling alone and empty. Consistently making relationships a priority will help us make wise and loving choices in all facets of our lives.

In 2009, I (Guy) went through an emotionally heartbreaking divorce after twenty-six years of marriage. I was blindsided. Getting a divorce was not on my radar; I truly believed I would be married to the same woman my entire life. The months following the divorce were like a biblical twenty-first century Job experience for me. Then one day, while in a sporting goods store, I rounded the corner of an aisle and staring me in the face was an entire wall of Wilson volleyballs. Chuck's friendship with Wilson in the *Cast Away* film came flooding back and I knew what I had to do…buy myself a Wilson. When I got home I looked up Chuck's quotes from the film and wrote them on Wilson. "I knew, somehow I had to stay alive. Somehow I had to keep breathing. Even though there was no reason to hope. I stayed alive. I kept breathing. And I know what I have to do now. I gotta keep breathing. Because tomorrow the sun will rise. Who knows what the tide could bring?"

Keeping Wilson in eyesight proved just as monumental for me as it did for Chuck. Being reminded to not isolate, but to stay close to my inner circle of support was nothing short of miraculous. My confidence soon returned along with my hope because I had my friends, my family, and my Wilson reminding me to keep breathing and to never give up.

Choice Filter #5: LONG-TERM CONSEQUENCES

In the well-known and loved classic holiday film, *It's a Wonderful Life*, Jimmy Stewart plays, George Bailey, a man who is contemplating suicide, because he has come to believe his life is worthless; he wishes he never had been born. As he stands on a bridge before attempting to jump off, he encounters his guardian angel, Clarence, (Henry Travers) who grants him his wish, and shows him what the world would be like had he never been born. Clarence points out to George the positive long term effects his life and his choices have made on the people and the small town of Bedford Falls. Some of his monumental life moments include saving his nine-year-old brother Harry's (Todd Karns) life when he fell through the ice while sledding. Had George never been born or had he not chosen to save Harry, Harry would have died and not been able to go on and win the Congressional Medal of Honor for saving many men in the war. George also prevented Mr. Gower, (H.B. Warner) the town druggist, from mixing cyanide with a child's prescription. Had George not stopped the distraught druggist, who was disoriented after learning of his son's death, the child would have been poisoned and died. Mr. Gower would have gone on to spend twenty years in prison, and afterwards become the town drunk.

George had dreams, big dreams to travel the world and attend college, but everytime he was just about to leave a crisis occured and he chose to stay and help. Through this journey, George is finally able to see his life does matter and comes to appreciate everything and everyone in his life. He pleads with Clarence to get him back to his life so he can spend Christmas Eve with his family and face all his troubles. To his surprise, the entire town comes to George's aid. Each of them thank George for what he has done for their lives.

What a gift to be shown the positive effects of our previous life choices. If we could only be given a day with our own personal guardian angel to see how each possible choice will pan out for us. Now that would be something!

Author, and twentieth century theologian, Harry Emerson Fosdick, said, "He who chooses the beginning of a road, chooses the place it leads to." When we consciously filter our choices, we must take the time to imagine or map out the road our choice will lead us down. If we work to train ourselves to instinctively make this an everyday practice, we will be better equipped to take control of our lives traveling on the road of our choosing. Without this form of conscious thought, we may eventually find ourselves in a place of despair and regret once the consequences of our choices have played out.

Sports Illustrated ran an article titled, *It's a Wonderful Life Story* in their April 3, 2006 issue. In the article, writer Steve Rushin tells the moving story of how Lance Randall, an assistant basketball coach at St. Louis University, quit his lucrative position to take over his father's Oshkosh West High School basketball team following his unexpected passing. Lance's fifty-three year old father, Steve, died on the operating table from what was supposed to be a routine angioplasty. The doctors had accidentally nicked one of his arteries.

In Steve's sixteen seasons at the small high school, he had developed an incredible reputation as a teacher and coach who cared deeply for his students. The local paper received hundreds of letters and well over three thousand people, including current and former players, came to pay tribute to the man who had impacted their lives so greatly. Observing this outpouring of love and the impact his father had on so many people, Lance knew what he had to do. Rather than leaving the Oshkosh basketball team without a coach midseason, Lance resigned his high profile and well paid position at St. Louis University to take over as head coach for his father's high school team. His decision turned out to be the Wisconsin feel-good sports story of 2006, as Lance took the high school team to their first ever State title. Oshkosh West became one of the smallest schools in state history to win the championship. Both Rushin and Lance said that Steve's life reminded them of George Bailey in, *It's a Wonderful Life.* Lance said to Rushin, "You're the first person outside the family to mention that movie. It's my favorite. My parents gave it to me when I was little. I cry just taking it out of the box. You're exactly right: my dad was the richest man in town."

Implementing the five choice filters into our lives teaches us to become conscious and intentional in our decision making process, setting in motion positive results in all areas of our lives. After seeing these results, we are then able to comprehend more clearly the long term implications of negative life choices and our desire to choose wisely greatly increases. We can do our best to strive for perfection by using the five filters: a noble value system, our inner voice, our self-talk, our relationships, and the weighing of the long term consequences. We do need to acknowledge there can be circumstances beyond our control. When we consider natural disasters, strange occurrences, fate, destiny, disease, and the fact we share the planet with over seven billion other choosing souls, we can see how so many factors influence how our lives play out. Since we cannot live in a plastic bubble protected from all adversity and harm, we must take outside factors into consideration.

In May of 2001, Marvin and Sharon McMordie were returning from a weekend conference in Edmonton to their home in Grande Cache, Alberta, Canada. They had traveled the same 250 mile stretch of road without incident for the past thirty years. Marvin was driving when they came across one of the few blind spots along the mountainous section of the highway. Two women in an oncoming car just happened to witness the strange occurrence. They reported seeing a moose running up a steep hill and then jumping over a guard railing to cross the highway at the exact same moment the McMordie's car drove past. The four thousand-pound moose landed on the roof of Marvin and Sharon's car, killing Marvin instantly. Investigators said the chances of someone driving by a remote blind spot and a moose jumping over the railing at the same time, had to be a one in a billion possibility. They also reported, had the moose landed on the hood of their car, or even the side of their car, the chances of survival would have been so much higher. Questions flourished! What if they had been traveling five miles per hour faster or slower? What if Marvin and Sharon had had a second cup of coffee at their last stop or not stopped at all? What is the likelihood a four thousand-pound moose would land on a car going seventy miles per hour? And miraculously, Sharon who was sitting in the passenger seat of the car, made the choice to lean down and pick up her sunglasses at the exact moment the moose landed on the roof of their car. She walked away physically unharmed.

We can question life occurrences similar to this story, but really there are no definite answers other than some circumstances are just out of our control. This does not imply we should simply accept life in some fatalistic fashion, because these outside factors are still the exception rather than the rule. If any of these tragic events do occur for us, apart from death itself, we still have the freedom to choose how we go about handling them. As long as we are able to find a way to get back on the path of discovering the masterpiece within, these experiences can make us stronger and wiser.

Having the five choice filters available to us can be a tremendous supplement in learning to become living works of art. When using these filters, we begin to see the progression of how one affects the other. If we have a noble value system in place, we are most likely listening to our inner voice. When we listen to our inner voice, our self-talk becomes much more positive. When our self-talk is positive, we develop a stronger self-image. When we have a strong self-image, we are able to maintain healthy relationships. When our relationships are healthy, our overall life perspective will be much clearer and our desire to make wiser choices increases in order to live a long healthy life. But, if we have an ignoble value system in place, the progression will naturally play out in a negative manner. We most likely are not listening to our inner voice, our self-talk is most likely negative and our relationships are most likely suffering. This downward spiral causes us to lose interest in making wise choices, because we have begun to feel our lives no longer matter. Adopting the five choice filters into our lifestyle will not guarantee perfect choices every time, but using these filters will increase our ability to make wiser choices, because they are rooted in a strong foundation of integrity and love.

Far too often choices are made abruptly without much thought put into them, leaving us with choices we regret in the long run. Making choices out of fear, resentment, impatience or insecurity will make wise, loving choices extremely difficult to achieve. The more we strive to make wise conscious choices, the wiser our unconscious choices will naturally become. An illustration for choosing wisely comes from a question comedian Jerry Seinfeld posed as part of his stand-up routine. Seinfeld asked, "When did everyone get so thirsty?" He was referring to the influx of bottled water available everywhere and how we are willing to pay top dollar for filtered water. Unfortunately, recycling these empty plastic bottles has not been a priority as a high percentage have made their way into our landfills. Being introduced to the convenience of filtered bottled water allowed us to acquire a taste for it. The demand for water filters at home and the office increased sharply as well. Once awakened to the health benefits and taste of filtered water, most of us can no longer tolerate bad tasting, chlorinated tap water. In the same sense, once we have tasted and experienced the difference between conscious choice and unconscious choice, we find we cannot imagine ourselves settling for unfiltered choices ever again. The decision to make wise choices, like the decision to drink filtered water, results in an overall healthy, meaningful, and fulfilling life experience.

CHAPTER 6

WORKBOOK CHALLENGES II

GET TO KNOW ME

1. Do I consistently make wise choices? Yes _____ No _____ Sometimes _____
   If not explain why? _____

2. Do I believe I can take responsibility for my life with the gift of choice?
   Yes _____ No _____ Somewhat _____

3. Do I tend to make more conscious or unconscious choices on a daily basis?
   Conscious _____ Unconscious _____ Somewhere in between _____

4. Do I currently live as a victim? Yes _____ No _____ Sometimes _____
   What victim traits hold me back? _____

5. Do I currently live as a warrior? Yes _____ No _____ Sometimes _____
   What warrior traits would I like to develop? _____

6. Which of the five choice filters do I need to further develop?
   Noble value system _____ Inner voice _____ Self-talk _____ Relationships _____
   Long term consequences _____

7. What brick wall philosophies do I tend to fall victim to?

    Economic _____   Narcissism _____   Religion _____   Quick Fix _____   Science _____

    Status or Titles _____

PRACTICAL POWER TOOLS

1. Make a list of your most significant accomplishments which have had long term positive effects on your life. Review the path of choices that brought you to the desired outcome. What lessons can be applied to your life today?

2. Read a biography or memoir, seek out programs, films, or documentaries based on the life of someone you admire. Record the lessons they learned in regards to their successes and failures in making life choices.

3. Take a major life choice or decision you are currently facing and work it through the five choice filters to help make the decision.

4. Create a Choice Journal. Document the choices you face and the lessons you learn from filtering your choices and making wise choices. Refer back to your Choice Journal to help with future choices and to encourage others.

5. Examine your self-talk. Is it healthy or unhealthy? Is it positive or negative? Is it helping or hindering you in making wise choices? Ask yourself if you are being too hard on yourself? Make a list of ways you can improve or sustain your self-talk.

BRAIN MEDICINE

1. I make wise, conscious choices
2. I choose to be a warrior
3. I listen carefully to my inner voice
4. I filter my choices
5. I release my brick wall philosophies

PERSONAL BRAIN MEDICINE

1. _____
2. _____
3. _____
4. _____
5. _____

It is our choices that show what we really are, far more than our abilities.

J.K. Rowling

LIFE SKILL #2

BECOMING THE HERO OF OUR OWN LIFE STORY

Everybody loves a hero. People line up for them, cheer them, scream their names. And years later, they'll tell how they stood in the rain for hours just to get a glimpse of the one who taught them how to hold on a second longer. I believe there's a hero in all of us, that keeps us honest, gives us strength, makes us noble, and finally allows us to die with pride.

Spider Man 2

CHAPTER 7

CHOOSING TO BE A HERO

Life is either a daring adventure or nothing at all.

Helen Keller

Once upon a time...

For many of us, regardless of age, this magical phrase immediately grabs our attention and sets our minds racing with visions of excitement and grandeur. For centuries, children have been entertained with fairy tales and stories of grand adventures that have been passed down through the generations. Not only are we drawn to fairy tales and stories because of their entertainment value, but also because each of our lives is a story in progress. It is only natural we begin to emulate and model our lives after these larger than life heroes, because they fuel our optimism for a bright future and teach us some of our most valuable foundational life lessons. Life can be an exciting adventure! Magical moments are possible! We have the ability to overcome obstacles and to be brave no matter how small or frail we may feel! In spite of life's adversities, if we remain patient and live a life of integrity, a positive outcome may be right around the corner! And of course there is always the possiblity of finding true love and a happy ending to our own life story!

When facing negative circumstances in our own lives, we often look to our favorite fairy tales for answers. For example we may ask ourselves, "How did *Cinderella* overcome her plight?" or "How did *The Little Engine That Could* make it through his difficult times?" The heroes in both tales, as in most heroes in stories and fairy tales, teach us no matter what obstacles we encounter, when we take responsibility for our lives and strive to make wise choices, we too can become the hero of our own life story. Fairy tales also prove we are never too young, never too old, never too small, and never too large to be considered a hero. In J.R.R. Tolkien's, *The Lord Of The Rings* trilogy, Frodo Baggins, a 3'6" Hobbit, is given the responsibility of safely transporting a powerful and evil ring back to the land of Mordor. Along the journey, Frodo begins to question whether or not he should return home to the safety of The Shire, where he has lived all his life, or to continue on his dangerous quest. He seeks advice from Gandolph, the Grey Wizard, and Galadriel, the Queen of the Elves. The wise sage, Gandolph, tells Frodo, "All you have to decide is what to do with the time that is given to you." Galadriel tells Frodo, "Even the smallest person can change the course of the future." Frodo ponders their advice and makes the choice to remain on the journey even if it costs him his life; it almost does. Frodo successfully returns the evil ring to its volcanic origins at the end of the story and saves Middle-Earth from impending gloom.

After a brief period back home, he decides to leave The Shire with a group of friends and continue on with his adventures. Frodo never considered himself a hero, but he lived as a hero in his heart. He was commited to following his dreams and to make the most loving choices for those around him. Funny how the two, following our dreams and loving others, are so often connected when someone has a heart like Frodo.

HEROES VS. SPECTATORS

To become the hero of our own life story (whether we make headlines or not) and most often we will not, means we have chosen to become an active participant in life. We can learn many lessons from watching and listening to children who are natural participants. How many times have we heard children say enthusiastic statements such as, "I want to be a nurse...a doctor...an astronaut...a professional baseball player... a lawyer... a scientist...a movie star?" Too numerous to count! Do we ever hear children say negative statements such as, "I want to work three jobs and still not make enough money to live, drop out of school, make minimum wage for the rest of my life working at a job I hate, and only support the dreams of others?" No, Never!!! Children innocently and instinctively treat life as a joyful adventure with endless opportunities just waiting to be seized and conquered. For children, living life as a participant is a given. The thought of living their lives on the sidelines as a spectator is not remotely present in children's minds.

So what would happen to cause innocent children to grow up and lose their desire to be a participant and to stop dreaming of becoming heroes? Does the desire naturally fade away with age? No! The desire to be heroes of their own life stories is always hiding in the shadows waiting to be resurrected. Their childlike innocence gets clouded when shame, fear, and doubt are introduced and embraced into their lives in the same way our masterpiece within becomes concealed. Dreams can be discarded for many years, similar to the giant block of marble Michelangelo used to create the *David*. Some may have completely given up on their own dreams and settled for so much less than they are capable of achieving, because of a lack of emotional support, self-esteem issues, blame-shifting, lack of funds, feeling like too many years have passed, unwillingness to take risks, addictions, laziness, paralyzing phobias, or just plain old bad luck. Each and every one of these factors has the power to influence a person towards settling into spectator status. Unless a spectator is willing to regain their innocent desire to become a hero of his or her own life story, they will never attain a truly meaningful life experience. Fulfilling the prophetic words of Henry David Thoreau, "The mass of men lead lives of quiet desperation and go to the grave with the song still in them."

I (Guy) have found in my sports writing far too many fans get more excited about their favorite players or teams than they do about what is happening in their own lives. Some fans can talk for hours about sporting events, but they seldom, if ever get excited about what is going on in their own lives. The fans that impress me the most are the ones who draw enjoyment and inspiration from their favorite sporting event. For many of these fans, watching an event motivates them to incorporate the same excellence into their own lives.

Upon hearing the word "spectator," the first thought that usually comes to mind is someone who is an observer of an event, rather than someone who participates in an event. Spectators will often live vicariously through others' dreams and successes rather than risking the possibility of failure when trying to pursue their own dreams and goals. In order to provide themselves with a pseudo sense of self-worth, they may become consumed with supporting a friend's dreams, a favorite team, or a cherished celebrity. By doing so, they may feel they are making a contribution to their own lives. The reality is, rather than being the hero of their own life story, they are becoming the cheerleader and hero worshipper of someone else's.

Of course being a spectator for entertainment purposes is fun and relaxing, but when it becomes our primary source of gaining self-esteem we begin to tread on dangerous ground. Cheering on others' dreams may feel personally gratifying for a short period of time, but the feeling is merely a temporary sense of worth, because our own personal dreams and aspirations remain hidden away in the closet. Participants will have good times and bad, but what separates them from spectators is that participants have made the commitment to remain on their hero paths no matter what roadblocks come their way. Participants or heroes take risks, make sacrifices, have determination, patience, courage, passion, and hope to carry them through even the very toughest of times.

Vince Lombardi, of the Green Bay Packers, is one of the most respected professional football coaches of all time. He led the Packers to five NFL Championships in eight years. Lombardi used the term, "hinky dinky," for players who were content to settle for second best or mediocrity. He was referring to one of his deepest frustrations as a leader. He explained, "The difference between a successful person and others is not a lack of strength, not a lack of knowledge, but rather a lack of will." Lombardi went further to explain that a hinky dinky attitude is when one tries to live up to their potential every now and then, but not on a regular basis. He continued, "Winning is an attitude and is not a sometime thing. It's an all the time thing. You don't win once in awhile. You don't do things right once in awhile. You try to do them right all the time." He firmly believed everyone has potential, but each individual must take responsibility to develop their gifts and talents.

Lombardi could easily have used the term "spectator" to define hinky dinky players. He had high level athletes trying out for his teams, yet many arrived to camp as spectators in their prevailing way of thinking or living. Lombardi was dealing with maybe the most subtle form of spectators, those who know they are talented, believe they are participants, yet in reality they are living as spectators. He spoke throughout his career about this hinky dinky mindset while trying to motivate underachievers. We might ask, "How could someone make it to nearly the top of their profession without being a participant?" Extremely gifted spectators can occasionally achieve high levels of outward success, but their spectator attitude will eventually catch up with them, resulting in negative consequences. When adverse times or pressures come their way, pseudo-participants either give up and quit, or are content to settle for second best. A mature participant or hero is able to face head on the inevitable challenges of life and uses these obstacles as motivation to reach an even higher level.

HERO TRAITS

If we are going to remain commited to discovering the masterpiece within, we must constantly nurture our childlike desires to become the hero of our own life story. In studying heroes, whether they are fictional superheroes or real life heroes, we find there are certain core traits they all possess. Without possessing these traits to a satisfactory level, we run the risk of living in the shadows or on the sidelines as a spectator. The four key traits of an archetypal hero, which we believe are vital to becoming the hero of our own life story include bravery, dedication, humility, and being a visionary.

Hero Trait #1: BRAVERY

We can thank the creators of comic book superheroes for characters such as Thor, Captain America, Superman, Spiderman, X-Men, and Batman. When we think of these well-known and loved comic book heroes, often the first word that comes to mind to describe them is "brave." These superheroes bravely risk life, limb, and reputation to save everyone from a little old lady crossing a dangerous intersection to saving the entire world from a major catastrophy or an evil villain.

Daring archaeologist, *Indiana Jones* has been one of the most loved characters in film for more than thirty years. Indy played by Harrison Ford, bravely stares danger in the face around every corner. We love him because of his flair, wit, determination, and romantic nature, but we love him even more for his flaws, humanness, cynicism, and ability to bounce back after getting beat up. Oftentimes, after watching a film of this nature, one is inspired to live life more bravely.

Developing a strong spirit of bravery is essential to becoming the hero of your own life story. We may imagine these superheroes or even real life heroes are born brave, but the reality is bravery rarely comes naturally to anyone. Bravery is developed by taking small risks and building our way up to grand acts. Heroes are those willing to continually take risks even if they've had a succession of failures. Instead of being discouraged and retreating to spectator status, they have the ability to refocus on their goals, shake off their failures, and remain a participant.

Having small positive growth experiences builds a strong foundation and enables us to persevere through any test. To further develop a hero mindset, we must learn how to listen to our hearts and its pull in the direction of participating rather than sitting on life's sidelines. Developing this independence through trial and error helps stabilize one's belief in personal capabilities, and keeps the seed of faith alive and growing.

Hero Trait #2: DEDICATION

While on vacation with my husband in the British Virgin Islands, I (Claudia) watched as a little blonde girl began to build a sand castle all by herself on the white sand beach. Two other young children were walking down the beach toward the blonde girl. When the children came upon the girl they stopped and asked, "What are you doing?" She answered, "Building a sand castle, want to help?" The boy and girl responded, "Sure." They exchanged names and with unbridled joy proceeded to work together. Even as a wave came ashore practically destroying their work of art they were not discouraged, they simply sighed in unison and went right back to work rebuilding the castle until their parents called for them. Once again we can draw a great deal from observing children's behaviors. Even in times of opposition, children may become disappointed over an obstacle, but the disappointment usually lasts for a very short period of time. They possess the dedication of a hero to start over from scratch rather than feeling defeated and giving up. Animator, Walt Disney coined the phrase "stick-to-it-tive-ness," which perfectly describes the dedication it takes to be a hero of our own life story. And the most effective way to develop stick-to-it-tive-ness, is to take responsibility for our own lives.

We can draw many applicable life lessons from studying parenting skills in nature. Parents in the animal kingdom instinctively teach their young necessary survival skills and then at the appropriate age send them on their way to take responsibility for themselves. The young animal must learn to fend for themselves, rather than become handicapped by a parent who is willing to soften every blow in life. For example, when young penguins reach six or seven months of age, their parents begin to encourage them to swim. The dedicated parents of the small penguins get in the water first, and call for their young to jump off the ice and into the water. Some jump in quickly while others take their time. The ones left on the ice eventually are led into the water by the currents and are forced to learn even if they are reticent. They all inherently know how to swim, but they must discover this capability for themselves. The parents remain dedicated to challenging their young until the lesson is learned. Around thirteen months of age, the penguins become completely independent of their parents. Making this transition is not always easy in nature or humanity, but any parent who babies or spoils their offspring rather than giving them the freedom to learn for themselves, is actually doing damage or handicapping their young.

We are the master of our life story. Constantly reminding ourselves of this fact and renewing our dedication or stick-to-it-tive-ness to achieving our life dreams is key to becoming the hero in our life story. In 1989, while modeling in Chicago, my (Claudia) roommate Sharlene introduced me to an extremely beautiful young woman who wanted my advice on how to get more modeling jobs. This woman was struggling to make a living while I just happened to be doing quite well at the time. Right away it was very clear her dedication to succeed with her dreams was enough to keep her going but her heart was torn, because all the signs seemed to be pointing to a dead end road and an imminent return to her hometown in Ohio. I had developed a reputation at my various agencies and with my model friends for helping others so I was happy to help her as well. After hanging out with her a few different times and feeling like I had given her all the advice and encouragement I could on how to book more modeling jobs, we made plans to get together often as friends.

The next time I saw her, she was lit up with excitement and hope. She had auditioned for a new television show and had made the callback, which was to take place in Los Angeles. I was so thrilled for her, because she stayed in Chicago rather than giving up and moving home. Because of her dedication, opportunities were finally coming her way.

We lost touch with one another, but I watched with great pride as Halle Berry accepted the Academy Award for best actress for her performance in *Monsters's Ball* in March 2002. I found a quote by her recently where she said, "I take care of myself, because I learned early on that I'm the only person who's responsible for me. It's all up to me."

Hero Trait #3: HUMILITY

One of the main traits endearing us to superheroes or even real life heroes is their high level of humility. We are often drawn to these heroes, because of their eagerness to give without expecting anything in return, their ability to relate to the common man, their readiness to admit they do not have all the answers, their lifelong willingness to learn, and their steadfastness to remain on the hero path regardless of failure or success.

Actor-Philanthropist, Paul Newman embodied the humility we see in heroes. His commitment to family, his legendary acting career, and his humanitarian efforts are all prime examples of why he is someone to be admired. His most well known philanthropic venture began in 1982 with *Newman's Own* salad dressing. Since establishing the Newman's brand, close to half a billion dollars and counting in charitable contributions have been distributed worldwide and the company has expanded to include numerous other food products. Newman did not set up the company to contribute a portion of their company's profits to charities; instead, he chose to contribute one hundred-percent of the companies profits after taxes. A very rare feat. Referring to his company, Newman said, "We are very effective recyclers; we take the money and we give it back." If it were not for the popularity of these products, we might not even be aware of his generosity due to his humble spirit. His other less publicized humanitarian efforts include his numerous camps set up around the world for children with life-threatening illnesses and conditions. Founded in 1988, Newmans' *Hole in the Wall Gang Camps* provides nine free, fun-filled camp sessions every summer along with family weekend programs serving more than twenty thousand children and family members annually.

Newman was often self-deprecating with his humor, but his confidence in his convictions endeared him to us. He clearly showed us that feeling insecure about one's self is not a requirement or that one needs to think less of themselves to be considered humble. Heroes do not allow failure, an occupational hazard, to drag them down or success to go to their heads. When encountering one or the other, heroes like Newman are able to learn from experiences and move on to the next task. They have the understanding that failure and success are part of everyday life on the job.

Humility is often one of the most difficult of the hero traits to fully embrace and may be the most necessary of all the hero traits. Renowned English author, C.S. Lewis, emphasized again and again in his writings that humility is the foundation to personal or spiritual growth and without humility our growth will be severely stifled. And we know from Lewis' works, such as *The Narnia Tales*, he championed the concept of the "hero" and the importance of a hero possessing a high quotient of humility. Yet in our humanness, almost all of us can be stubborn and prideful to such a strong degree that we must relearn, and relearn, and relearn the importance of humility until we genuinely embrace it, much like in the classic film, *Groundhog Day*.

Bill Murray plays Phil Connor, a self-consumed, hyper-cynical, and arrogant weatherman who is assigned to cover the annual Groundhog Day celebration in Punxsutawney, Pennsylvania. A brutal snowstorm forces Phil to remain in town. When he awakes thinking it is the morning of February 3rd, he quickly discovers he must relive Groundhog Day over again. Morning after morning, Phil awakes to find himself yet again stuck reliving the day. At first, he decides to use the opportunity to feed his own selfish ego, until he gets bored and goes after the affections of his co-worker Rita, played by Andie MacDowell. He learns quickly what a good person she is and tries to pretend he is a good person as well to win her affections. Unable to succeed with Rita, he tries to kill himself numerous times; even that does not work. Tired of getting nowhere while pursuing his own selfish needs, Phil decides to show a little kindness to others. To his surprise, he realizes he becomes genuinely concerned with the needs of others and that he is actually enjoying himself. A new and more humble Phil has begun to emerge. Rita soon notices what a kind and loving man Phil has become and begins to see him in a different light. Having successfully transformed from a selfish and arrogant loser to the hero for many of the townspeople, Phil has finally learned the value of humilty. The next morning he wakes up a new and improved man next to Rita realizing he has finally made it to February 3rd. He begins his day by lovingly asking her, "Is there anything I can do for you today?"

Hero Trait #4: VISIONARY

What is the key ingredient or motivation sparking an individual to continue living life as a hero well into the twilight years of life with passion and joy? Why do others choose to become spectators without the hope of ever becoming the hero of their own life story? Heroes possess an optimistic attitude or strong belief in themselves, which appears to be lacking in spectators. Most spectators seem to be waiting in the wings for all the perfect elements to line up, but in most cases the elements never do. They make excuses for not taking the first step, but these excuses often remain for the duration of their lives unless a more optimistic belief in themselves is established. Spectators are primarily governed by doubt and fear while heroes are primarily governed by a positive belief in their abilities and potential. How can someone foster or establish a vision for life, which is essential to walking the hero path? Creating this vision is a process that starts small and grows very quickly if nurtured properly; just as a small seed can grow into a nutritious fruit or vegetable if given the proper care. This transition is set in motion by planting one seed at a time. As we bear the fruits of our labor, each accomplishment helps establish a positive belief blueprint. Our blueprint provides a strong foundation to continue the journey on the hero path. Too often we wait for life to come to us, or someone or something to set the agenda for our lives. A visionary learns to set their own goals and takes the initiative to fulfill them.

I (Claudia) had dreamed of being a model from about ten years of age. After high school, instead of moving to New York or Los Angeles, I chose to move to Dallas after reading how the city was becoming the next big hub for modeling. Since my parents insisted I get a college degree, I enrolled at Bauder Fashion College and chose Fashion Merchandising for my major. I was able to do a few modeling jobs during my first year of college and because of my success, I felt it was time to move onto the next step, signing with a professional modeling agency. After the end of my first year of studies, I went with five college friends to an open inteview day at the Kim Dawson Agency. To my great surprise, I was immediately accepted and decided to stay in Dallas during the summer to begin my career as a model. To my disappointment, I was the only one of the six of us accepted into the agency. Needless to say, I lost a few friends.

The next few months proved to be tough. I was trying to make enough money to pay the rent and build my model's book in order to book modeling jobs. I finally made it through with a handful of photos of which I was really proud. I even switched agents briefly after hearing the Tanya Blair agency was better with new models. The vision for my career was right on track when Tanya informed me the famous founder of Elite Models, John Casablanca, was coming to find models to take to New York and Paris.

The day of the interview, I patiently waited in the lobby five hours before I was finally brought in to see him. He flippantly browsed through the first few of my hard earned photos and to my utter surprise he asked, "Why are you even trying?" I innocently responded, "It's been a dream of mine for a very long time." He said, "You're wasting your time, you will never make a dime." I quickly asked, "You mean after I've worked this hard and spent so much money, you are saying I will never work as a model?" He responded, "No, never." Without time to think of anything else to do, I snatched up my model's book and looked him right in the eye and confidently said, "I'll prove you wrong." I then turned and walked out. I had such a strong vision for my career I decided right then and there that no one would be allowed to squash my vision even if they were one of the most famous agents in the industry. The small victories and hard work before and after this encounter helped me gain the confidence to remain motivated for the next seventeen years as a successful model. I eventually worked with Elite Models in Chicago and Atlanta for many years.

A healthy challenge can motivate us to either remain on our hero path or it can send us spiraling down and retreating into the life of a spectator. If we make the choice to see challenges as opportunities to renew our belief in ourselves, they can help empower and strengthen our self-worth. This empowerment helps maintain a hero mindset and keeps us motivated to remain on the hero path. If we allow obstacles to overtake us, we run the risk of becoming discouraged to the point of giving up on our dreams and settling to live the rest of our lives in a protective shell. Cocooning ourselves in this so called, "safe place" is actually an excuse not to take responsibility for our choices or our lives. Spectators tend to retreat to these safe places while heroes are visionairies who are willing to keep moving toward new challenges rather than away from them.

> *Each day you get to make a choice whether you are going to take*
> *a step forward, remain the same, or take a step back.*
>
> Kirk McCaskill

I (Claudia) just happened to be in London on August 31, 1997, the day the world's beloved Diana the Princess of Wales passed away from a tragic car accident in Paris, France. Wanting to honor her passing and the humanitarian she was, my husband and I felt led to leave flowers at the gates of Diana's home, Kensington Palace, alongside a few other flowers already there. Witnessing the outpouring of sadness unfold throughout the week was quite spectacular. As each day passed, we were awe struck as more and more flowers were brought to the Palace grounds in tribute and memory of the "People's Princess." Soon after her passing, the Spencer family created an exhibit in tribute of Diana at the family's Athorp Estate. I had hoped many times upon returning to London to make the trip to Northampton to see the exhibit, but time never permitted me to travel outside the city.

In the fall of 2005, while visiting my brother Kevin in Houston, Texas, I was thrilled to discover the exhibit just happened to be at the Houston Museum of Natural Science. After viewing the almost two hour exhibit of Diana's personal items from her childhood, her wedding to Prince Charles, her involvement in over three hundred worldwide charities, her untimely death and her heartbreaking funeral, I found myself wondering. "If I were to die, what kind of life to death exhibit would my life look like?" As the days passed, I could not help but ponder this question. I even shared the challenge with my closest friends and family members and in doing so saw how profound the question truly was. Some said their exhibit would last ten minutes while others joked they better get busy or theirs would be even less than a minute. I found these thoughts served as a healthy challenge to take responsibility for my life, to use all the opportunities given to me, and to take advantage of all the gifts with which I was born. Humanitarians and heroes like Princess Diana inspire each of us to become the heroes of our own life story. We can challenge ourselves by asking what would our life exhibit look like? How long would the tour last? Have I made my mark in the world? Have I become or am I on the path to becoming the hero of my own life story?

CHAPTER 8

HERO DEMOTIVATORS AND REMOTIVATORS

Empower me to be a bold participant, rather than a timid
saint in waiting, in the difficult ordinariness of now.

Ted Loder

We have the power to create a life filled with excitement, passion, and joy or to settle for a life of mediocrity. If we make the choice to defy mediocrity and learn the necessary skills which help to keep us motivated on the hero path, we build a reservoir of hope from which to draw when facing demotivating obstacles or circumstances. Without hope, our motivation can quickly evaporate and cause us to regress back into living as unfulfilled spectators.

Dee Owens of Houston, Texas, runs a very successful business teaching swimming lessons to area youth. Dee put together a highly effective training guide from her many years of experience for aquatic instructors. Her guide stresses the importance of removing obstacles or demotivators from the students' paths so they will be able to learn at an accelerated pace. She states, "*Learning is a natural part of the maturing process, meaning that humans are born with a desire to learn. People do not need to be motivated to learn. One has only to remove the demotivators for learning to be a positive experience. Imagine you are taking a journey and the highway is filled with potholes to dodge, old tires to drive around, heavy traffic that slows you down, the wrong map, or construction work detouring you from your destination.*"

We will all encounter demotivators throughout our lives, but if we educate ourselves to be prepared for them when they come along, we will be able to remotivate ourselves to stay on the path without being affected in a devastating manner. Learning to manage these demotivators can create a secure environment, whether in a swimming pool or in the arena of life. In this chapter we have identified major demotivators, which can stifle our desire to live as full-fledged hero participants. Along with these demotivators, we have also provided twelve practical remotivators as antidotes that will help keep our motivation fresh and strong.

DEMOTIVATORS AND REMOTIVATORS

Demotivator #1: FEAR OF REJECTION

For the majority of us the fear of rejection is the hardest demotivator to overcome, because completely eradicating fear from our lives is humanly impossible. The good news is we can educate ourselves to better manage its vice-like grip. Since we are all born with an innate desire to be loved and accepted, it comes as no surprise the possibility of rejection is at the root of most fears. Retreating to the safety of our own environment may be our initial knee jerk reaction after feeling the pain of rejection, but responding in this manner only serves to magnify the problem. The lyrics of, *I Am A Rock*, by singer/songwriter, Paul Simon, articulates how we often respond to rejection. The essence of the song tells when we isolate we become hard and cynical on the inside. And it is sad to say, we begin to die a slow emotional death.

Retreating from the world will not solve any fear-driven predicament even though logic or the voice of reason often tells us that if something or someone hurts us we should not attempt the action or engage the person who caused the hurt ever again. If we allow this philosophy to govern our actions, we will never experience the many joys life has to offer. Resorting to this behavior has the potential to cripple us as heroes, to stifle our creativity, and to hinder our willingness to take risks. To help keep fear in proper perspective we can remind ourselves fear is often a figment of our imaginations. Once we experience the fear and survive the fear, we are able to see how the fear was never as bad as we imagined.

Remotivator: FACING THE FEAR

On one occasion while writing this book, we as authors, became quite discouraged over one particular rejection letter and its comments. We always knew we would receive our fair share of rejection letters, after all, *Chicken Soup For The Soul* was rejected 146 times and Louis L'Amour was rejected 350 times before his first sale, but for some reason this person's comments were quite demotivating. We realized we needed to work through the disappointment so we decided to release some of our frustrations at a local batter's cage in Calgary. Letting off some steam helped to get our minds off the sting of the rejection letter and back to a clearer perspective. Instead of becoming bitter and cynical, we chose to write our rejector a thank you e-mail for taking the time to look at our project. In the letter, we also asked her a few questions regarding our book, hoping to tap into her publishing expertise. To our surprise, she was quite encouraging regarding our material and actually helped us improve our direction for the book.

Rejection is disheartening and is always difficult to work through, but when addressed immediately, not only does it prevent grudge holding from happening, but often personal benefits are achieved. The best approach in dealing with the fear of rejection is to tackle the fear head on as quickly as possible, instead of avoiding it altogether. When we face our fears, we diffuse its stronghold over us and we rediscover a sense of faith and hope. Experiencing small victories over our fears furnishes us with a renewed sense of self-worth and the confidence to take on more challenging risks. We are then better prepared to manage any additional obstacles placed upon our path, which have the potential to demotivate us and cause us to live as fearful spectators.

Demotivator #2: ISOLATION

If we do not take the time to seriously address the fear of rejection, isolation can get so out of control we suppress our chances of ever becoming the hero of our own life story. If we make the choice to remain isolated, we run the risk of opening the door toward a continual downward spiral of loneliness, depression, hopelessness, and suicidal tendencies. Isolation is an intended defense mechanism to prevent further hurt from occurring. However, instead of preventing more pain, we actually inflict more pain on ourselves than the original hurt. In turn, we become our own worst enemies.

The Washington Post reported Japan as having the largest isolation problem in the world. The article revealed as many as one million shut-in's, mostly young males, have been in self-imposed isolation for a period of six months to ten years. Forty-one percent of these shut-ins were isolated for a period of one to five years. Refusing to work or have any social contact, the vast majority of those in isolation showed no signs of psychiatric disorders. Japan's diminishing economy is believed to be the direct cause of this growing problem. Having lived in Japan on two separate occasions, I (Claudia) witnessed the emphasis of honor in the Japanese culture. The pressure to succeed is immense, due to the belief that if a family member does not achieve career success it is a dishonor to the family.

In another study, the Harvard School of Public Health in Boston completed a ten year study of more than twenty-eight thousand socially isolated men and found fifty-three percent were more likely to die from heart related causes, and more than twice as likely to die from an accident or suicide than those who maintained a large network of family, friends, and community involvement. Isolation does not occur overnight. There are numerous dynamics that can lead us to a chronic level of isolation, but the demotivating root cause begins with feeling alone without anyone to connect with on an intimate emotional level.

Remotivator: MAKING AN EMOTIONAL CONNECTION

Writing off all future relationships due a few bad encounters, regardless of the severity, can cause us to miss out on the beauty of experiencing life's deepest pleasures. We must challenge ourselves to resist isolation, because through relationships we have the greatest opportunities for personal growth and fulfillment. However, we must take into consideration establishing a large number of acquaintances will not necessarily help us emotionally; we can still feel alone in a crowded room. Making intimate one on one connections with others can nurture and motivate us to return to society. If we succumb to an isolationist mindset, we can begin pulling ourselves out of this trap by heeding some valuable advice from the film, *28 Days*. After leaving rehab, the patients are advised to begin life anew by buying a plant, which they must keep healthy and alive. This exercise is meant to teach personal responsibility and to take the focus off of themselves. Once they have been able to nurture and keep the plant alive for a year while working the 12 Steps and attending meetings with other recovering addicts, they are free to move onto pets and romantic relationships.

In order to break down self-imposed walls of isolation, we must be brave and risk exposing our hearts to possible rejection again. If we do not take risks to establish meaningful relationships, we put ourselves at a greater risk by hiding away as permanent spectators of life. The act of pulling ourselves out of our perceived comfort zones and searching for ways to connect with others is vital. We can start by taking extended education courses, joining a recreational sports team or gym, volunteering in a passion area, or if necessary, signing up for group therapy. When making an emotional connection with others, we are able to resolve feelings of being alone in the world without anyone to care for us. We once again become a functioning member of society and approach life from a place of joy.

Another example comes from an experience I (Claudia) had with my daughter Carrie, when she was struggling with math her junior year in high school. The math teacher had phoned to ask for a parent-teacher-student conference, so I asked Carrie what was going on in the class. I found out she did not understand the material, she did not particularly care for her teacher, and she had chosen to hide in the back corner of the classroom. I told Carrie I thought if she were to find an emotional connection with her teacher, she would be able to make better grades. During the meeting, I purposely asked the teacher in front of Carrie about her life. She revealed her love of teaching kept her from doing much else in life. She had cats but did not get to see them very often, because she was never home. She lived a good distance from the school, because she did not make enough money to live nearby. So, she spent almost two hours driving to and from work. She lived alone and had no time for a relationship, because she volunteered after class to coach one of the school's sports team. The teacher even joked with Carrie saying she herself had been a horrible math student until her college years, so she understood the dislike for math. Thankfully, the idea proved to be a success.

On the way home, Carrie could not stop talking about how she never knew what a great person her teacher was and how she felt bad for not listening to her in the past when she was giving up so much to teach. Having gained respect for the teacher, along with an emotional connection, Carrie not only agreed to sit in the front row of the classroom, but she also brought her math grade up from an F to a B. The dedicated math teacher ended up becoming one of Carrie's favorite teachers.

Demotivator #3: LIFE SETBACKS

Even though we would all like to avoid obstacles or life setbacks, they will always be a fact of life. Setbacks may feel extremely demotivating, but they are not always negative. As a matter of fact, the Chinese symbol for crisis is actually the symbol for opportunity and the symbol for danger combined. Even when setbacks are negative, they can be turned around for our own good, just as in the famous Friedrich Nietzsche phrase, "What doesn't kill you will only make you stronger," which made a resurgence in 2012, by Kelly Clarkson's hit song, *Stronger.*

Our perception of setbacks is the key to whether or not they will break us or strengthen us to carry on with our dreams. For example, Thomas Edison was asked by a reporter while trying to invent the light bulb, "After 9,999 tries, Mr. Edison, are you going to have 10,000 failures?" Edison replied, "Young man, I didn't fail 9,999 times. I discovered 9,999 ways not to invent the light bulb." For Thomas Edison each failure was just one step closer to fulfilling a goal. He also said, "For every wrong attempt discarded, is another step forward." If we allow setbacks to paralyze us, we begin to lose hope, become cynical, and our lives suffer mentally, emotionally, physically, and spiritually. Only we can decide for ourselves what path we are willing to take, the path of a hero or the path of a spectator.

Remotivator: PERSEVERANCE

One of the best ways to remotivate ourselves when setbacks come along is to research successful people throughout history who achieved great accomplishments and study how they dealt with these setbacks. A classic and often quoted example, would be Abraham Lincoln, who persevered through adversity his entire life.

He was born in 1809.

His mother died in 1818.

His sister died in 1828.

He failed in business in 1831.

He was defeated for Illinois state legislator in 1832.

He tried his hand at a grocery business in 1833 and failed.

He was elected to Illinois legislature in 1834 and served four terms.

His fiancee died in 1835.

He suffered a nervous breakdown in 1836.

He became a law partner in 1837.

He married Mary Todd in 1842.

He ran for Congress and was defeated in 1843.

He ran for Congress and was defeated again in 1846.

He retired from politics in 1848.

His four year old son Edward died in 1850.

He returned to politics in 1854.

He ran for the Senate and lost in 1855.

He ran for Vice President and lost in 1856.

He ran for the Senate again and was defeated in 1859.

In 1860 he ran for President and won becoming America's 16th President.

Today, Lincoln is still considered to be one of the greatest leaders in world history. The heart of a hero in any field of endeavor lies in the ability to never give up on dreams no matter what obstacles are placed along the path.

When we begin to realize setbacks and obstacles along our journey are life's greatest teachers, we are able to remain motivated and steadfast on the hero path. Baron Pierre de Coubertin, founder of the modern Olympic Games, also created the Olympic Creed which states, *"The important thing in the Olympic Games is not to win, but to take part, just as the important thing in life is not the triumph, but the struggle; the essential thing is not to have conquered, but to have fought well."* Once we learn the art of perseverance, we gain many valuable benefits: self-love, self-respect, wisdom, and integrity.

Whatever we set out to achieve in life should not fall into an all or nothing category, because a failure can be considered a success and a success can be considered a failure. It all depends on the internal outcome. If we learn and grow through the process and become better human beings through these setbacks, we are successful. If we have gained success but become despicable human beings in the process we have actually failed. It would be virtually impossible to find anyone in history who has achieved great feats without facing adversity or setbacks.

Demotivator #4: DISAPPOINTMENT

Disappointment often stems from unrealistic expectations we have placed upon ourselves or from unfulfilled expectations in the pursuit of a goal. If we allow disappointment to cloud our thinking, we are left paralyzed in frustration, confusion, and discouragement. We can become demotivated to the extent we may give up on our dreams and goals altogether, and revert back to being spectators. Setting high standards and goals is a healthy practice but setting unrealistic expectations can be very damaging. Disappointment is almost always the inevitable end result. We must risk being truly honest with ourselves and re-evaluate why the disappointment occurred in the first place. We must ask ourselves, "Do we truly possess what it may take to achieve the desired goal?" If not, can we further train or educate ourselves to attain the goal or is it time to let go of the dream and find a more realistic goal?

Letting go of a dream or goal when it is genuinely unrealistic should not be thought of as giving up, but instead this act should be seen as making a loving and wise life choice toward remaining on the hero path by pursuing other realistic options. We should also ask ourselves if we are truly putting in the work required to attain the goal. If not, we must prioritize and create a better plan for achieving the goal. If we are putting in the necessary work and we are still not getting anywhere, we should seriously consider whether to remain on this path and create a new plan of attack or change the goal entirely.

The most emotionally demotivating disappointment comes when we possess the talent, knowledge, skills, and work ethic to achieve our goals yet still come up short of the mark. These unfulfilled expectations usually occur when our perceived A to Z path toward our goal takes us in an unexpected direction. How we deal with disappointment is the key to whether or not we are able to remain on the hero path. We can either choose to give up on our dreams and become disillusioned spectators, or we can choose to see these unexpected obstacles or detours as valuable life lessons, and become even more determined to continue pursuing our dreams. Even though we may have suffered a major disappointment the reality is we may be closer to the fulfillment of our dream than ever before. And, it is important to remember even if our dreams never reach the climax we expect, just being on the hero path may open the door to a more promising future. We often hear about people who almost gave up on their dreams a short time before a breakthrough occurred. If handled correctly, disappointment can actually teach us determination and resiliency.

Remotivator: PERSONAL BEST

Any athlete who has ever medaled in the Olympic games has experienced the disappointment of defeat at the regional, national, or international level. In order to keep disappointment to a minimum, a wise coach will encourage his athletes to focus on achieving their "personal best" rather than focusing on achieving a medal. After all, ninety-eight percent of the athletes who compete in the Olympic games will not receive a medal. The philosophy of personal best reduces the stress of an all or nothing mentality, and places the focus on constant athletic improvement while building personal integrity and character.

Carla Samuelson was a nationally ranked swimmer in Canada who eventually earned a spot on the national team at the age of twelve. Her coach constantly stressed the importance of his athletes achieving their personal best at every swim meet in which they completed. His goal was to get Carla and her teammates to reach their full potential as athletes and to give them a realistic chance of qualifying for the Olympic games. Carla's most memorable lesson in her swimming career occurred when she won two gold medals at the Alberta championships to qualify for Nationals. In one of the finals, Carla knew she could hold back and still easily win even if her personal best was not achieved. In the other final she had to swim her personal best to win the gold. Her coach allowed her to enjoy the victory of her two gold medals for the remainder of the weekend.

When she returned to practice on Monday morning, he praised her for achieving her personal best in one event but then chastised her for underachieving in the other event even though she had won a gold medal. His concern was that she had taken a step back in her overall development by allowing a complacent attitude to creep in. He knew this type of attitude would cost her any chance of making the national team. Yet, when she finished eighth in all of Canada, at only thirteen years of age, her coach was ecstatic and could not encourage her enough, because she had shattered her personal best against other swimmers who were two to eight years older than herself.

Placing importance upon doing our very best regardless of the outcome serves as a healthy remotivator. Disappointment does not come along quite as often and when it does, if we remind ourselves we are performing to the very best of our capabilities, we are able to remain motivated and on the road to becoming the hero of our life story.

Demotivator #5: BEING OVERWHELMED

People of all ages struggle with burnout due to the stress and pressure of living in our fast paced world. The ever growing necessity for a dual family income leaves us working a required fifty plus hour work week while juggling family, home, and community responsibilities. In most situations the needs of others come first and our needs are placed at the end of a very long list. If we continually give, and give, and give to satisfy other's needs, our energy will become depleted, our immune systems will begin to fail, our passion for living will cease to exist, and we settle to live a life of a frustrated spectator. We may believe we are over participating in life, but in actuality we are over participating in other's lives. Without sufficient personal time management to take care of our own health and well being, the stress can be extremely overwhelming and even debilitating. We cannot keep up this level of output and live a quality life on five hours of sleep a night, and a few vacation days once every decade. Family, work, and community commitments can greatly enrich our lives, but if we allow any of them to take complete control not only do we suffer, everyone involved suffers. When we begin to feel we have no choice of escaping out of the quagmire, we must stop and remind ourselves we always have the power of choice to find a more peaceful, balanced solution.

Remotivator: REST AND RENEWAL

When I (Claudia) married into a ready made family, I found myself not only juggling the demands of a busy career, but also managing a household, instantly taking on an unfamiliar role as a mother to four daughters, and actively creating a strong relationship with my husband. I often discovered I placed myself last in order of priorities trying to be a super woman for everyone and everything. One day I had an epiphany! I realized if I take care of myself first, maybe I would have more energy to take care of others without resentment. And really, the world would not end if all the towels in the house were not washed, folded, and put away in the linen closet. I began this new mindset by once again scheduling in solitude time for myself. As a single woman for many years, I had scheduled and valued my solitude time, but I let it slide when marital responsibilities took over much of my personal time. I also found if I made sure my work was done, my clothes were washed, my bed was made, and my bathroom was clean first, the feelings of being overwhelmed went away. I had the same amount of time in the day, but for some reason I felt like I had twice as much time as before. I also found I was more creative, I was less tired, I was more loving and giving, I gained a stronger sense of self-confidence, and in the long run I set a better example for my new daughters.

Unless we take the time and initiative to make necessary life changes when we feel overwhelmed, we will forever remain in a cycle of frustration. We can take the time for rest and renewal by scheduling in a weekly one to three hour solitude date, and by taking mini fifteen to twenty minute solitude breaks throughout the week. If a solitude date is not feasible, due to a crisis in the middle of the day or week when certain commitments must be honored, taking mini timeouts can help bring back peace of mind and prevent us from being snowed under by stress and pressure. Going for a short coffee break by ourselves, taking a quick walk or nap, finding a quiet place at home or work, hiding in the washroom with a favorite magazine or book, or whatever it takes to pause in the day can be an oasis for our minds or souls to be renewed.

Creating A Solitude Date

1. A solitude date must be fun!
2. We must spend the time alone.
3. A solitude date must be at least 1-3 hours weekly or every other week.
4. We must make our solitude date a priority writing it into our weekly schedule.
5. A solitude date must feel rejuvenating to us.

Benefits Of A Solitude Date

1. We become reacquainted with ourselves.
2. Resentments are kept in check.
3. Renews our drive to attain our goals.
4. Improves our time management.
5. We appreciate significant relationships more.
6. Our creativity comes alive.
7. We become a joy to be around.
8. People respect us more, because we respect ourselves more.
9. Clears our thinking.
10. Gives a sense of inner peace.

Claudia's Solitude Dates

1. Seeing a newly released film.
2. Taking a drive in the countryside and pulling over to take photographs.
3. Walking in nature or swimming laps in a pool.
4. Browsing through magazines and books in a bookstore or library.
5. Writing in my journal and pulling out my datebook to plan what is ahead for me.

Guy's Solitude Dates

1. Going to the curling rink and throwing rocks up and down the long sheet of ice.
2. Going to the batters cage to get rid of mental clutter and frustrations.
3. Browsing book stores and soaking in the atmosphere.
4. Going to a movie for inspiration or just for fun.
5. Taking a long drive or walk into the country.

Demotivator #6: WING CLIPPERS

We will all encounter at least one individual during our lifetime who will publicly or privately demean us, ridicule us, shame us, or put us down. As we mentioned earlier, these wing clippers are insecure individuals who attempt to build up their own self-esteem by attempting to clip our "wings" whenever we talk about ourselves, our hopes or our dreams. If we have already experienced success, they often try to knock our accomplishments down to feel better about their shortcomings or fears. A wing clipper can affect their victims in various ways: some may retreat into a protective shell rarely sharing their dreams, others may be so demotivated they will not ever venture out onto the hero path again, or they may choose to bravely stand up to the wing clipper and challenge them.

Remotivator: EMPOWERMENT

With our core need in life being to love and to be loved, we can unknowingly look for approval from toxic people. So how can we survive and thrive around someone who appears to find joy in clipping our wings? It may be surprising and helpful to know the greatest teachers on love, i.e., Moses, Mother Teresa, Jesus, Buddha, and Ghandi all suggested to avoid this type of person as an act of love to ourselves and as a quiet wake up call to the one trying to hurt us. Sometimes keeping a physical distance from a wing clipper is the healthiest route to take. But many times these people live under the same roof as us, go to the same schools, or work right along side of us. In these situations learning how to keep an emotional distance is the key to retaining our hero wings. This includes restricting our conversation to surface issues and being careful not to share our hearts, dreams, or accomplishments, unless these people have a sudden growth in maturity or a kindness revelation.

I (Guy) was leading a conference at a Young Writers Conference in Calgary when the topic of toxic people came up. An eleven year old girl who was nearly in tears shyly put up her hand and asked how she could deal with her best friend who had just told her earlier in the week she was never going to make it as a writer. This cute little girl revealed she had been journaling since she was six years old on a daily basis and it was obvious she had a passion for the pen. She revealed to the group the only reason she came to the conference was her school had given her a scholarship and she felt obligated to come. I mentioned how sometimes good friends can be toxic without even knowing it, because of a selfish agenda or jealousy. She then said her best friend wanted her to go shopping on the day of the conference and was upset she would not go with her. I asked her if she thought the only reason her friend discouraged her from writing was that she wanted her to go shopping. It was as if the lights came on for this little girl and she completely understood the reason behind the surprise attack. I talked about why we need to be cautious with whom we share our dreams, and how timing is crucial as well. She came up to me after the class and you could see the renewed hope in her expression when she said, "I am so glad I came today. I was thinking of giving up on my dream of writing and now I want to keep on going. Thank you!"

Maintaining our motivation is difficult when confronted by wing clippers unless we are feeling particularly strong and empowered. If we search to find the reasoning behind wing clippers' actions, we will often be very surprised. These wing clippers can discourage us for reasons as selfish as a shopping trip or as inconsiderate as someone who desires to become the hero of their own life story but is not willing to put in the hard work. There are those who insist we remain in spectator mode so they will have a spectator buddy.

Demotivator #7: GRUDGE HOLDING

We have established throughout *The Masterpiece Within* that relationships are at the core of who we are as human beings. Very often the emotional state of our relationships determine our level of motivation to become full-fledged heroes. For example, if we feel we have been wronged or hurt by someone, instead of focusing our energy on our own hopes and dreams, we tend to shift all our energy and attention on the person who hurt or wronged us. Choosing to hold a grudge limits our ability to think rationally, and shuts down our creativity and our capacity to love. The sad reality is that whenever we hold a grudge we actually end up hurting ourselves in the long run far worse than the person whom we are holding the grudge against. In many cases the person we feel has harmed us does not care or even know the extent of how consumed we have become by the hurt or disappointment. The Alcoholic Anonymous 12 Step program stresses over and over again if addicts do not complete steps eight, nine and ten, which involve forgiveness of self and others, there is a ninety-nine percent chance the addict will relapse into drug or alcohol abuse. Unless we work to resolve our grudges through the act of forgiveness, we run the risk of reverting back to spectator status.

Remotivator: FORGIVENESS

I (Guy) have a friend, Steve Parrish, who teaches junior high school English in Calgary. He not only understands the power of forgiveness, but he attacks grudge holding in a very unique manner. Steve has observed over the years whenever students are holding onto grudges they may as well not even come to class, because their motivation for learning is almost nonexistent and their creativity is blocked. If he knows of students in his class who are not getting along, he will take them out into the hallway and ask them to work out their differences before they return to his classroom. When the students have resolved their differences and forgiven each other, they are then invited back into the classroom. This process usually takes about five to ten minutes, but Steve is willing to give the students the entire class period if necessary. After completing this exercise, the students' creativity is restored along with their ability to participate and learn. Steve and his wife Gillean have also practiced this same principle in their home for over the past ten years with great success.

My (Claudia) mother, Mary Church, was great at teaching her four children how to resolve differences in this same manner. Whenever any of us would fight with one another she would put us in a room and close the door until we kissed and made up. She would open the door and ask if we had resolved our differences. If we said yes, she would ask us to prove our forgiveness by letting her see us hug and kiss each other. Well of course if we were telling a fib, we could not hug and kiss until we had resolved our problems. Today, to the amazement of many of our friends, the four of us are so close we even take yearly vacations together.

The power of forgiveness is one of the most potent tools we have at our disposal. Choosing to practice forgiveness of self and others constantly remotivates us as heroes, and we become a positive influence for those around us; often motivating others to follow our lead.

> *You will know that forgiveness has begun when you recall those*
> *who hurt you and feel the power to wish them well.*
>
> Lewis B. Smedes

Demotivator #8: LOW SELF-ESTEEM

We all struggle from time to time with insecurity and self-esteem issues, whether we are on a hero path or a spectator path. If we permit these insecurities and short comings to dominate our thoughts, becoming the hero of our life story will become an extremely difficult task. In order to build confidence or to retain a hero mindset, we must focus our energy on our strengths, talents, and accomplishments rather than magnifying our limitations, disappointments, and weaknesses. This not only enables us to calm the negative chatter inside our heads, but this practice also enables us to gain a balanced perspective of our current life situation. If we are not vigilant in attacking self-esteem issues head on, the internal battle will remain constant. When we get to the root of low self-esteem, we often find negative opinions of others come from our own unfulfilled expectations. Why is it on any given day we can hear a handful of positive comments about ourselves and not really remember any of them, but the minute we hear a negative comment regardless of the source we tend to dwell on it for days and sometimes even years severely damaging our self-esteem? Constructive criticism can be viewed as an opportunity for personal growth as well as a motivational tool, but unless we are mature or evolved enough to learn grow from the criticism, the effects will be extremely toxic. Thankfully we have many outlets to bolster our self-esteem whenever we are ready to use them, helping us to remain on the hero path.

Remotivator: BUILDING SELF-RESPECT

Back when I (Guy) was working as a youth counselor near Edmonton, Alberta. I developed a program to teach young teens life skills, self-worth, and a sense of community through fun creative activities. One afternoon I received a frantic phone call from a mother whose seventh grade son, *Thomas (*named changed to protect his privacy) had just been caught shoplifting. She asked if I would be willing to counsel him as part of his rehabilitation. I agreed. After meeting Thomas, I realized he suffered from numerous self-esteem issues including the additional embarrassment of being arrested. To say he was reluctant from the onset would be a huge understatement. I discovered he was the only male in a single parent home where he had to compete with two sisters who were high achievers, attractive, and very popular. He on the other hand, had zero self-confidence, struggled with a "D" average, and was an overweight teen.

Our core group of teens were very open to embracing newcomers, so I believed we stood a good chance at making a difference in Thomas' life. Through time, he was eventually able to let down his guard, willingly participate in weekly activities, and enjoy his newfound friends. I felt he needed a strong male role model so we introduced him to a local man whom we knew would make a great mentor, because of his reputation for building self-confidence in others. To further support Thomas, we as a group, began to show up at his baseball games cheering him on, which really seemed to light him up. He had a definite charm about him and everyone grew to love him despite his occasional setbacks and quirkiness. Little by little we began to see his self-esteem improve. His mother, who was extremely grateful for our support and Thomas' progress, was still quite concerned for her son's future. She decided to take him to an educational specialist to have him evaluated for learning disabilities, and to also find out what vocational possibilities might be right for his personality type. Because he had a history of underachieving, she braced herself for bad news.

His assessment included IQ and achievement tests, and to the surprise of everyone the results revealed he was actually at a genius level. His mother's initial reaction was reserved, because of his troubled past. She even suggested maybe he should be retested, but the evaluator assured her the findings were accurate. The counselor then met with Thomas, explaining the test results and his hidden potential. He walked out of the meeting a changed young man, believing for the first time in his life he was smart and had just as much potential as his two "straight A" sisters. In all my years as a counselor I have seldom seen someone's self-esteem make such an about face in what seemed to be an overnight transformation.

Within a few weeks, Thomas turned his grades around and was able to maintain his honor student status throughout high school. He also went on to graduate from two different colleges and as a result of his increased participation in sports he was able to get into very good physical shape. Following a short missionary stint in Latin America he decided to pursue his dreams of being a radio DJ. Today, Thomas is a very popular DJ at a radio station in Western Canada, and continues to live as the hero of his own life story.

We may not all find out we are geniuses but placing ourselves on a hero path, looking for taking advantage of opportunities as well as surrounding ourselves with positive role models, is a legitimate method to discover our talents and to begin rebuilding our self-esteem. Once again we are reminded of the famous African proverb, "It takes a village to raise a child."

Demotivator #9: DENIAL OF HUMANNESS

Actor/Comedian/Author Steve Martin stated, "The problem today is that the only success is a total success, and a lot of things don't fall into that category." What causes us to have this belief in the first place? There are three main sources which greatly contribute to this belief: our parents, our religious upbringing, and the entertainment culture to which we are exposed. These sources are intended to guide and enrich our lives, but if we begin to live under the misconception that we are not allowed room for human error, we will develop unhealthy expectations of perfection.

As children, we desire to please our parents, not only because we do not want to disappoint them, but also because we do not want to face punishment. The religious traditions we are exposed to and the laws society tells us we must abide by help foster our innate sense of right and wrong. The fear of God and authority can take root to such an extreme we begin to believe if we do not follow the rules to a tee we run the risk of eternal damnation or of being thrown into the slammer with all the other evildoers. Today, more than any other time in history, we are bombarded daily by the world of entertainment. If we assume these images are the "norm" and we must perfectly emulate the lives and physical attributes of movie stars, music stars, sports stars and supermodels, we may become overwhelmed and demotivated to the point of feeling like not even trying. Anytime we get caught up in comparing our lives with other's accomplishments or outward appearances we set ourselves up for disappointment or failure. If we believe we have to live in a way that totally denies our humanness or requires us to follow in someone else's footsteps in order to be successful, we will eventually break under the pressure. Our dark side will act out in inappropriate ways: hypercritical intolerance of others, rebellion, angry outbursts, hypocritical or self-abusive behavior, or even giving up on our dreams altogether.

Remotivator: CLEAR PERSPECTIVE

One of the most helpful lessons we can learn as heroes of our own life story is how to allow ourselves room for our humanness. We must first understand being human means we will make mistakes, and we will have insecurities, doubts, and fears. Secondly, it is important to gain a clear perspective on the three major sources that can cause us to believe we must deny our humanness: parenting, religious traditions, and our entertainment culture. None of these three sources were ever meant to make our lives unbearable, but sometimes they can inadvertently demotivate us if we do not fully understand their intent. In most cases, parents want what is best for their children, and the boundaries adults set up are meant to keep children safe and to give them a strong foundation. Authentic religion is intended to develop the spiritual aspect of ourselves, and to open our hearts to give and receive love. Our entertainment culture is meant to inspire us, to provide fun and excitement, and to offer a necessary break from everyday life. Unless we are reminded or made aware of these basic truths, we can easily get caught up in expectations of perfection for ourselves.

According to many leading sociologists and pop culture experts, the entertainment culture is the primary culprit for promoting this unrealistic perfectionism causing us to deny our humanness. An article titled, *The Prozac Kids*, from an issue of *People* magazine revealed the number of children on antidepressants has tripled in the past decade to as many as one million. Dr. Peter Whybrow, the head of Neuropsychiatric Institute at UCLA was quoted in an article saying,

"We've defined for them what is the good life. Having the right pair of sneakers, wearing the right clothes, having the right friends. All of those things are so complicated in adolescents, who are trying to create themselves and we've increased the pressure to do that by commercializing their lives more than ever before."

These adolescents will grow up and continue to live under the same illusion and pressure unless they are taught a clearer perspective. Companies are trying to turn a profit and the more attractive people appear in their movies, television shows, videos, and commercials the more we are led to believe we will look the same if we buy their products. The bottom line is these companies are willing to use whatever smoke and mirrors they deem necessary to convince consumers to spend their hard earned money. Because of this, we are left believing movie stars, sports heroes, music icons, and supermodels are flawless and have all the confidence in the world. This is a complete fallacy! These stars, whom we idolize and emulate, are just as human with insecurities and self-doubts as we are.

Claudia and I (Guy) have had the opportunity to work with or befriend numerous celebrities throughout our careers, from Grammy and Academy Award winners, to international supermodels, to professional athletes and Olympic medalists. A common trait amongst these top entertainers is they are quick to acknowledge their humanness, and are often the most humble people anyone could ever meet. A large majority of their successes have occurred because they have learned how to accept their humanness, and to persevere through failure, self-doubt, and rejection, rather than allowing these potential demotivating setbacks to throw them off the hero path.

Demotivator #10: PRIDE

Pride is one of those terms which needs to be properly defined or we can easily misjudge the context of its use. We can look at pride in two very different ways, as either healthy or unhealthy. Used in a positive context, pride is needed in building a strong sense of self-worth. For example, we can be proud of an accomplishment that took a lot of extra effort, or parents can be proud of their children's good grades in school. Healthy pride cultivates and maintains our character and integrity. Used in a negative context, pride eventually breaks down our self-worth. Unhealthy pride is rooted in selfishness and stubbornness, and usually manifests through unwise decision making. For our purposes in this chapter, we will be referring to unhealthy pride because it is one of the major demotivators in preventing us from walking the hero path.

I (Claudia) have always been dedicated to living out my dreams no matter what hard work is required of me. As a preteen, I began babysitting for neighborhood families. The day I turned sixteen, I immediately went out and got a job in the bakery department of a local grocery store. This same strong work ethic has proven to serve me well through many years of career success and life fulfillment. One spring while working in Chicago, I came upon a movie set and I stopped to see what was going on. A couple of men in business suits, who looked like they were in charge, came over to ask if I was an actress. I told them yes, but at the moment I was in town doing some modeling work. It began to rain so they asked if I wanted to come inside to the set to talk further, because there was a role in the film they thought I would be right for. I thanked them for the offer, but because I felt like I had not earned the opportunity the hard way, I told them I needed to get going to my next modeling interview. As I walked away, I asked what the film was called so I could look for it. They replied, *The Untouchables*. Rounding the corner I saw a very long line of Paramount Pictures movie trucks, and remember wondering for a moment if I was truly making the right choice.

The Untouchables, starring Kevin Costner, Sean Connery, and numerous other well-known actors went on to become a huge blockbuster hit. A few years later, I began to realize the huge opportunity I had missed, and wished I had not been so prideful. Some would say I made an honorable decision, while others would tell me I missed out on a once in a lifetime opportunity. I now realize the opportunity was a godsend, and I did not take advantage of it because I was too prideful to accept any career help, and too fearful others would think I had not earned my success. I am also now fully aware of the millions of dollars at stake for movie studios when shooting a film, so had I not been right for the role I would have never been cast. This life lesson still serves me well in that I am more open to opportunities and accepting acts of kindness, rather than being stubborn and stuck in an honorable but faulty belief system.

Remotivator: HUMILITY

A prideful heart acts from a place of fear, is selfish in nature, and is closed down while a heart of humility acts from a place of love, is courageous and committed to remaining teachable. Time and time again, throughout our journey on the hero path, we will be reminded of the value of humility, especially when we experience the negative consequences of a choice made from a prideful state. When we choose to embrace humility over pride, we open ourselves up to a wealth of resources and opportunities for growth and development.

Take the classic example of a family that has never faced a problem of poverty in the past, but finds themselves in temporary financial hard times at Christmas. In their dilemma, do they remain prideful and unaccepting of gifts of money or food from friends and neighbors who are aware of their plight, or do they courageously choose humility and bring food to their table and gifts to place under their tree? If they choose a prideful path, the family will still be without food and most likely the parents will remain stuck in bitterness, anger, and left feeling like failures. If they choose the path of humility, their children will be able to see a very human side of their parents and everyone in the family will learn valuable life lessons in humility, gratitude, and a sense of community.

Making wise choices often requires a tremendous amount of courage, especially when pride rears its ugly head. Choosing for the highest good of ourselves and others regardless of how ashamed or embarrassed we may feel at the time is a true act of humility. When we continually remind ourselves to run our decisions through the five choice filters found in Chapter Five; noble value system, inner voice, self-talk, relationships, and long term consequences, we become more likely to face pride in a healthy way and to remain motivated to continue on the hero path. Prideful choices made from a place of fear will often play out in regret, where choices made from a loving place of humility, will often play out in a positive manner.

Demotivator #11: LAZINESS

Laziness is a lack of motivation to take responsibility for our lives. This demotivator can stem from being overly pampered and protected as a child, from unfulfilled expectations, from experiencing negative ramifications of an unwise choice, or from simply being content to coast by in life on minimal effort. When we allow laziness to take up most of the waking hours in our day, our behavior must be addressed as quickly as possible, because this mindset will only perpetuate itself into more laziness and lethargy. In order to get out of this mindset, we must find some form of motivation to wake us up. We could start by granting a friend or family member permission to challenge us or by creating the motivation on our own. If we choose to remain in this self-destructive state, we may never rekindle our passion to live as a hero.

Remotivator: REWARDS

One of the best remotivating catalysts for laziness is receiving some form of a reward in exchange for labor exerted. Of course the fruits of our labor will never be realized if we cannot find the motivation to get off the couch in the first place. Only we can decide for ourselves if we want to put in the work and sacrifice necessary to live as the hero of our life story. Developing and applying a strong work ethic can quickly become habitual when we set up the proper reward system. When we feel we have done well at a job and are appreciated for our efforts, we will naturally apply ourselves more. We can take this lesson and apply it to our own lives by offering ourselves small but motivational rewards for a task well done.

In my (Guy) desire to continue curling on a highly competitive level, I know I must practice at least twice a week. To make practicing more motivational over the years, I created a little one on one game with myself. If I make a certain percentage of my practice shots, I usually reward myself with a new book to read or lunch at my favorite fish restaurant. If I throw under a certain percentage, I take my rewards away and just head back home for lunch instead. This reward/punishment system helps to keep me motivated and looking forward to my next required practice. Unless we ascertain ways to daily motivate ourselves, we will settle for a life of skipped practice sessions, laziness, and mediocrity.

Demotivator #12: LOSS OF A SENSE OF HUMOR

If we find ourselves irritable, quick to anger, stressed out, and frustrated this may be an indication we are taking life too seriously. When we get into this state of being, our mind, body, spirit, and emotions begin to feel depleted. Our quality of work diminishes, our relationships become strained, our health is threatened, and our motivation declines. We can ask ourselves, "When was the last time I laughed, really laughed out loud?" If we contemplate for too long, most likely we have hit our limit and need to take a much needed break to find our humor again. Famous humorist, Will Rogers, was quoted as saying, "The times you don't feel like laughing are the times you need to laugh the most." Anybody can laugh when they are having fun. It is the times when things are not going so well that we need to engage humor. Unless we intentionally take the time to become reacquainted with our sense of humor, our energy to live as a hero will eventually dry up.

Remotivator: REESTABLISHING JOY

Many of us have heard for years the age old adages, "Laughter is the best medicine," and "To be joyful in all circumstances." But until we actually experience the loss of joy or the inability to laugh, these phrases are not as powerful. We all get caught up in the seriousness of life at various moments and need to be reminded how important joy is to our sanity. Rarely does something or someone come along and instantly help us restore our joy and snap us out of our doldrums. It is our own responsibility to come up with a plan to remotivate ourselves. Some of the ways we can restore a sense of joy or fun to our lives include watching a comedic film, spending time with someone who has a knack for cheering us up, reading a light-hearted book, or even looking for the humor in how serious we have taken life lately. Making a list of things that bring us joy and drawing from this list to get us back on track will always be worth the effort.

To live as a hero and to have a meaningful life, we must learn how to remotivate ourselves when the temptation is strong to give up and settle in as spectators. Demotivators will strike even the most solid heroes, but they do not have the power to completely demotivate us unless we allow them.

One morning while working on this particular section of *The Masterpiece Within,* we were writing at a Starbucks in Calgary when a married couple who both happened to be "little people" came in and sat down at a table next to us. We could not help but being drawn into their conversation, because the husband was noticeably distraught. The defeat he felt was obvious in his body language even before they sat down. His concerned wife was doing her best to encourage him in a loving, non condescending manner. Nothing seemed to cheer him up until she said, "Take a step of hope, honey." This remotivating statement was exactly what he needed to hear, because his countenance immediately lit up. He optimistically responded, "You're right, you are absolutely right." We were reminded at that moment how crippling the loss of hope can be. If we lose our hope, we lose our motivation. If we lose our motivation, we risk stalling or being thrown off our hero path. During times of struggle, regardless of our demotivating circumstances, we must put into practice the remotivator which will counteract these obstacles. We must bravely take a step of hope.

> *Every trial endured and weathered in the right spirit makes*
> *a soul nobler and stronger than it was before.*
>
> James Buckham

CHAPTER 9

WORKBOOK CHALLENGES III

GET TO KNOW ME

1. When I was a child I dreamed of growing up one day to become? _____
    _____
    _____

2. I believe I can become the hero of my own life story.
    Yes_____ No_____ Sometimes _____

3. In reviewing the twelve demotivators, the ones that hinder my growth to becoming the hero of my own life story most are...
    Fear of Rejection _____   Isolation_____   Life Setbacks _____
    Disappointment _____   Laziness_____   Being Overwhelmed _____
    Wing Clippers_____   Grudge Holding_____   Pride_____
    Low Self-Esteem_____   Denial of Humanness_____
    Loss of A Sense of Humor_____

4. In reviewing the twelve remotivators, the ones that inspire me to become the hero of my own life story?
    1. _____

2. _____

3. _____

PRACTICAL POWER TOOLS

1. Create a plan for incorporating a solitude date into your weekly schedule. Design the date specifically around what you enjoy doing. List possible ways to spend your solitude date.

    1. _____

    2. _____

    3. _____

    4. _____

    5. _____

2. Find a hero mentor.

    a. Who do you look up to in life? _____

    b. List the qualities you admire in them.

        1._____ 2._____ 3._____

    c. Make an effort as soon as possible to get together with someone who is a hero of their own life story and mine their wisdom. Ask if they have the interest and time to become a mentor for a specified amount of time.

    d. Find a hero mentor from history and research their journey through biographies, memoirs, film, and the Internet. Learn from their mistakes and their successes.

3. An extremely helpful tool is to observe spectators and the mistakes they are making which cause demotivating life consequences. We are then able to take these lessons and apply them to our own lives without going through all the personal trauma and life setbacks. If done in a constructive and objective manner, we can see the logic and value of applying remotivators to our lives.

    Spectator(s): _____

    Demotivating Life Consequences: _____

    _____

4. Perform a vow ceremony. Rituals and ceremonies throughout time have symbolized commitment. A vow ceremony is a commitment to love and honor yourself. It is similar to a marriage ceremony, but this is performed alone and symbolizes love of self. You may purchase an item such as a ring, necklace, or bracelet to serve as a symbol and reminder of this powerful vow to yourself. Arrange for the ceremony to take place in a comfortable, safe, and private location. Lighting a candle can help create a sacred surrounding. Either write your own ceremony or use our example.

I _____ vow today and this day forward to be completely committed to the nurturing of my soul, to love, honor, and respect myself. I will not allow toxic people, habits or others to control my thoughts, feelings, happiness, or my life in general. I will use this symbol (purchased item) as a reminder of my commitment to my own self-love.

5. Create a hero mission statement. Writing a hero mission statement helps define what we desire to achieve in our lifetime. In the same way many large companies have a business mission statement.

My hero mission statement: _____

_____

_____

_____

_____

_____

BRAIN MEDICINE

1. I am the hero of my own life story
2. I continually achieve my personal best
3. I deal with obstacles head on
4. I make solitude dates a priority
5. I am full of hope

PERSONAL BRAIN MEDICINE

1. _____
2. _____
3. _____
4. _____
5. _____

You may not control all the events that happen to you,
but you can decide not to be reduced by them.

Dr. Maya Angelou

LIFE SKILL #3

DISCOVERING AND DEVELOPING LIFE BLISS

If you follow your bliss, you put yourself on a kind of track that has been there all the while, waiting for you, and the life that you ought to be living. Wherever you are- if you are following your bliss, you are enjoying that refreshment, that life within you, all the time.

Joseph Campbell, *The Power of Myth*

CHAPTER 10

LIFE BLISS CHARACTERISTICS AND TOOLS

A musician must make music, an artist must paint, a poet must write,
if he is to be at peace with himself. What a man can be, he must be.

Abraham Maslow

Throughout history, man has pondered the question, "What is the meaning of my life existence?" Austrian psychologist and author, Dr. Viktor Frankl, built an entire career around this school of thought when he created the concept of "Logotherapy." Frankl believed when we discover our life meaning, we are able to heal our emotional ailments, addiction problems, relationship disputes, spiritual dysfunctions, and most psychological disorders. Of the thirty-two books he wrote during his lifetime, *Man's Search For Meaning*, was voted by the Library of Congress in 1991 as one of the ten most influential books in America. It was not only translated into twenty-nine languages, but has sold more than four million copies in the United States alone.

Many cultures down through the centuries have created their own terminology to define meaning or purpose in life. In ancient Sanskrit, the world's oldest known language, "dharma" is often used in the translation. In Latin, the word "avocatio" is used to express the root of our true vocation. In French, the word "metier" refers to living out our specialty or role in life. In Greek, the word is translated as "logos," in which Frankl derived his term logotherapy. In theological circles, logos is translated as "the will or word of God," but in the broader sense it can be viewed as "that which gives reason for being." Our modern language contains numerous words or phrases that carry the same connotation: our avocation, our life purpose, our passion, our calling, and our bliss. The term "bliss" has been used often over the years with various meanings but did not come into vogue to describe purpose in life until the latter part of the twentieth century when Joseph Campbell coined the phrase "follow your bliss." In more recent years, the word bliss has gained popularity in advertising, business, the entertainment world, and news media.

We, as authors, carefully researched myriad terms and phrases to find the ideal term or concept to describe "having found our life meaning." We chose the term "life bliss," because we believe the term precisely encompasses the contemporary and multi-dimensional attributes for which we were searching. When we are living our life bliss, the four primary attributes of energy, joy, meaning, and love will be present. We are naturally energized, because our endorphins are being triggered. We experience joy and often lose track of time. We have a deep sense of meaning and self-worth in the world when we are using our talents and gifts. And, we feel a sense of self-love, because we strongly believe in our hearts our life is making a difference, giving us the determination to press on regardless of the obstacles we encounter. When these four characteristics are present, we gain a sense of purpose because we are living up to our fullest potential.

LIFE BLISS

There are two forms of bliss that will occur throughout our lives: bliss encounters and genuine life bliss. Genuine life bliss is rooted in our identity. Our true identity is not so much what we do, but what motivates or energizes us to feel our life matters. Genuine life bliss is a sustained, deep holistic sense of inner fulfillment, because all four characteristics of love, joy, meaning, and energy are present. When having a bliss encounter, all four characteristics may or may not be present but there is a sense in our hearts these characteristics will not be present for an extended period of time. Bliss encounters can be seen as life signposts, pointing us toward a greater destination. They are fun, adventurous, memorable, and often life altering, but they are only meant to be seen as a pitstop or seed of hope to serve as motivation to continue down the path of discovering our genuine life bliss. When we experience a bliss encounter, we are feeling totally alive and energized, similar to children playing and losing all sense of time. This is why a man can get excited about playing recreational slow pitch if he feels his presence is making a difference or why a mom feels alive when asked to help her daughter plan a fairy-tale wedding. For those two short hours playing a game, or the months it takes to plan a wedding, these individuals feel alive, and their lives have meaning and worth. We will eventually come to realize these bliss encounters, as good as they are, are lacking a sustaining element because they are temporarily fulfilling in nature.

Actor, Dustin Hoffman, captured the passion behind finding ones genuine life bliss when he was interviewed on the television show, *The Actors Studio*. He shared with the viewing audience his passion for acting can best be described as Picasso described his passion for painting, *"If they took my paints away, I'd use pastels. If they took my pastels away, I'd use a crayon. If they took my crayons away. I'd use a pencil. If they stripped me naked and put me in a cell, I'd spit on my finger and draw on the wall."*

Witnessing others living in their genuine life bliss can inspire us to discover the same excellence for ourselves, because they are exuding a captivating and all encompassing joy. Bob Costas interviewed Paul Newman shortly before Newman passed away for his HBO show, *Costas Now*. Costas spoke with him about the various sports films in which Newman starred and about his love of film making and race car driving. Toward the end of the interview, he asked Newman what was part of the allure of sports for him. Newman responded, *"It's the part of excellence, I mean excellence and I don't care where you see it. Whether it's in a restaurant with a waiter or a guy directing traffic and he really knows what he's doing. I could watch him for an hour. So that's the only thing I look for… excellence in anything."*

When we are living in our genuine life bliss, we will experience an inner "sense of rightness" in our mind, body, spirit, and emotions that will reflect outwardly as well. This feeling will remain constant for a very long period of time. It is not that we will never have struggles or insecurities, but we will have an innate sense our lives are moving forward in the right direction. Our anger subsides or is kept in check. We feel deeply joyful. We have energy and passion to persevere when life becomes difficult. The faith we have in ourselves will be tested, but there is a constant sense of underlying hope. We are more open to giving and receiving love. Money is not our main motivation. And, we inspire others to also find their genuine life bliss.

In the hit film, *City Slickers*, Billy Crystal stars as the film's lead character, Mitch Robbins, who is stuck in a mid-life crisis and has lost his bliss. Mitch is celebrating his thirty-nineth birthday, sending him even deeper into his plight. He is not only struggling to find life meaning, but he is beginning to feel the spark in his marriage flickering and he has lost his enthusiasm for his radio station job. While cleaning up after Mitch's birthday party, Barbara, Mitch's wife played by Patricia Wettig asks him, "Are you not happy?" He responds, "No, I just feel lost." Barbara encourages her husband to go on the annual vacation his buddies have arranged, instead of a family trip to Florida so Mitch can, "go and find his smile."

This year's adventure takes them on a real life cattle drive from New Mexico to Colorado where they can pretend to be cowboys for two weeks. The trail boss is a crusty old cowboy named Curly, played by veteran actor Jack Palance. Mitch is enamored by Curly's character, who seems to be everything Mitch is not: confident, strong, and at peace with himself. He develops a friendship with Curly and begins to feel comfortable enough to ask him a few heart to heart questions. One of the questions he asks is, "Do you know what the secret of life is?" Curly holds up his index finger and replies, "This. One thing. Just one thing. You stick to that and everything else don't mean anything." Mitch excitedly says, "That's great, but what's the one thing?' Curly responds, "That's what you've gotta figure out."

Mitch goes on to experience numerous mishaps, heartwarming moments, and obstacles with his buddies, including the death of his new friend, Curly. After almost drowning in a raging river while trying to save a calf, he announces he finally knows what Curly meant. *"It is something different for everybody. It's whatever is most important to you. For me, when I was in the river I was only thinking about one thing. All the other stuff just went away. Only one thing really mattered to me."* When he arrives home he tells Barbara he found his smile and that he is not going to quit his job, he is just going to do it and everything else better. Mitch discovers, to his surprise, he is already living his genuine life bliss and the only change he has to make is his perspective.

There are so many different versions of bliss that no two individuals will ever describe their genuine life bliss in the exact same manner. Some may say their life bliss is spending time with family members, working a maximum of eight hours a day and having time to be involved in church or social activities while someone else may describe their life bliss as spending time alone with their spouse, working a minimum of ten hours per day and making time to develop a particular hobby. Life bliss can be any combination of life passions and should be seen as a state of mind versus a specific activity or occupation.

When striving to discover our genuine life bliss, we must also consider the long term ramifications of our choices. Often times we have a fairy tale version of a profession or lifestyle in our minds versus one of reality especially if we have never truly lived it. For example, we may be determined that being a fireman is our life bliss, but if we have not done our homework to know the job requirements, which includes a twenty-four hour shift, we may be quite surprised after investing our time, energy, and money. Or we may dream of having an adventurous single life without thinking through the amount of time spent alone. Throughout our lives, our life bliss may go through many transformations, as our lives are ever changing. Therefore, making the cultivation of our bliss a continual lifelong process.

TOOLS TO DISCOVER AND CULTIVATE LIFE BLISS

Each and everyone of us has our own unique life bliss just waiting to be discovered and cultivated. Some may feel completely lost as to what their life bliss is or even where or how to start looking. While others may have already tasted life bliss, but are going through a bliss crisis and are in need of a little clarity to make sure they are on the correct path.

The path to discovering or clarifying our life bliss does not have to be as overwhelming as we sometimes make it out to be. The journey can be a fun and exciting adventure. We have put together a number of tools to help us discover our genuine life bliss. We may choose one tool at a time or pick out a few tools that seem to spark our interest. Having these tools at our disposal helps to jumpstart the development of our genuine life bliss and energizes us to continue discovering the masterpiece within.

LIFE BLISS TOOLS

Life Bliss Tool #1: OUR INNER VOICE

As we have mentioned throughout the book, our inner voice is ready, willing, and waiting patiently at all times to lead us in the best direction possible. We can all relate to statements such as, "I have a feeling," "My intuition tells me," or "I can feel it in my gut." In cultivating life bliss, our inner voice will always be our primary ally. Getting into the habit of asking ourselves pertinent life questions will speed up the process in clarifying our life bliss and is a good exercise to sharpen our inner voice. What comes to mind first when we ask ourselves these questions will most likely contain the answer we are seeking. "What do I really love doing with my life? What are some of my most meaningful and fulfilling life moments? Or What gives me energy and gets me really excited about life?"

Co-founder, chairman and CEO of Apple Computers, Steve Jobs, delivered the commencement address at Stanford University in June 2005. In his speech he said, "*Your time is limited, so don't waste it living someone else's life. Don't be trapped by dogma – which is living with the results of other people's thinking. Don't let the noise of other's opinions drown out your own inner voice. And most important, have the courage to follow your heart and intuition. They somehow already know what you truly want to become. Everything else is secondary.*"

Life Bliss Tool #2: SOLITUDE DATE – RETREAT

> "*Every now and then go away, have a little relaxation, for when you come back to your work your judgement will be surer; since to remain constantly at work will cause you to lose your power of judgement. Go some distance away because the work appears smaller and more of it can be taken in at a glance, and a lack of harmony or proportion is more readily seen.*"
>
> Leonardo da Vinci

Taking time to quiet our hearts and minds is critical in hearing our inner voice and discovering our life bliss. We can always find ways to keep ourselves occupied with "stuff" day after day, or to make excuses in order to avoid being alone, but solitude should never be treated as optional in cultivating life bliss. Creating solitude time is one of the most beneficial habits we can ever adopt. Planning a weekly solitude date and having a yearly retreat or two is something most of us feel we just do not have the extra time, energy, or money to do. We need these breaks to realign ourselves with our life bliss, and to reenergize our lives with passion. Having solitude time allows us to take care of ourselves, to think, pray, cry, walk, meditate, journal, release anger, or to do whatever works best to reconnect with our hearts. There are many creative ways to have low cost one to three day retreats. Besides saving nickels and dimes, we can explore many opportunities through low cost overnight monastery/retreat centers, by having friends/spouses take care of our children, or by searching websites such as Priceline to bid for high end hotel rooms at a reduced price.

Life Bliss Tool #3: EXPERIMENT

Hearing about someone else's life bliss experience can be inspiring, but if we just adopt their ideas without cultivating our own life bliss we may be setting ourselves up for disappointment. Mother Teresa would make it very clear to potential workers that not everyone is called to live and work in Calcutta. She would challenge them by saying, "Find your own Calcutta." If they still believed they were making the right choice, she would arrange for a short term trial for them to work with the, Sisters of Charity. This temporary arrangement would usually settle the issue or open a new and clearer door for the volunteers' authentic life bliss. The fact that these workers were on a path to discover their bliss was an aid to bring them even closer to their genuine life bliss.

Copying or following in other's footsteps that we admire can be a good kick start in our search for our own life bliss, even if we find their life bliss is not ours in the long run. Another valuable method in cultivating our life bliss is to experiment with various life directions on paper by writing out what our lives would be like hour to hour and day to day in this situation. This exercise is a great help in taking away the glamour or romance we have created in our imaginations before we put a large amount of energy or time into it. After completing the exercise, if we find we are still passionate about pursuing this path, we will then feel more confident in our choices.

Life Bliss Tool #4: NEVER TOO YOUNG - NEVER TOO OLD

Who made the rule that once we reach a certain age we have nothing left to contribute and that we have to retire from life? Or, if we have not reached a certain age of maturity we have to wait for adulthood or permission to go after our dreams? Some of the greatest feats in life have been achieved by those who refused to place restrictions on themselves because of their age.

Never Too Young

1. Joseph Armand Bombardier invented the snow mobile- Age 15
2. Sacagawea took Lewis and Clark on a yearlong expedition to the west- Age 16
3. Mary Shelley wrote the classic story, *Frankenstein*- Age 18
4. Wayne Gretzky won the National Hockey League's MVP award- Age 19
5. Malala Yousafzay won the 2014 Nobel Peace Prize- Age 17

Never Too Old

1. Colonel Harlan Sanders started franchising his Kentucky Fried Chicken recipe- Age 65
2. Jessica Tandy won the Best Actress Oscar for *Driving Miss Daisy*- Age 80
3. Ichijirou Araya conquered Mt. Fuji- Age 100
4. Sisters "Sadie" and "Bessie" Delaney co-wrote their first book, a best seller- Ages 104 & 102
5. Equestrian, Ian Miller after competing in nine Olympic games won a silver medal- Age 61

One of the most passionate people I (Guy) have ever encountered is Reg Schjerning. Reg was an entrepreneur at heart who never lost his excitement for taking risks. When he retired in his mid-sixties, he stumbled upon his childhood passion of drawing and painting, which he had not considered exploring since he was a teenager. One day, while watching television, he discovered a local art instruction show around which he soon began to religiously plan his life. Within five years, Reg began showing his art, making hundreds of dollars on many of his pieces. He continued to paint full time right up to the time of his death. I have had the honor of seeing first hand how Reg has inspired many in his sphere of influence to also follow their own life bliss.

Twenty-years old and already nominated for three Nobel Peace Prizes! Craig Kielburger and his twenty-eight year old brother, Marc co-founded *Free the Children*, the largest network in the world in which children help children through education. When Craig was only twelve years old, an article in his hometown Toronto newspaper about a young Pakistani boy who was murdered after escaping and speaking out on the abuses of child labor, moved Craig to make a difference. Craig and Marc never dreamed in only eight short years they would be able to raise enough funds for medical supplies and to build over four hundred primary schools in forty third world countries. Marc, a Rhodes scholar and graduate of Oxford University, was quick to support his brother and has now become the organization's executive director. These two passionate young men have written four books to help educate young people around the world on the importance of getting involved in humanitarian endeavors. To inspire more diversified humanitarian services they established a network called, *Me to We*, which is also the title of their best selling book and their company motto stating, "Regardless of age, one person can make a world of difference!" In addition to their Nobel Prize nominations, Craig and Marc have won numerous international humanitarian awards and have appeared on *CBC, BBC, CNN, Oprah,* and *60 Minutes*.

Life Bliss Tool #5: EDUCATE OURSELVES

I (Claudia) had the pleasure of having dinner one evening with NFL Hall of Fame great Gale Sayers, during an annual *Wednesday's Child* golf tournament in Dallas, Texas. In getting to know each other, we were discussing our current career projects so I shared the premise of *The Masterpiece Within*. I explained how we were gathering quotes for the project and that I would love to get a quote from him because of his inspiring life story. He kindly agreed, sharing his most heartfelt life philosophy; "As you prepare yourself to play, you must prepare yourself to quit. How do you do that? A high school diploma then a college degree, because that gives you something to fall back on and to be a productive person in the community." He went on to further explain one of the biggest problems for players in the NFL is knowing the right time to quit and knowing what they should do with their lives when they retire, since the average career only lasts about three and a half years. We can all relate to this advice, whatever life direction we may choose. Preparing ourselves for change, when change is necessary, will leave us more productive and less frustrated for the next chapter on the horizon.

We may be reluctant at first because a new direction may seem frightening, but having a strong educational background will give us the confidence to face any phase of our lives. There are many educational resources: local college and university classes, Internet sites, libraries, new and used book stores, audiobooks, DVD's, magazines, newspapers, and television programs that contain a plethora of information. We must always remind ourselves life teaches us on a daily basis, and every phase in our lives is just as significant as the last. A helpful tool is to keep an ongoing journal to record these life lessons and observations. Along our journey, it is so important to pay attention to the lessons, to absorb the lessons, and to apply the lessons.

Life Bliss Tool #6: REVISIT CHILDHOOD DREAMS

Taking the time to go back and revisit our childhood dreams can be one of the most beneficial methods to discover our life bliss, similar to Mitch in *City Slickers* when he revisited his childhood dream of being a cowboy. Although he had no desire to become a cowboy full time, the cattle drive allowed him the opportunity to rediscover his life bliss. As we have emphasized in prior chapters, children dream without boundaries and adults have the tendency to place limitations on their dreams and aspirations, causing the innocence of childhood idealism to flicker out. More often than not, when revisiting our childhood dreams, we will find our life bliss turns out to be what we were most passionate about when we were children. If we have forgotten our early childhood dreams, asking family members or childhood friends what we aspired to become may spark our memories. Another way to access our youthful passions is to search back into our past and make a list of dreams we have had over the years. The key is to get our minds into a childlike state and to do whatever it takes to dream without boundaries.

Life Bliss Tool #7: BRAINSTORM

If we feel our creativity needs to be sparked or we need a little help with our life direction, brainstorming is a great exercise. We can approach brainstorming in a couple of ways, either with a group or on our own. Having a brainstorming party and inviting a few trusted friends or family members can help open our eyes to options and possibilities we may have never considered previously. We should make it a fun activity by providing drinks, snacks, as well as pen and paper for others to make a list of our talents, gifts, and strengths. As a side benefit they may ask for the same advice in return. Oftentimes, others are able to see our gifts and strengths much easier than we can. When we are on our own, we can brainstorm by keeping a note pad handy at all times as we experience life, or by keeping a running list of interests that sound exciting or inspiring. These ideas can come from strangers, radio, television, films, books, billboards, music, magazines, or even newspaper want ads. Asking ourselves questions can once again be very enlightening. "What do I find myself daydreaming about doing? If money were not an option what would I choose to do with my life? What do I enjoy doing so much that I lose track of time? How can I transform these things I enjoy into my genuine life bliss."

Life Bliss Tool #8: RESOLVE CONFLICTS

One of the biggest hindrances to living up to our full potential is our inability to address unresolved conflicts. These conflicts can either manifest within ourselves or with others. Reliving conflicts over and over again in our minds sucks up emotional energy that we could put to better use. If not addressed, these unresolved conflicts will produce even greater fear, frustration, and shame and will eventually overtake our thoughts causing us to become tentative or to steer us away from pursuing our genuine life bliss.

There is an old Jewish proverb that says, "To be afraid of a man creates a trap, but he who trusts in God is kept safe." Meaning, if our emotional focus is on someone we are afraid of or intimidated by, we will become trapped into living well under our potential. Some theologians even imply that our personal growth will plateau at the juncture where we allow the person we are fearing to influence how we make choices. But, if we can keep our focus on living by our convictions, we will be kept safe in the sense that we are free to live as we were intended to live; making life choices based in love and not in fear.

In order to heal a conflict, we must either let go of or work through the issues we have with this person until we are able to gain peace of mind. Working through the conflict would involve confronting the conflict or individual head on either in person, through a phone call, or in a letter. Ideally, a conflict should be resolved in person, but if a face to face meeting is not an option, a phone call is the next best choice. A letter should be considered as our third option especially if we feel a meeting could cause us possible harm. We also highly recommend never trying to resolve the conflict through electronic communication tools, such as texting, emails or social media. More often than not, these exchanges have the potential to become a breeding ground for further misundertandings and even greater hurt.

If the situation calls for simply letting go, because the person causing us emotional distress has no clue a conflict even exists, or if approaching them would clearly complicate matters further, we recommend a simple letter writing ceremony. This ceremony consists of writing down all our feelings against the offender until we feel we have addressed every issue. We then take the paper and burn it in a safe place while repeating, "I release (insert name here) completely of my conflict," until we feel at peace and no longer a prisoner to the strife. Whether the conflict is unresolved within ourselves or with another person, this letter writing exercise is often therapeutic because it helps us clear the air, regain a clear perspective, and carry on cultivating our life bliss.

Life Bliss Tool #9: GENEROSITY

Actor Sharon Stone, and former NFL coach Sam Wyche, have spoken often during interviews about how active they are volunteering in soup kitchens and inner city relief centers. They both believe generosity helps them maintain tender hearts, helps them gain perspective on how blessed they are in life, and helps them clarify their life purpose. On the other end of the spectrum, nothing can stall our life progress like a closed heart.

I (Guy) have seen this shift happen over and over again in the ministry profession. The majority of ministers start out with the good intentions serving others and to live a life of generosity. Sadly, however, for some a shift in focus begins to emerge from love and service to "What's in it for me." When a secure paycheck or the not so attractive addiction of prestige or ego stroking becomes the primary motivator in the minister's life, he or she will inevitably lose their edge. When this shift occurs, cynacism, emptiness, and disillusionment will often take over and the ministers focus swings from love and service to maintaining status quo. Unless a minister is able to rediscover their original intentions, not only will their inner life suffer, but a real subtle form of self-serving spirituality will be promoted within their sphere of influence, rather than one of unselfish love and generosity. Making a conscious effort to be more generous with our time, money, and resources will provide room in our hearts to freely explore and come to a deeper understanding of our life bliss. Hopefully we will inspire others to do the same. We can exhibit generosity in small ways, i.e., opening doors for strangers, letting someone in front of us on the freeway, volunteering in an area of passion or where we know a need exists.

Life Bliss Tool #10: JOURNAL

There are those who love to journal while others feel it takes a special disposition. If the privacy factor is an issue, our recommendation is to write anyway because of its therapeutic value. One way to deal with these fears is to buy a small lock box or to release our feelings on paper and safely dispose of the pages upon completion. The most obvious benefits of journaling we are looking for with this exercise is to help us to discover our life bliss. However, additional benefits include keeping us organized, providing a safe place to vent our feelings, to clarify our thoughts and goals, and to increase our creativity. Some of the approaches to journaling include scheduling a certain time of day to journal, and to make a list of our goals, fears, insecurities, failures, successes, and dreams. We can start by choosing a journal that appeals to our sense of self, one large enough for a briefcase or purse, or small enough to fit in a pocket. Consider purchasing one containing some of our favorite quotes, or made of our favorite color. Bookstores seem to carry the most extensive collection. Writing first thing in the morning may help us set the tone for our day, or writing at night before bed may help us to relax and unwind, even if we only write a few lines. After a short period of time, we may find this exercise not only helps us identify our life bliss, but the activity becomes more therapeutic than we ever imagined.

In his book, *The Success Principles*, Jack Canfield provides his insight on journal writing; "*Many people have their greatest success accessing intuitive information through journal writing. Take any questions that you need an answer to and just start writing about it. Write down the answers to your questions as quickly as they come to you. You will be amazed at the clarity that can emerge from this process.*"

Life Bliss Tool #11: REMAIN OPEN-MINDED

Taking my (Claudia) nieces, Sydney and Hannah, and nephew Zak on a yearly summer adventure is one of the highlights of my year. In the summer of 2013, after making our way back to Nashville, I discovered a man who owned a glass blowing shop in the quaint downtown area of Franklin. I called and made an appointment with Jose Santisteban for the four of us to take a class with him. The experience was new for all of us as we marveled at Jose's technique and mimicked his skills as best we could. In getting to know him, we asked how he discovered glass blowing. He revealed that he was attending Vanderbilt University and was two weeks away from graduating as a double major in Literature and Philosphy when a friend invited him to a lecture on campus by famed glass artist, Dale Chihuly. Jose was fascinated. Upon graduation, he met a friend of a friend, who studied under Chihuly. His new friend was intrigued with Jose's excitement and invited him to come live above his studio in Seattle to learn his craft. Jose went on to study glass blowing at Washington State and in New York, Alabama, and Italy before moving back to Tennessee and opening his own shop. Jose said, "Literally the first day working with glass, I knew it was what I wanted to do the rest of my life."

Life Bliss Tool #12: SUPPORT TEAM

We have all been around people who love to smile, laugh, enjoy living, and have a positive outlook on life. We rarely, if ever, walk away from these people without feeling energized and refreshed. On the other end of the spectrum, when we have been exposed to individuals who are grumpy, angry, resentful, and negative about almost everything, they often leave us feeling cynical and uninspired. The environment we place ourselves in has the power to profoundly affect our moods and attitudes. In the process of cultivating our life bliss, it is vital that we monitor our surroundings very carefully. Negative influences have the potential to stall our growth while positive influences can accelerate our growth.

In the film, *Bend It Like Beckham,* Jess, a very talented soccer player, played by Parminder Nagra, finds support in an unconventional manner. She has no parental or family support, because they believe a young Indian woman should be raising babies instead of playing sports, so she places posters of British soccer star, David Beckham, on her bedroom ceiling and walls to serve as inspiration. Although she has never met him, whenever Jess feels discouraged, she goes into her room and talks to Beckham as if he were in the room with her. He is the only one in the house who understands her dreams. Time and time again, after venting to Beckham, she is able to find her motivation to continue on despite her family's lack of support.

A good way to begin forming a support team is by identifying friends or family members who always pull for us as our own personal cheerleaders. We can spend more time with them by asking for their wisdom or gaining their insights on life, and in exchange we can help to encourage them with their dreams. Joining groups with like-minded people, such as local art classes, recreational sports teams, community associations, and charity organizations can provide new friendships, which will naturally influence us to clarify our life bliss. Remaining open-minded and personable with others is key to forming strong relationships.

> *You gave me the greatest gift of all… you believed in me.*
> Rodney Copperbottom to his father Herb, in the film, *Robots*

Life Bliss Tool #13: STEPPING STONES

Sometimes we are lucky enough to discover our life bliss early on in life. We may have a certain dream job in mind, but due to circumstances or limited opportunities, we may feel we will never have the privilege of working in our ideal career. Finding jobs or opportunities, which supplement or parallel our life bliss, will serve to keep our passion and creativity alive. Harrison Ford realized upon taking a drama course in college that he was destined to be an actor. In his journey to becoming a full time actor, he worked diligently to hone his craft. He set his goals and would not sway from his beliefs and principles.

He moved to California and began to pursue his career as an actor. He refused to take roles in anything other than film and theater. Ford had always enjoyed making things with his hands, from stage sets to signs to model trains so he decided carpentry would provide his creative outlet while paying the bills. His first job was building a recording studio for musician Sergio Mendes, a job he had heard about through a friend. When Mendes talked to Ford about the project, he was so impressed with his enthusiasm and detailed blueprint that he hired him on the spot. He became known as "carpenter to the stars," due to his high quality workmanship. He worked his way up to leading man status while using his creative outlet as a stepping stone. He was also able to put his carpentry skills to work in numerous films such as, the barn-raising sequence in the film, *Witness*. He has often said he could have easily remained a carpenter and still have been extremely happy, because he loved carpentry so much. Sometimes we may feel stuck in a career that is not our lifelong dream, but if we understand it is providing an outlet and possible stepping stone to finding our genuine life bliss, we will have more patience with the process.

While on the path to discovering our genuine bliss, we will need to embrace patience and determination. If we are experiencing dead end roads, after many attempts to cultivate a specific direction for our life bliss, it may be time to re-evaluate our plan of attack. Not that we have to completely give up on our dreams, but we may simply need to fine tune or readjust them, because we do not have the skills or internal makeup to see them into fruition. Continually using the tools in this chapter can help us gain the clearer vision we may need. Enjoying and savoring every moment of the journey is extremely important, because of all the beneficial lessons we will learn along the way aiding us in cultivating our genuine life bliss. As long as we remind ourselves to always follow the yearnings of our heart, we will be lead in the right direction.

In the Brazilian fable, *The Alchemist*, Paulo Coehlo beautifully illustrates the story of Santiago, a shepherd boy who yearns to travel and follow his dreams. Night after night, Santiago has the same reoccurring dream of finding his riches near the Pyramids. He makes the courageous decision to leave his homeland, and set off on a mystical adventure to Egypt. On his journey he finds wisdom in listening to his, "Never quiet heart" and comes to understand that no heart has ever suffered when it goes in search of its dreams. Each person Santiago encounters plays a key role in getting him closer and closer to Egypt. When he finally reaches the Pyramids, he meets a man who tells him he too had a recurrent dream. *"I dreamed that I should travel to the fields of Spain and look for a ruined church where shepherds and their sheep slept. In my dream, there was a sycamore growing out of the ruins of the sacristy, and I was told that if I dug at the roots of the sycamore, I would find a hidden treasure. But I'm not so stupid as to cross an entire desert just because of a recurrent dream."*

Santiago's heart was bursting with joy because the stranger had just described an abandoned church near his home; he now knew where he could find his treasure. After years of being away, he returns home and does indeed discover a treasure chest filled with Spanish gold and precious stones, just where the stranger had told him. He placed trinkets he had collected on his journey into the chest to serve as reminders of the lessons he had learned. Through reflection on his adventure, he came to understand many things: love, faith, letting go of fear, and "It's true; life really is generous to those who pursue their destiny."

CHAPTER 11

MAJOR LIFE BLISS BARRIERS

A man does what he must, in spite of personal consequences,
in spite of obstacles and dangers and pressures.

John F. Kennedy

In 1937, Karoly Takacs of Hungary won the World Pistol Shooting Championship almost assuring himself the chance at a spot on the 1940 Hungarian Olympic team. Then in 1938 while serving in the Hungarian army, Takacs had a grenade explode in his right hand, his shooting hand, destroying it completely. Determined to compete in the sport he loved and to return to a world caliber level, he taught himself how to shoot all over again, this time using his left hand. Unfortunately World War II broke out canceling both the 1940 and the 1944 Olympic Games. In 1948, the Olympic Games resumed in London. Takacs, at the age of thirty-eight, qualified for the games and entered the competition as an expected underdog. He surprised everyone when he won the gold medal by a large margin, setting a new world record. He went on to repeat his gold medal performance in Helsinki at the 1952 Olympic games.

Karoly's story is an illustration that shows us how we all have the ability to overcome barriers when the desire and commitment to live in our life bliss is strong. Recognizing these barriers is often half the battle in eliminating them from our lives, much like a wise therapist knows how to get his client to talk at least fifty percent of the time in order to identify their problems and to accelerate the healing process. The client learns to find solutions by venting and talking his way into healing through self-discovery and awareness. In seeking to discover our life bliss, there are a number of barriers that need to be dealt with effectively. In the following pages, we have identified major barriers and have included concise solutions to manage these barriers. Once we identify and begin to manage the key barriers in our lives, our genuine life bliss will become clearer and more achievable.

MAJOR LIFE BLISS BARRIERS

Life Bliss Barrier #1: EXPECTATIONS OF PERFECTION

One of the most lethal barriers to discovering our life bliss is striving for unrealistic perfection. We are often lead to believe that if we achieve a certain level of perfection, we will be considered successful. These self-defeating expections can whitewash the entire purpose of the human experience, because no one should expect constant perfection from themselves. Life should be thought of as a continual learning and growing process, but our current society fools us into thinking we can rely on various quick fixes to achieve happiness and the perfect life experience. Out of desperation, we anxiously hope and pray for "aha" moments or accelerated personal growth experiences to relieve us of our pain. The desire for quick fixes explains one of the major reasons we see massive sales of lottery tickets, increased fast food options, continual new fads in diet books, miracle-claiming exercise programs, psychic hot lines, get rich quick schemes, sex hot lines, and fountain of youth products. When we ask ourselves what have we bought into lately hoping for an immediate life changing miracle, we may realize how focused we have become on quick fix solutions that yield only temporary results. Therefore the, "why even try" attitude eventually creeps in and dominates our thoughts. With this kind of pressure and endless cycle yielding lackluster results, no wonder domestic violence, alcohol and drug abuse, eating disorders, obesity, shopaholic tendencies, credit card debt, and the breakdown of family is at an all time high.

The fashion industry has taken hits for years over how thin models appear in magazines, and lately, the focus seems to be expanding to include film and television stars. The camera typically adds ten pounds to one's physical appearance, so imagine how thin some performers actually are in person. Of course, fashion manufacturers and film and television producers are not concerned about the emotional issues of their stars, or their consumers when a negative bottom line could cost them their jobs. Profit is their priority. If the general public feels pressure to look thin, imagine the constant scrutiny those in the entertainment arts go through who are expected to appear physically lean to keep their jobs. We as a society have not only come to expect perfection from ourselves, but we have placed even greater expectations on our sports heroes, movie stars, music idols, and supermodels.

Pro golfer, Ben Hogan, was known as the most fanatical perfectionist on the Professional Golfers' Association (PGA) Tour during his era. Midway through his career while playing in a tournament, Hogan returned to his hotel room complaining once again to his wife, Valerie, his frustrations over not being able to achieve perfection in his game. She finally had enough of Ben's unrealistic expectations and cried out, "You'll never be perfect, nobody is perfect. Can't you just be satisfied with being the most consistent golfer on the tour?" For Hogan this was revolutionary! He realized Valerie was right. No human can be perfect. He then understood that although he may never golf the perfect round, he could now strive to be the most consistent golfer at minimizing his mistakes. He believed this epiphany was the turning point in his career even though he was already one of the best golfers in the world. He was able to sleep better, practice just as hard but more efficiently, play more consistently, treat his wife with more respect, and appreciate the little things in life. Ben Hogan finally began to enjoy life and to live in his life bliss more effectively.

Solution

The notion of unrealistic perfection can intentionally or unintentionally come from many different sources, i.e., family members, school teachers, coaches, and music instructors. For many of us the primary source comes from being brought up in a religious environment. Whenever we are made to feel like there is very little room for human error or that God is ready to pounce on any little misstep we make, the end result is unnecessary and exaggerated guilt, shame, and fear. Experiencing this overwhelming desire to be flawless places undo pressure on us, which can be so great that we feel like giving up on discovering our life bliss, and on developing a deeper relationship with family members, friends, co-workers, and especially an ogre for a God. When confronting those close to us, we will often find expectations of perfection are not as strong as we imagined. When we study major religions, we find the core teachings do not imply this unrealistic view of perfection. There are realistic standards to live by in authentic spirituality, but does God really expect us to be perfect? It is interesting when the concept of "perfection" is examined from a Hebrew and Greek study of biblical words, the connotation simply means "consistency," which makes more sense of what a loving God would want for us. There is no implication of absolute perfection.

When we strive for consistency, we take the all-encompassing pressure of perfectionistic expectations away, allowing us the freedom for our talents to blossom. We should take pride in knowing we are on the path to becoming a living work of art and applaud and reward ourselves for consistent effort and progress. Rather than investing time, money, and a great deal of hope in dead end quick fix solutions, we would be wise to remind ourselves long-term results require a long-term commitment of consistant hard work.

Life Bliss Barrier #2: THE ENTERTAINMENT CULTURE

The Scott Newman Foundation was formed by Paul Newman and Joanne Woodward in memory of their son Scott, who died of a drug and alcohol overdose in 1978. Their daughter, Susan Kendall Newman, has spoken frequently for the foundation at alcohol and drug abuse symposiums around the continent, sharing her research on how the effects of media and entertainment have impacted our culture. She found that with the advent of television in the mid 1950's a major paradigm shift began to occur. The pre-mid 1950's culture milieu was more predisposed for people to develop their life bliss, because more time was devoted to reading, thinking quietly, and interacting with others. This created a more favorable environment for a hero-participant way of life and the pursuit of life bliss. The cultural adjustment to television moved the pendulum from a participant mentality to more of a spectator mentality that said, "Sit back, relax, and let us entertain you."

We, as a culture, love to be entertained. Every year film box office receipts escalate to an all-time high and sports teams around the globe continue to grow out of their venues, driving the need for larger and grander stadiums. Entertainment can be fun, it can be inspiring, and it can be a great stress reliever, but like anything else in excess, it can be detrimental to our lives. If the pursuit of being entertained becomes an escape, do we escape so far on a regular basis that it leaves us without any time to discover our life bliss? If we are not careful, a subtle way of thinking can creep in where we believe we are following our life bliss when, in fact, we are vicariously living through and faithfully supporting our heroes from our couch at home or our seat in a stadium; we never become the hero of our own life story. This "couch potato" lifestyle could be referred to as, "spectator virtue," because we erroneously believe we are making a considerable contribution to our own lives by cheering on our heroes' successes from our living room. The world around us suffers, because our own gifts and talents are never given the opportunity to come into fruition. It is not so much that we are overtly abusing our world, but if we allow forms of entertainment to consume our lives, we will never find the time to cultivate our own life bliss.

Solution

Resist a spectator virtue lifestyle and be proactive in our own lives. Cheering on our favorite sports teams, watching our favorite television shows, actors, musical artists, reality show stars, etc. is by all means fine in moderation, but if we find ourselves without any time left in the day to develop our own personal growth, valuable life seconds, minutes, months, and eventually years will tick away to our detriment. Schedule in allocated periods to take care of ourselves and to map out forward growth on our masterpiece path. Seek out a friend who desires to discover their masterpiece within and hold each other accountable.

Life Bliss Barrier #3: TRIBAL THINKING

Everyone belongs to a cultural group, whether they are aware of it or not. These groups generally consist of family, work or social groups where people interact on a regular basis. A healthy group or tribe will embrace and encourage those who are following their life bliss even if their paths mean breaking away from the fold. But some members of the tribe may begin to feel threatened when someone wants to break away from unspoken rules governing the group. The main reason this occurs is that the threatened members instinctively know they are falling short of living up to their potential. It is as if a mirror is being held up exposing fear in other tribal members. They are afraid their safe group may break up or they may be held accountable for discovering their own life bliss. A deep fear of abandonment, judgment, and anger may be directed toward the member who wants to break away from the tribe. The end result of tribal thinking, at its worst, is that it can develop an isolated subculture with minimal positive influence in the overall culture. Unless major risks are taken to pursue our life bliss, creativity and learning to think outside the boundaries are stifled. Often it takes a crisis, a dissolution of a tribe, or a tragedy to inspire us to risk change.

Society tends to set us up to believe how our lives should progress: birth, school, college, marriage, children, middle age, retirement, old age, reflection, and then death. These stages in themselves are beneficial for life's learning process, but unless we consciously choose the progression our lives take, we may never find our life bliss. Middle age is sometimes the first time we seriously consider asking ourselves if we are happy with the direction of our lives. This awareness can be a positive reality check causing us to reconsider whether or not we are living as the hero of our life story. Or, it can be a negative jolt where cynicism consumes us and pursuing our life bliss may never be considered again, because we instinctively know that for life to have substance, there must be a connection to living in our bliss.

Solution

The most basic psychological truth is that we as humans have two primary needs: to love and to be loved. For some of us, the biggest hindrance to breaking out of tribal thinking is the fear of being alone. We are afraid the tribe may cast us out, and if that occurs we fear we may never be loved or be part of another tribe again. Whether we want to admit it or not, one of the biggest barriers in pursuing our life bliss is searching for the approval of others first rather than putting our needs and dreams first. Always keep in mind, the responsibility to remain on the path to becoming a living masterpiece, lies in our own hands. Seek out approval from ourselves over the approval of others. Surround ourselves with those who will encourage our hopes and dreams, even if their support has to become long distance in nature. Risk change and reevalute often where we are in our growth on the path of discovering and developing our life bliss.

Life Bliss Barrier #4: VICTIM MENTALITY

Very seldom, if ever, do we find people living fully in their life bliss who consider themselves victims. A victim is a blame-shifter, who feels wronged by their world, and victimized by perceived injustices. Problems are always someone else's fault or the result of circumstances beyond their control. This destructive mind-set prevents them from taking responsibility for their lives, or pursuing their own life bliss.

Actors and screenwriters, Ben Affleck and Matt Damon are excellent examples to show how rejecting the victim mentality can prove to remove boundaries and life restrictions. Over and over again, Hollywood casting directors told Affleck and Damon they were not handsome enough to be cast as leading men. Rather than remaining victims to the auditioning process, they co-wrote a screenplay for the two of them to star in the leading roles. *Good Will Hunting,* went on to win an Oscar for best original screenplay, and the film catapulted Affleck and Damon into instant movie stars. There are always ways around restrictive circumstances, it is only a matter of being patient with the process, being open to alternative options, and creating means to break through limitations set by others.

The victim mentality manifests itself in many different ways. We must first recognize whether or not we are functioning in a victim state, and then identify what excuses keep us there. If we give in to these excuses, we sabotage discovering and cultivating our life bliss. This mentality is the antithesis of choosing wisely and taking responsibility for ourselves. Fear will always be the underlying fuel feeding victim mentality. We can be lead astray from our life bliss when we are seduced by any of the excuses we have identified.

Common Excuses Of Victim Mentality

Excuse #1: LACK OF SKILLS: *"I have absolutely no talent."*

Response: We are all born with many unique talents. We must simply apply the work necessary to unearth our gifts and talents and put them into practice.

Excuse #2: NO CLUE: *"I don't have a clue how to find my talent."*

Response: Having no clue how to uncover our talents is one of the main reasons for writing this manual, particularly this section of *The Masterpiece Within*. Other resources available are through friends, educational institutions, personality tests, and competent counselors.

Excuse #3: ENVIRONMENT: *"You have no idea of my dysfunctional family upbringing or the dead beat town in which I grew up."*

Response: Research has shown that the highest achievers in life tend to come from adverse backgrounds and that second generation children from higher income families tend to under achieve. Sometimes adverse conditions can be the perfect foundation for growth. Remember the ABC's of life, Adversity Builds Character. Low cost therapy is available in many forms through local YMCA's, social service agencies, or self-help books at our neighborhood libraries if we feel we need to go that route first. We may be surprised by what we find when earnestly searching out opportunities in our own communities.

Excuse #4: EDUCATIONAL OPPORTUNITIES: *"I have never had the opportunity to expand my education."*

Response: We have more resources at our disposal than at any other time in history. Consider book stores, libraries, the Internet, affordable community colleges, resource manuals for scholarships, and low interest loans. As the saying goes, "Where there's a will, there's a way."

Excuse #5: FINANCES: *"My family can't and I definitely can't afford to do anything that would give me opportunities to succeed with my dreams."*

Response: When we sincerely pursue our life bliss, we will be amazed at how the door of opportunity often swings wide open. There are many scholarships available that are never even claimed. We can start by talking to counselors at local state schools to find out how to apply for grants, scholarships, and low interest loans. If our life bliss does not require further formal education, yet finances are an issue to continue developing our life bliss, approaching financial backers who are sympathetic toward our dreams may be an option to explore. If we are not comfortable asking for help from others, it may just be a matter of saving our own money until we have the necessary capital.

Excuse #6: NO CONNECTIONS: *"I just don't know the right people and everyone knows it takes connections to get a break in life."*

Response: Sometimes just expressing our talents can create opportunities that we never knew existed. People notice hard workers, because they stand out in a crowd. A strong work ethic and commitment to cultivate our life bliss will attract others who want to encourage and possibly participate in helping us climb the ladder of success.

Excuse #7: COMPARING: *"You don't know the pressure I feel to live up to the success of my family and everyone around me."*

Response: Comparing our lives to the lives of others is unfair and self-deprecating. Each person has his own unique path. Anytime we compare our lives to other's lives, we will be left feeling defeated because there will always be others, whether in our family or not, that are doing better than we are. Seeking to be an original creation is much more fulfilling and admired than settling to be a follower.

Excuse #8: LACK OF SUPPORT: *"How can I ever achieve anything in life? No one ever encourages me in any way."*

Response: Many times we must be our own cheerleader in life. Continually looking for outside moral support and approval will only slow us down. People who live in their life bliss are those who take responsibility for their own dreams. History teaches us that leaders from every era were men and women who withstood long periods of isolation and rejection, yet never lost sight of their dreams.

Excuse #9: RACE: *"My ethnic background works against me."*

Response: We can study examples of other people in our ethnic group that have made a positive impact while being oppressed. There are many impressive examples in all ethnic backgrounds of people who have overcome the grandest of obstacles. Oprah Winfrey has often stated, "Excellence is the best deterrent to racism or sexism."

Excuse #10: GENDER: *"There are few opportunities for my gender."*

Response: We should never underestimate our talents and strengths. If we are really going to live in our calling, we must look for numerous ways to find and seize opportunities when they present themselves, be willing to take risks, and find creative outlets. Hiding our talent behind bitterness and resentment will only serve to sabotage our potential. Hard work and talent, regardless of gender, will eventually get noticed. Studying biographies and memoirs can demonstrate how others were able to take control of their lives.

Excuse #11: COSMOS ALIGNMENT: *"I'll wait for the stars, God or fate to put everything in place."*

Response: There will always be an endless number of excuses that can create a dormant individual. Resolve to live life without regret; sometimes we are too patient and polite. Make everyday count. Take risks. We cannot always wait for permission to take a legitimate chance in life when our dreams are involved, or we may miss out on a moment of opportunity. These excuses are all based around laziness or indecision, and they are mostly rooted in deep-seeded fear. If we are not willing to face our fears head-on, they will rob us of our opportunities for bliss, and will lead to disappointment in our later years. The time is now! We cannot wait a second longer.

Excuse #12: OBVIOUS INJUSTICES: *"No one realizes the hurt and pain I have experienced."*

Response: There is great freedom in the expression and release of internal grief and the act of forgiveness. Not only forgiveness of ourselves for past mistakes and bad choices, but forgiveness of others as well. Some of the most compassionate, caring people have suffered the worst of injustices, yet they have not allowed the causes of their pain to hinder the pursuit of their bliss.

Excuse #13: NO ENERGY: *"I just don't have the energy to do the work, but I wish I did."*

Response: Our energy can become depleted whether from overwork, grief, trauma or just plain laziness. Rest and relaxation is necessary to rejuvenate our bodies, but if we sit back and do nothing for long periods of time, laziness becomes an easy habit to acquire. The longer we sit back and do nothing, the more we reinforce tiredness and a lethargic state of being. People who follow their life bliss have learned how to wear many hats and to juggle their time. As former NFL coach, George Seifert, has said, "A secret to handling a busy schedule is to not get caught up in unnecessary life minutia, but in staying focused on what our primary jobs and priorities in life are. A lot of it is learning to say no and prioritizing."

Solution

An example of someone who refused to live in a "victim mentality" is Oprah Winfrey. Her life could have been a story of tragedy, but instead has become one of miraculous triumph. Born to an unwed mother, raped at nine by a cousin, and soon after by an uncle, Oprah became pregnant at the age of fourteen, giving birth to a son that only lived a short time. Due to her unhealthy surroundings, her mother's frustration, and Oprah acting out in anger, she was sent to live with her biological father Vernon, a move which would prove to be a major turning point in her life. Her new family life had a strong positive influence and much needed structure. She quickly began to turn her life around. No longer did she act out in a destructive, self-abusive manner. She broke free from the barriers and excuses that were obstacles in finding her life bliss.

Oprah has come to be one of the most influential women in the world, creating numerous life changing programs such as the *Angel Network, Oprah's Book Club, and the National Registry for Sex Offenders,* which alerts neighborhoods when convicted sex offenders move into their areas. Oprah is a modern-day warrior who teaches the importance of taking responsibility for ourselves rather than living the victim mind-set. In what Oprah calls her, "full-circle moment" she started a program on her television show in 2005 to capture accused child molesters. She herself offered one hundred thousand dollars to the person or people who turned in these sexual predators. Within the first week, when the first two were captured, she said, *"Raped and molested at nine and fourteen I now get to put behind bars who did to me what they've been doing to others. I am going to keep going until I am able to change the laws in this country state by state by state. I heard the call as if God himself said it to me, and he probably did."*

When we find ourselves venturing down the road of a victim, resist the victim mindset, resist the mind chatter of anger, resist the litany of excuses with all the strength we have, and put a stop to these thoughts as soon as possible. Taking a moment to feel sorry for ourselves is healing but soaking in a pity-party bath for too long will stunt our growth. So why not take a couple of hours or even a full day to fully celebrate our pity-party? Why not buy ourselves a balloon, a small cake, feel the emotions, and acknowledge that we are hurt or deeply disappointed about something? Then after no more than twenty-four hours, let it all go and move on.

Taking control of our thoughts or life circumstances by stepping out with acts of personal power will not only help to make us the hero of our own life story, but we change the lives of those around us for the better in the process. Instead of allowing our anger, resentments, and discouragement to harm us, choose to take the high road, and use the anger we feel as fuel to drive our actions toward living in our genuine life bliss. Make the choice at every turn to be a warrior rather than a victim.

Life Bliss Barrier #5: TOXIC RELATIONSHIPS

We are all exposed to people in our lives who put us down or make light of our dreams and accomplishments whenever we are around them. In some cases, they can be people whose opinion we value, in other cases, they can be people who just do not like us. The bottom line is they are not treating us with the dignity we deserve. Some present themselves as arrogant, but if we get to the root of their behavior, we will be most likely surprised to find they are insecure and jealous of our gifts, talents, or life circumstances. If we are not careful how we interact with toxic people, we can become too discouraged to continue cultivating our bliss. We are not asking to avoid these people at all costs, but for our own mental health it may be necessary for a brief period of time. When walking away from people we believe to be toxic, we should ask ourselves, "How does this person make me feel when I am around them? Do I feel comfortable or irritated? Do I feel bad about myself when I leave their presence? Do I feel less of a person?" We will always encounter toxic people, especially when we are making positive changes in our lives and are energized from living in our life bliss. Our life success and positive example challenges them to take more responsibility for their own lives.

Different Types Of Toxic Relationships

1. Dream Killers: These are the people who try to talk us out of our dreams. They can come up with every excuse why we should not pursue our dreams and they are very pushy with their own ideas for our lives. Again this stems from jealousy, insecurity, and envy. This person may have the same dreams as we do, but lack the talent or drive we have. Thus the jealous attitude of, "If I can't do it, no one in my life will do it either." When people feel they have to belittle our dreams, it is as if they are trying to steal our souls. We must be careful when sharing our hopes and dreams with others. Dream killers are spectators just waiting to destroy our enthusiasm by trying to bring us down to their levels so they will not feel like failures themselves.

2. Energy vampires: If we encounter certain types of people who drain our energy by just being around them, chances are they are energy vampires. Usually these people feel negative about their lives and are not willing to work on their own life bliss. They survive on the stories of our success by draining us with questions every time we are around them. Another form of an energy vampire is someone who is not satisfied unless he has one-upped everyone in the room. He believes his stories, life experiences, projects, and dreams are better and more interesting than anyone else's on the planet. Although energy vampires may appear very confident with their outward demeanor, their inner reality is that they have very low self-esteem and are dominated by their insecurities.

3. Fixers: Fixers are those who have the answer for everyone else's lives, yet they never seem to focus on taking care of their own life issues. Telling others what to do gives them a sense of importance. Fixers make us question our choices, question our dreams, and can cause us to feel stupid, sad, lost, and worthless by their toxic behavior. These people seldom, if ever, put in any effort to develop their own life bliss, because it is too much work or too painful to face their own reality.

4. Abusers: Abusers can be the most dangerous people to have in our lives. Not only do they attack us emotionally and mentally, but our physical lives may also be at risk. We must take steps to eliminate this kind of person from influencing or having an effect on our lives. These people mirror their own self hate back to us. They are steadfast in the belief that someone needs to take the blame for their failures and it certainly will not be themselves.

5. Negative social groups: As long as we feel a sense of comfort, security, and acceptance from a group, we may feel a sense of responsibility to remain a part of it, regardless of whether it is healthy for our personal growth or not. Alcoholics Anonymous coined the term, "stinkin' thinkin'" to describe this kind of unhealthy behavior. This statement refers to when we know we should remove ourselves from a bad situation, but we feel trapped, and for whatever reason we will not take the necessary steps to get out. Sure signs of a toxic social group appear when our needs are never validated, when we cannot be honest in a group, and when there is an atmosphere of denial.

Solution

In our quest to discover and cultivate our life bliss, one of the toughest barriers to break through is in the area of toxic relationships. This task can be difficult when dealing with people who have underlying jealousy issues with us, especially when they belong to our inner circle and with whom we have continual exposure. We can either work to resolve the negative issues, or we can keep an emotional or physical distance at all times. For example, sometimes we are feeling healthy in our emotional and mental state and we can handle being around certain toxic people. We have the energy to be cordial, yet we are strong enough to keep an emotional distance. At other times, we might have to remove ourselves physically for a period of time from the toxic situation or person to protect ourselves during vulnerable times. Choosing our circle of influence must be done with great care and consideration.

Dick Vermeil, the highly successful football coach and television analyst stated, "Finding good character players is vital; eliminating bad character players is even more vital." Vermeil stressed the importance of firmly dealing with toxic people in order for individuals or teams to reach their desired goals. This process takes time and diplomacy, because wide sweeping changes of this nature cannot be put into place over night. The elimination of these toxic influences must begin immediately. Surrounding ourselves with positive people and those on the path of discovering their own masterpiece within provides us with allies to advise us and protect us from those who wish to do us harm.

Life Bliss Barrier #6: UNDISCIPLINED TALENT

There are many individuals with obvious talent, but when discipline is neglected, talent remains dormant. Those who are willing to pursue their life bliss tend to become very frustrated with this kind of individual, especially if they long for the same gifts the undisciplined individual is abusing.

I (Guy) was counseling a man who was struggling with how to deepen his spirituality and to bring the spark back into his marriage. He is a multi-talented individual who seems to master whatever he tries. Yet, his discipline from a spiritual and marital perspective was in an underachieving mode. I was brainstorming for ways to challenge him, so I went outside for a walk. Remembering he was a big hockey fan, an idea crossed my mind to go down to the local sports collectors store and buy him two hockey cards. One was Jaromir Jagr, who has played for teams such as the Pittsburgh Penguins and the Washington Capitals, and who is a five time points scoring leader in the National Hockey League. The other player was Petr Klima, a multi-year veteran of pro hockey who has bounced around from team to team. Both players grew up in former Communist Czechoslovakia and came to North America as two of the top blue-chip recruits ever to play in the NHL.

When they broke into pro hockey, there were little if any discernible differences in their skills. Their potential was evident even to the casual fan. As Jagr's skills and talents grew into superstar status, Klima never seemed to live up to his potential. He could be a human highlight reel one night and barely noticeable the next. Jagr did live up to his potential and beyond. Many consider him the best player in the world in the 1990's, while Klima bounced around the NHL and minors for over ten years. No one ever doubted his ability, yet he so underachieved. In purchasing these two cards, I asked the store owner the price. He found a beat-up Jagr card for six dollars but told me a mint condition card could run up to one hundred dollars or higher. He then said, "I should just give you the Klima card, because it is only worth five cents."

The difference between the two talents was summed up by then Edmonton Oiler General Manager, Glen Sather, "Jaromir Jagr is an extremely talented hard worker who knows the value of discipline and commitment. Petr Klima is always, and I mean always, the last player on the ice for practice and the very first player off the ice." Jagr is headed for the Hall Of Fame, and Klima may be remembered as one of the most underachieving talents in hockey history.

I shared this story with the man I was counseling. He took it better than expected and placed the two cards in a plastic covering, keeping them in his wallet as a reminder of the necessity to link discipline with talent. Seven years later, he brought out his wallet to show me he still used the two cards as inspiration. To his credit, he incorporated definite steps of discipline to improve his life, and because of this, he deepened his spirituality and created a stronger marital bond.

Solution

Thomas Edison said, "Opportunity is missed by most people because it is dressed in overalls and it looks like work." All the talent in the world can only take a person so far. Without discipline, one underachieves, cheats themselves, and also cheats those around them who could benefit from their gifts. We need to continually challenge ourselves to be, "can-doers" and to put in the hard work necessary to live up to our fullest potential. And, always keep in the forefront of our minds, to strive to beat our personal best through consistant hard work.

Life Bliss Barrier #7: UNHEALTHY EGO

A healthy ego can act as a protective shield along life's journey, driving us to accomplish our dreams and goals. An unhealthy ego can lead us down a self-serving, self-consuming empty abyss. Living in the height of total selfishness in an unhealthy ego state can be enjoyable for a short length of time, but after this deceptive state runs its course, and it always does, we are left feeling empty and alone. Most of us have had moments of feeling like a big fish in a little pond and also feeling like a minnow in a large lake, but unless we are able to handle this power or insecurity with maturity we will never be able to discover or cultivate our life bliss.

My (Claudia) friend, Jedd Hughes, a talented songwriter and musical artist from Australia, was telling me about the popular phrase, "tall poppy syndrome" used in his homeland when referring to those with an unhealthy ego. Poppies grow with such a long stem that whenever they are among other flowers, they will always stand out as the tallest in the field. It is as if the poppy or person is saying, "Look at me I'm over here and I'm the most important in the field or crowd." We all want to feel important in the world, but if we allow an unhealthy ego to dictate our thoughts, actions, and interaction with others our false sense of self-importance and arrogance will create a barrier between us, other people, and our life bliss.

We can also explore an unhealthy ego from the flip side as if someone has a "short poppy syndrome" if you will. There are those of us who for one reason or another hide from life in a multitude of ways. We do not want to stand out in a crowd and if we ever do receive attention, we are mortified and wait months or even years to risk being in a public setting again. We spend our lives watching others have fun and engage in social activities, all the while wishing we could be a part of a cool and accepting crowd.

Solution

We need loving and supportive relationships in order to attain our life bliss. Unless we take a more humble approach with others, the barriers to bliss will continue to grow. And, unless we break out of our own self-imposed prisons, we may never be able to fully discover and develop our life bliss. It is vital to challenge ourselves to be team players and to wholly embrace that we are all equals. We all face a new day with new choices to make. Learning to be honest and real with ourselves in making our choices and honing our people skills, allows a clearer and more supported path to our life bliss. A genuinely beautiful poppy will always be recognized and appreciated. And, we will always be recognized and appreciated if we choose to live with passion, integrity, and character.

Life Bliss Barrier #8: CONFIDENCE CRISIS

Having worked in the entertainment industry for most of my adult life, I (Claudia) have experienced my own fair share of rejection over the years leaving my confidence bruised and occasionally shattered. Somehow I have always managed to find ways to regain my confidence. I often dreamed of the time when my confidence would no longer go through these low periods, and expected once I was able to achieve a certain level of success my confidence would remain steadfast and strong no matter what negativity came my way. I also imagined when I had the honor of meeting A-list actors, sports stars, and music stars they would not only have a high level of confidence, but these stars would never experience low or crisis moments in their confidence. Meeting numerous celebrities over the years, I quickly discovered just because someone has achieved a high level of success, does not make them immune to experiencing a crisis of confidence. Cindy Pearlman, of the *Chicago Sun-Times,* interviewed actor Matt Damon. He discussed this very subject saying, "You can look at me and think this guy has it all, but let me tell you, I don't think anyone in the business feels secure. Ever." It has been my experience that no matter what level of success a person achieves, we are still human and will have times when we feel insecure, particularly those of us in the entertainment business, because our work is constantly being scrutinized in the public arena.

In 1983, I (Guy) went through a crisis of confidence and faith, where my doubts about my own inner confidence and God's reality were questioned to the point of utter despair. St. John of the Cross referred to this kind of experience as, "The dark night of the soul." This period of my life lasted for almost six months, and was easily one of the toughest emotional times of my life. I would walk for hours and hours, talking to myself and to a God I was not even sure existed, trying to get answers and soul relief. What eventually helped me get through this inner crisis was reading some ancient wisdom I found in Psalms 77 where the writer, Asaph, describes his own dark night of the soul. He was able to pull himself out of his dark night when, "He remembered the deeds of the Lord." I immediately sat down and divided a piece of paper into three columns. In the first column, I recorded times in my life where I had achieved significant accomplishments, or the times when God seemed very real to me. In the second column, I recorded stories from people I knew and trusted who had overcome adversity through their faith in God, or had experienced modern day miracles. In the third column, I recorded stories from books I had read or speakers I had listened to that gave me hope my life really did matter, and that reinforced my faith in God. The majority of my list was in column one. This exercise did not completely restore my confidence overnight, but it did restore a strong element of hope in my life.

The original piece of paper has evolved into a fairly thick book, which I now call my, "Hope Journal." I can honestly say since beginning this journal, it has been my primary tool to help me sustain hope when my confidence was hanging by a thin thread. And, believe me, I have been tested many times.

In a real dark night of the soul it is always 3:00 in the morning.

F. Scott Fitzgerald

From February 2008 until November 2012, I (Guy) went through a series of intense setbacks and angst that tested my confidence and hope, like I had never experienced. St. John of the Cross explained such a season of life as, "Phase two of the dark night of the soul." He explained that this season of setbacks or traumas are generally not self-induced, although they are co-mingled with our choices and reactions, through this season of purification and intense personal growth. Thankfully, prior to "Dark Night II," during a time of prayer, I had what can only be explained as a sacred encounter warning me of a challenging time ahead. The message, felt deep in my soul, gave me reassurance I would not be alone, but that I would experience loneliness and feelings of being forsaken at a level I had never encountered before. If not for his harbinger, I do not know how I would have coped with the next four years. Let me explain…

This day began during the 2007 Grey Cup in Toronto, where my favorite sports team since I was a kid, The Saskatchewan Roughriders, were playing for the championship of the Canadian Football League against their fiercest rival, the Winnipeg Blue Bombers. Roughrider defensive coordinator and friend, Richie Hall, called and asked me to join him for breakfast. I felt honored, as he had his entire family, his fiance, the coaching staff, and the players to choose from. We had one of the best heart to heart talks about life we had ever had. No football talk. My time with Richie almost seemed sacred, so maybe the stage was being set for what happened to me later that night.

The Grey Cup was a beauty! I was able to witness rare history as my one hundred-plus year old football team won their third championship in a last minute victory that led to a celebration of players and fans like I had never seen before. Nobody wanted to leave Rogers Skydome. This was easily one of my best days ever. I was sitting beside an eighty year old man who had traveled two thousand miles, and had witnessed all the heartbreak the Roughriders had given fans over the years (think Cubs or Red Sox and their history). With tears streaming down his cheeks, he wore a look of satisfaction that if he died that night his life was complete.

A few hours after the celebrations had died down, I went back to the house where I was staying, knelt by my bed and thanked God for the gift of a wonderful day. Thoughts of gratitude flooded my soul, mixed with feelings hard to describe. It was not ominous but more like an old friend wrapping their arms around me. These are the words that captured my mind clear as a bell, "This weekend was a gift for your faithfulness. This next little while is going to be really hard, but trust Me you will be okay, and you will be a better person because of this next season of life."

The blows were harsh. After twenty-six years of marriage my wife asked me for a divorce that I truly never saw coming. I never knew the depths of loneliness a person could feel. Then I lost a dream job as the communications manager for the Billy Graham Association, due to the economic crisis in 2008 that set me on a path of dusting off my resume on more than a few occassions. I had to bury two wonderful dogs fours years apart. It was gut wrenching to be by their sides as they passed on. In both cases, they were in pain and crying out to me for comfort. A week after my second dog died, I lost one of my favorite cousins, who died after a lifelong battle with addictions. I then experienced another failed relationship due to my own poor decision making. Years of bittersweet, but the one word that sustained me like no other, Hope!!

I do not know how many times in the next handful of years the, "hopeful moments" listed in my Hope Journal, served as my anchor. Looking back, I almost doubled the items during my "Dark Night II" years. In August 2012, I shared the idea of my Hope Journal with a teenager in Colorado named, Kiley Thomas. She thought it was the coolest idea ever and wanted to start her own. A few months later on my birthday, Kiley surprised me with one of the most cherished gifts I have ever been given, a new handmade Hope Journal.

My Hope Journal is always near me at home and is usually one of the first things I pack when going on a trip. I may not even open this journal for a couple of months or add anything to it, but just knowing it is close by at all times seems to bring reassurance that I am not alone and that my confidence can be rejuvenated.

Solution

Two-time Nobel Prize recipient, Marie Currie so eloquently stated, "Life is not easy for any of us. But what of that? We must have perseverance and above all confidence in ourselves. We must believe that we are gifted for something and that this thing, at whatever cost, must be attained." We are all fragile beings. Whether our confidence wanes for a fleeting moment or even on up to a full blown crisis, the sooner we address this barrier head on, the easier it will be to remain on the path to discovering and cultivating our life bliss. If left unmanaged, we stand a greater chance of becoming cynical or completely paralyzed in self-doubt. Our choices and behaviors will then become completely irrational and often destructive in nature or overly cautious where we retreat to a pseudo sense of safety. One way to prevent a crisis of confidence from occurring in the first place is to resist any form of negative sponsoring thoughts. These thoughts are the opinions we carry with us about ourselves. If we can train our sponsoring thoughts to be more positive in nature on a daily basis, via brain medicine and the principles in this book, when we come anywhere near the right conditions for a confidence crisis to break out, we will be better equipped to resist opening the door to disaster.

Life Bliss Barrier #9: REGRET

Initially we had planned to address eight major barriers, but after conducting interviews, surveys, and seminars we found many people felt that regret was a huge emotional barrier to overcome in order for them to discover their life bliss. Often the reason given was the older they became, the harder it was to bounce back from life failures or setbacks. They were often left feeling numb, paralyzed, and overwhelmed. There is nothing more frustrating when it comes to regret than getting caught up in the "woulda, shoulda, coulda syndrome. " Where we find ourselves saying, "If only I could have...What if I would have...?" There is no need to beat ourselves up and allow the feelings to eat us up to the point of sickness or terminal disease. We must remind ourselves everyone experiences failure and disappointment, and that if we had developed the skills or had more information at the time to make better choices, we would have acted accordingly. As one studies biographies and memoirs, we learn very quickly that no one has a completely smooth ride through life. It is impossible. If someone says they have never had any regrets in life, they are not looking hard enough, or they are the kind of person that puts a positive thinking spin on everything for fear that they will jinx themselves. Even the most highly successful person will tell us that their successes were more often than not preceeded by failure.

Solution

While struggling with regret one day, I (Claudia) became determined to find a way to turn my pain into power. I decided instead of reliving my regretful moment with the negative outcome playing over and over inside my head and torturing myself emotionally day after day, what if I relived the moment in my mind, choosing a better direction this time? I was amazed at how effective this exercise proved to be. I decided to run moments of regret from my entire life due to the lack of choice education through my new process and discover my power in each situation.

I have to say this exercise was not only monumental in working through past regret, but when facing current moments of decision making, I was able to act from a place of power, instead of the role of victim. As a wonderful proverb I found states, "A man is not old until his regrets take the place of his dreams." I cleared room in my thoughts to focus on my future dreams rather than my past regrets. Much like when Alexander Graham Bell said, "When one door closes another door opens: but we so often look so long and so regretful upon the closed door, that we do not see the ones which open for us." We must learn to address and feel the feeling, grieve over past choices, dust off our failures, move them out of the way, and try over again.

No matter what barriers are thrown upon our life path, overcoming or removing them is our personal responsiblity. No one else can do the work for us. We must be willing to take one day at a time and deal with each obstacle immediately when it comes our way. The sooner we learn to manage the barriers in our lives, the easier it will be to live in our life bliss.

Sociologist and author, Malcolm Gladwell, makes a great case for spending ten thousand hours developing our craft in his book, *Outliers*. He believes that the greatest athletes, musicians, scientists, and entrepreneurs spend at least three hours daily honing and mastering their craft. The beauty of this is, when we discover our life bliss, we naturally want to constantly develop it. The daily development of our bliss is simply a matter of managing our time and any obstacles in our way.

CHAPTER 12

WORKBOOK CHALLENGES IV

GET TO KNOW ME

1. Am I living my genuine life bliss? Yes _____   No _____   Somewhat _____

2. My genuine life bliss is _____

   _____

   My bliss encounter includes_____

   _____

3. Identify the major barriers that tend to hold me back the most.

   Expectations of perfection____   The entertainment culture____   Tribal thinking____

   Victim mentality____   Toxic relationships____   Undisciplined talent____

   Unhealthy ego____   Confidence crisis____   Regret____

4. Identify the tools that I can embrace to minimize these barriers.

   Inner voice____   Solitude date/retreat____   Experiment____

   Never too young-never too old____   Educate ourselves____   Revisit childhood dreams____

   Brainstorm____   Resolve conflicts____   Generosity____   Journal____

   Remain open-minded____   Support team____   Stepping stones____

5. What major barriers have I overcome in the past that I can learn from now?

    1. _____

    2. _____

    3. _____

6. Who are the toxic people in my life or what excuses are negatively distracting?

    1. _____

    2. _____

    3. _____

PRACTICAL POWER TOOLS

1. Review, "Tools to Discover and Cultivate Life Bliss." Choose three or four that you can try out as soon as possible.

2. Spend time with a child. Children play and think freely without any boundaries. They dream about, play, and act out their bliss. Observe their childlike qualities and maybe even join in. This should trigger your memories as a child, reminding you what seemed really exciting to do with your life at an early age when life possibilities were without limits.

3. Volunteer. Volunteering in an area of interest can reignite your passions, or help you rediscover what they really are. At the very least, you have softened your heart to become more passionate by doing this good deed. According to the Sioux Nation, "Generosity keeps the heart tender."

4. Ask an elder. Find someone who has lived in their bliss. Discover their attitudes, sacrifices, inner characteristics, and how they dealt with adversity and mistakes. You can learn from their work ethic, maturity, insights, and life wisdom. As King Solomon stated, "He who walks with the wise, becomes wise."

5. Create a Hope Journal. When we find ourselves in a confidence crisis we will need a tool of encouragement to get us back on track. Creating this journal will prepare us for times

of crisis when our confidence is low or nonexistent. The journal could include a list of accomplishments, the times our lives have really made a difference, answers to prayers, encouraging words from others, and whatever we have done in the past that makes us proud of ourselves. Adding entries when they occur will help us get into the practice of recognizing good things that happen in our lives. Referring back to our Hope Journal on a regular basis, will help prevent the onset of a confidence crisis or keep them to a minimum.

BRAIN MEDICINE   **PERSONAL BRAIN MEDICINE**

1. Anything is possible   1. _____
2. I am extremely talented   2. _____
3. I have a clear path to my genuine life bliss   3. _____
4. I have all the tools I need to cultivate my   4. _____
   genuine life bliss
5. I live my life bliss daily   5. _____

You can't use up creativity. The more you use, the more you have.

Dr. Maya Angelou

LIFE SKILL #4

BALANCING EMOTIONS, SPIRIT, MIND, AND BODY

The self-renewal process must include balanced renewal in all four dimensions of our nature: the physical, the spiritual, the mental, and the emotional. Although renewal in each dimension is important, it only becomes optimally effective as we deal with all four dimensions in a wise and balanced way. To neglect any one area negatively impacts the rest.

Stephen R. Covey, *The 7 Habits of Highly Effective People*

CHAPTER 13

CREATING BALANCE IN THE 21ST CENTURY

Happiness is not a matter of intensity but of balance
and order and rhythm and harmony.

Thomas Merton, French Monk and Poet

In 1997, my (Guy) family and I were privileged to have, Claire Carver-Dias from the Canadian National Syncronized Swimming team, come and live with us for almost five months while she trained in Calgary. Claire was Canada's number one ranked swimmer for a couple of years leading up to the 2000 Barcelona Olympics Games and for the two years following before she retired from the sport. Getting to know Claire, observing how a top level athlete trains for world competition and seeing the importance of seeking to achieve wholeness to maximize high performance was a real education. During a weekend retreat in preparation for the 2000 Olympic Games, the syncro team's coaching staff challenged Claire and her teammates to come up with a mission statement that represented what made them successful in prior competitions and what their overall life goals should be. Their mission statement was as follows:

"Our purpose is to be a team that is strong and true: a team of complete women who are centered by their physical, emotional, mental, and spiritual well-being. We choose to constantly pursue new heights in our quest for Gold Medal Performance at the 2000 Olympic Games and beyond. We believe in honesty, trust, and hard work. We know greatness will result from our passion."

Claire and her Canadian teammates went on to win the bronze medal in the extremely competitive syncronized swimming event in Barcelona, and during her tenure with the national team they always placed on the podium at international events, including World Championships.

As humans, we are integrated beings comprised of four dimensions: mind, body, spirit, and emotions. Many philosophical and spiritual belief systems, through the ages and today, emphasize this school of thought. For example, Judeo-Christian teachings use heart, soul, mind, and strength, Buddhist and Hindu traditions refer to the four dimensions as our body, mind, and soul/spirit, with the mind being a mix of intellect and emotion. The Native American culture uses the Medicine Wheel, which represents the four dimensions coming together as one. The central thought is, in order for us to be "whole" and function at our highest level, we must have a harmonious balance in all four dimensions. In continuing to discover our masterpiece within, we must choose to embrace the art of balancing our emotions, mind, spirit, and body.

The concept behind syncronized swimming serves as an apt analogy to represent how the four dimensions work when they are in balance. When all eight team members are swimming in sync, the performance can be spellbinding because of the harmony of the routine. But, if any of the team members are thrown off for whatever reason, the routine begins to fall apart unless each team member is able to find their way back in unison. We can imagine the four dimensions of mind, body, spirit, and emotion as our personal team members. If we work to balance these "team members," our lives will soon become a well choreographed performance.

If there is a buzz word among elite athletes looking for an edge, it is, "balance." From the 1990's to the present, sports psychologists having been expounding the virtues of developing a more balanced approach towards all of life for athletes. The emphasis begins with primary life balance involving the integration of mind, body, spirit, and emotions, then moves to address the important underlying areas such as expectations, family, vocations, and finances.

The one attribute hockey superstar, Wayne Gretzky, admires when observing elite athletes is how they cope under pressure. Gretzky attended as many curling matches as he could during the 2010 Winter Olympics, in Vancouver. One of the athletes he requested meeting at the Games was Canadian curler, Cheryl Bernard, who became a media darling for her on ice presence, down-to-earth likablity, and coolness under pressure. Bernard's team members were the, "cardiac kids" at both the Canadian Trials and the Olympics. Cheryl had to win almost eighty percent of her games on her last shot, which is the equivalent to a last second shot in basketball. Gretzky said, "Cheryl Bernard is easily the best athlete I have seen at these Olympics in dealing with pressure." What Gretzky did not know, was the inner battle she fought to achieve life balance to get to the place in her life where she seemed to be performing at a whole different level while dealing with pressure.

Cheryl admits to striving for life balance in the years leading up to the Vancouver Games. She knew balance was critical, but was having a difficult time putting it into practice, as most of us do. Her team was one of the best in Canada, but was still considered a darkhorse or outside legitimate contender. Team Bernard had the breakthrough they were looking for when they won the Olympic qualifying tournament, a competition considered the deepest field in Canadian curling history. Cheryl, the skip (or captain) lead the team to a silver medal victory at the 2010 Vancouver Olympics. She talked with us about embracing balance:

"We were exhausted, burnt out. We weren't doing well in events. We were just hanging in, qualifying, but then losing out. Then we started to worry. We couldn't go into the toughest competition in our lives, The Canadian Olympic Trials, like this. Then the pressure started to get to us. The fear and concern were getting overwhelming, almost paralyzing. We were playing scared, playing not to lose. Then one day, I was walking my dog, trying to understand what was wrong. Why were we struggling? And it hit me. We didn't love the game anymore. We didn't love the practice - we weren't enjoying each other. We had lost perspective. WE WEREN'T BALANCED!

So we had a meeting, and we talked, and talked, and we got more and more excited, because it resonated with all of us. Knowing we need balance is one thing, finding it and sustaining it is another. I believe it's an on-going tension throughout life, but somehow we found enough of it, we really found it. Being on the same page with each other as teammates helped, but we also consulted our coach and brought in a sports psychologist. We worked diligently on finding perspective in all phases of the game both on and off the ice. This involved our value systems, along with the mental, emotional, and physical parts of ourselves and spilled into off-ice tensions like family, work, finances, and unspoken expectations.

We asked ourselves why do we play this sport? Because we love curling! What if we don't win the Olympic Trials? Well then we go back to our lives, which are full of great family, friends, and jobs. We all have great lives whether we win or lose. We made a deal to start having fun again, to remember why it is we play the game, to laugh more and to do this all without regrets. We needed to relearn how to want it, but not HAVE to have it. It's all about finding balance…and sustaining it!"

Great philosophers, psychologists, sages, scientists, creeds, cultures, and belief systems throughout history and around the globe have embraced the fine art of balance. Scientist, Sir Isaac Newton's third law of motion says, "For every action, there is an equal reaction." Psychologist, Carl Gustav Jung reminds us, "The word, 'happiness' would lose its meaning if it were not balanced with sadness." Diversely talented artist, Leonardo da Vinci created the famous, "Vitruvian Man" to show the importance of symmetry and balance in all things. Chinese philosopher Confucius used the term, "Chung-Yung" when referring to persistent balance between extremes. In nature we must have balance of sun and moisture for nature to flourish. To make beautiful harmonic music, there must be a balance between high and low frequencies. For our physical well-being, we must have the proper balance of nutrition and physical movement to be healthy and vital. For us to feel balanced with "love," we must give and receive love.

In the twenty-first century, one of the largest concerns for millions in the western world is learning to create balance between our professional and personal lives. On the job responsibilities are increasingly bleeding over into our personal lives leaving us with little time to devote to our family members or to ourselves. According to a survey of fourteen thousand US workers, conducted by The Heldrich Center at Rutgers University, "The desire for work/life balance is being championed not only by professionals with graduate degrees and other white collar workers, but particularly by low-to moderate income workers who are struggling to find ways to sustain economic opportunity at work, and take care of business at home." Work/life balance has become an issue for all economic classes. Americans put in an average of 1,986 hours at work per year, more than any other nation in the world. If we factor national holidays and vacation time into the equation, not available to every worker, we are on the verge of approaching fifty hours per week at work.

My (Claudia) brother, Kevin, who works as a controller for a very large corporation often talks about the twelve hour days, five days a week minimum that has become the industry standard for salaried employees in the corporate world. Of course, these sixty hours do not include overtime that is often required at various intervals throughout the year, or even the fact that employees are also expected to bring laptops home for additional work after hours. Our own personal time is becoming more and more precious. A large majority of us are hiring out services, not necessarily because we are making more disposible income, but because we have less time to perform common tasks such as lawn care or housekeeping chores.

Searching to go even deeper into the issue of work/life balance, we decided to poll nearly 1200 of our friends, family members, peers, and workshop attendees around the world to better understand the ongoing tension of this relentless struggle. Of all the surveys we conducted for *The Masterpiece Within,* we were amazed to find how passionate and amplified the responses were. Days and sometimes even weeks after replying to the poll, a number of respondents called or sent in additional commentary after having time to think through the questions on a more indepth level. We posed three simple questions, but often received quotes, which we have included.

Question #1: ***What happens to you when you feel your life is out of balance?***

Top 10 Answers:

1. Overwhelmed (loss of perspective)
2. Irritable (moody, angry, loss of humor)
3. Relationships suffer
4. Lower self-esteem (lonely)
5. Poor choices
6. Unhealthy (bad eating habits, not caring for ourselves)
7. Impatience
8. Creativity suffers
9. Spirituality suffers
10. Guilt

Tim, Computer Technician; Sault Ste. Marie, Michigan:

"I am not assured I'm doing things correctly. Things feel wrong. My self-confidence goes down and my decision-making skills are slowed. My time seems to be wasted easily, goals aren't met, things get put off. Frustration sets in which often causes impatience and in turn causes additional stress and anxiety. Not to forget my sleep is affected."

Marty, Stockbroker and Mom; Franklin, Tennessee:

"Anger seems to be the emotion that takes over my life when I'm out of balance. I get angry because I don't have the time to do the things I want to do. I tend to get frustrated very easily and feel tired and depressed. In a nutshell, I feel like I am living for everyone else."

Dean, Minister; Brisbane, Australia:

"When my life is unbalanced my tendancy is to isolate myself as I find any interaction with family brings a volatile response. My normal coping mechanism is shot."

Joanne, Film Producer; Venice, California:

"I feel unable to make decisions or think clearly. I disconnect from my inner voice, my confidence. I make snap decisions or say things I haven't thought through."

Question #2: *What are the benefits you feel when you are in balance?*

Top 10 Answers:

1. Clarity (perspective)
2. Confidence
3. Stronger relationships
4. More productive
5. Motivation (energy and creativity)
6. Peace (calm)
7. More loving and giving to others
8. Hopeful
9. Overall health is better (sleep better)
10. Patience

Jackie, English Teacher; Moncton, New Brunswick:

"When my life is in balance my perspective is so clear, I am much more patient, peaceful, more loving, more teachable, a better person-mother-wife-teacher when I am in balance. I also am much more creative when I am in balance with more energy."

Marty, Stockbroker and Mom; Franklin, Tennessee:

"My mood instantaneously becomes happy and loving. I share my happiness with others...my family, friends, and often complete strangers. I have tons of energy and am able to conquer any task that I may be facing. I can see the clearer picture of my life without the excess clutter in my mind."

Bill, Canadian Olympic Director of Curling Coaches; Sidney, British Columbia:

"When my life is in balance, my self-esteem is intact...I am much better at picking and choosing the important things in life. I know what is of immediate importance and needs my attention 'now' and those things that aren't going to change."

Question #3: *What do you do to bring balance back into your life?*

Top 10 Answers:

1. Physical/mental exercises
2. Read an inspiring book
3. Quiet time (bath, journaling)
4. Relationship time (confide, enjoy, play with kids)
5. Spend time outdoors
6. Pray
7. Get organized by creating a to do list
8. Go to a movie
9. Review favorite books or journals
10. Healthy living (sleep and eat well)

Amanda, College Student; Calgary, Alberta:

"I dance! Honestly, I turn on music and dance my brains out. It makes me feel so happy."

Gay, an Office Manager; Eau Claire, Wisconsin:

"I find a good book to read, listen to some music; either good ole' rock and roll, jazz or great Christmas music (sometimes even in July). Play with my cat. Find time for a nap. Call an old friend. Find a good movie (usually a comedy). Pound out some music on the piano."

Gerry, Music Store Owner; Maymont, Saskatchewan:

"I hug my child and realize how lucky I am to have her. I talk to a valued friend that I feel I can relate to and will understand me. I do my regular job duties to restore feelings of self-worth. I pray."

Achieving life balance is not easy, but it is possible. Do we ever achieve PERFECT balance in our lifetime? Probably not, because developing "wholeness" is arguably the ultimate human struggle until our dying day. Becoming unbalanced is easy, because our humanness is in constant tension with who we currently are and who we desire to become. Balancing our lives is a process filled with paradoxes and a life-long dance of a few steps forward and a couple steps backwards. But the good news is we can learn the skills to achieve the proper amount of balance to consistently function at our personal best. And, most important of all, the more balanced we become in body, soul, mind, and spirit, the greater our capacity to love ourselves and to love others.

> *Life is like riding a bicycle; to keep your balance you must keep moving.*
>
> Albert Einstein

CHAPTER 14

DEVELOPING EMOTIONAL MATURITY

Emotions are the color of life; we would be drab creatures indeed without
them. But we must control these emotions or they will control us.

John M. Wilson

In seeking to attain emotional, physical, intellectual, or spiritual growth, we must first be
stirred emotionally to create the momentum necessary to commit to the process. Our
emotions are the necessary spark to ignite the desire for growth in all four aspects of our
humanness. Educators teach us the most effective learning begins for a student when they are
stirred emotionally. If the student makes an emotional connection with the subject matter or
the teacher, they are more likely to be motivated to take the necessary steps to learn, therefore
absorbing the information at a greater rate. Many theologians teach that a genuine spiritual
awakening cannot occur until an individual is moved emotionally with a deep need to connect
with God. In the physical sense, we can take our bodies for granted for years by not eating
healthy and not getting enough physical exercise, but the moment we are given news of a life-
threatening disease, we will be naturally moved emotionally to make the necessary changes to
take better care of ourselves.

Even in the workplace, the importance of emotional maturity is playing a greater role when
employers seek to hire new employees. A person's emotional intelligence, or EQ, has quickly

become more important to overall job performance skills than simply having a high IQ or GPA. Dr. Daniel Goleman, author of the best selling book, *Emotional Intelligence*, tells us, "A person's EQ consists of self-awareness, impulse control, persistence, zeal, self-motivation, and social deftness." Goleman believes these are the qualities of those who excel in intimate relationships and who are the "stars" in the workplace. And, in order for our society to thrive, these qualities are becoming increasingly necessary.

My (Claudia) brother-in-law, Rod Stricklin, who works at Compassion International in Colorado Springs, Colorado, relayed to me the importance his company places on a healthy balance of IQ and EQ. He went on to tell me about a woman from Rwanda he and his colleagues recently interviewed for employment. Right from the start, they were quite impressed that she spoke five languages, because Compassion feeds and educates children in numerous countries around the world. After the initial stage of the interview revealed she had a high IQ, they then moved onto the EQ evaluation phase of the interview. For Compassion, this phase consists of a series of questions based on the three C's: character, competence, and chemistry. She openly shared with them possible reasons why she may not be a good employee for their company, which was a good indicator that she possessed a high EQ. Through careful evaluation they soon hired her, more so because of her high EQ rather than her high IQ, but the fact that she had both qualities was an added bonus.

In the early 1990's, the University of Calgary in Alberta, Canada, found itself flooded with new applicants in the education department. In order to limit the amount of students in this particular department, the faculty made the decision to admit only those with an eighty percent or higher high school average. Many of the veteran teachers within the province of Alberta were strongly opposed to this criteria being the sole requirement for entrance into the university, because this method would not serve as a healthy indicator for how well one would teach in a classroom setting. The teachers made the argument that having an educator in the school system with a high EQ was much more effective in communicating and working alongside students than someone with merely a high GPA.

In developing a mature emotional life, we need to understand the role our emotions play. Emotions are universal or cross-cultural in the sense that no matter where we travel around the world, even if we do not speak the same language, we can more often than not understand the emotion someone is feeling just by observing their expressions or body language. The word "emotion" comes from the Latin root, "emovere," which translates as, "to be in motion." If we combine Eastern and Western thought, we can define emotion as something that influences the mind and sets it in motion towards a constructive, neutral, or destructive path, due to the adoption of a particular outlook or action. In other words, emotions are neutral in nature, but how we choose to respond to the emotion, determines whether it will be constructive or destructive to us.

CONSTRUCTIVE EMOTIONS

In May 1995, actor Christopher Reeves, an accomplished horseman, was participating in a high-jump show in Virginia when he was unexpectedly thrown from his horse. The accident left him a quadriplegic, confining him to a wheel chair and respirator/ventilator for the rest of his life. Once an active athlete, the news of his condition threw him into a deep depression with thoughts of suicide. The former, *Superman* bravely and wisely made the choice to channel his feelings of anger and devastation into a constructive and positive direction. Through Reeves' passion and commitment, he helped heighten the awareness of spinal cord injuries and willingly used his own resources and body as a guinea pig to work towards a cure.

He set up, "The Christopher Reeve Foundation" raising millions of dollars for research, and labored year after year on new legislature to provide a voice for many patients who had no hope at all. Never asking for sympathy, Reeves worked diligently to exercise his body. He was able to gain sensation in over seventy percent of his body, a feat never heard of in prior spinal cord injury patients. Although labor intensive, Reeves also refused to give up on his acting career. He appeared in and directed numerous films, documentaries, and television programs. Right up until his death in October 2004, he was lobbying for the Christopher Reeve Paralysis Act for biomedic and rehabilitation research, as well as quality of life programs for those with spinal cord injuries. Reeves could have continued choosing a destructive route for his emotions and remained bedridden without helping himself or others. However, because of his desire to use his emotions in a constructive manner, he will go down in history books as one of the greatest actor-activists of all time. He proved to be the superhero he once portrayed to his friends, family members, and to new and old fans alike. The Christopher Reeve Paralysis Act was signed by President Obama in 2009.

We can imagine potentially destructive emotions as similar to toddlers. If these toddlers or emotions are left to run around a room without any adult supervision or healthy boundaries, chaos would eventually erupt, because each toddler or emotion would eventually attempt to gain their fair share of air time. Just as toddlers need proper structure to guide them, we also need guidance to learn to better manage our emotions or they will continue to control us. The more we train ourselves to transform our destructive emotions into constructive emotions, the higher our EQ will become, and the more balanced we will be in all four dimensions.

DESTRUCTIVE EMOTIONS

An emotion can only become destructive if we choose to embrace and act upon the negative behaviors associated with it. The classic film, *Ben-Hur*, shows how the path of destructive emotions can progressively worsen when we do not choose to alter their direction. *Ben-Hur* tells the story of Judah Ben-Hur, a rich Jewish prince played by Charlton Heston, who has a falling out with his boyhood friend, Messala, a Roman citizen played by Stephen Boyd, with whom he grew up in Jerusalem. As a young man, Messala is sent off to train as a Roman soldier, and he returns to Jerusalem as the commanding officer of the Roman legions based in Palestine. During Messala's initial return, he and Ben-Hur are extremely happy to see one another, but their reunited friendship quickly begins to disintegrate after Ben-Hur chooses not to support his friend politically. Feeling betrayed, Messala, now a powerful Roman officer, decides to take his anger down a destructive path by sending Ben-Hur off to the galleys as a slave on a Roman warship on a trumped up charge. To hurt him even deeper, Messala sends Ben-Hur's mother, Miriam (Martha Scott) and sister, Tizrah (Cathy O'Donnell) to prison.

While on the warship, Ben-Hur becomes consumed with hatred and revenge taking on the same destructive attitude and emotions as Messala and vows to get even with his former friend.

A few years later, Ben-Hur gets his opportunity. During a dangerous and bloody chariot race, which ends with only the two of them crossing the finish line, Messala becomes mortally wounded. After the race, Ben-Hur is called to Messala's death bed but instead of making up, which he expects, Messala cruelly gets in one last hurtful statement before dying. "Your mother and sister are still alive, they are not dead, look for them in the valley of the lepers if you can recognize them. The race goes on Ben-Hur, the race is not over."

Upon hearing this news, Ben-Hur's hatred and bitterness escalates even further. Esther, (Haya Harareet) his childhood sweetheart, lovingly and firmly challenges him by saying, "What has become of you Ben-Hur? You seem to be now the very thing you set out to destroy. Giving evil for evil. Hatred is turning you to stone. It is as though you have become Messala." Esther's words eventually begin to penetrate Ben-Hur's tough exterior. Finally able to grasp the destructive consequences of his anger, he chooses to take the constructive path of love and forgiveness. One of the most powerful life lessons this film teaches is that when we embrace an emotion into our mind and spirit, we take on the characteristics of that emotion, whether constructive or destructive.

We must be careful with whom we choose to expose ourselves, and with whom we choose to spend our time, because emotions can be contagious. For instance, in a positive light if we find ourselves around a humorous person who exudes joy and laughter, we will often be drawn into their world of joy. So much so, we may find ourselves joyous and laughing right along with them even if we started out in a bad mood or bad place emotionally. In the negative sense, if we find ourselves around someone who is gossipy or angry at someone with whom we have no ill-will, we may find ourselves without consciously realizing we have become angry and bitter toward the innocent party. A destructive emotion may seem fatal at first, but if we choose to use the emotion to propel us toward its positive alternative, we feel free, hopeful, inspired, more tolerant, loving, and peaceful.

> *When you are behaving as if you love someone, you will presently come to love him. If you injure someone you dislike, you will find yourself disliking them more. If you do him a good turn, you will find yourself disliking him less.*
>
> C.S. Lewis

THE GRADE "A" PLAN FOR DESTRUCTIVE EMOTIONS

While researching methods to effectively manage destructive emotions, we created what we like to refer to as, "The Grade "A" Plan." The goal of the plan is to receive an "A" grade in taking the destructive emotion to a constructive emotion while using the four A's : "Acknowledge," "Analyze," "Action Plan," and "Accountability." The strategy is to walk the reader through practical instructions and provide tools to help shorten the distance or bridge the gap from hurting to healing.

1. Acknowledge

In order to diffuse the destructive emotion, we must first acknowledge that a destructive emotion is present and affecting our lives in a negative manner.

2. Analyze

A. In this next step, we begin the process of diffusing the potentially destructive emotion by breaking it down until we get to its root cause. The first phase of analyzing begins with stopping or halting ourselves when we become aware that the destructive emotion is present. We have adopted this Alcoholics Anonymous (AA) formula, "H.A.L.T." as a helpful awareness tool for this phase. AA estimates that ninety percent of emotional issues can be identified when we ask ourselves, "Am I Hungry, Angry, Lonely, or Tired?"

B. If we feel the need to probe even deeper and move to the second phase, we will be able to discover the root cause of the destructive emotion and address it accordingly. For instance, we may think we are feeling lonely, but when we investigate further, the deeper emotion we may discover is fear. The analyzing progression continues as: I feel lonely-I feel fearful-I feel scared-angry-paralyzed-overwhelmed-tired-hopeless-not connecting with my spouse-rejected by my spouse-fearful they will judge me-fearful they will leave me-fearful I'll be alone-fearful of being rejected and alone just like I have been in all other significant relationships in my life.

C. The in-depth probe reveals the root cause of my emotion is fear: fear of being rejected and alone.

3. Action Plan

In the third step of the Grade "A" Plan, we take the destructive emotion and its discovered root cause, and begin to create a plan of action. We provide a variety of tools under each destructive emotion to teach ourselves how to move to its antidote or positive alternative.

4. Accountability

The fourth step is holding ourselves accountable to follow through with the action plan by listing a minimum of three tools from the tools' list and applying them to help bridge the gap between the destructive and constructive emotion. Holding ourselves accountable is to challenge ourselves to take any future destructive emotions through the Grade "A" Plan.

The goal of this chapter is to attain a higher level of emotional maturity in continuing to develop our masterpiece within. In the following pages, we will identify the four main critical areas or attitudes that most often hinder us from gaining emotional maturity. We will offer their antidotes and the Grade "A" Plan to assist us in attaining higher emotional intelligence.

EMOTIONAL ATTITUDES

Emotional Attitude #1: LOVE - FEAR

Throughout my (Claudia) adult life, I have been a student of human behavior, to enrich my writing or acting skills, to examine marriage and family therapy groups, or to prepare material for the writing of this book. The number one most life-changing lesson I have learned revolves around the idea or school of thought that our actions stem from one of two places: either from a place of love, or from a place of fear. If we act from a place of love, we are more secure in ourselves, humble, relaxed, joyous, and a pleasure to be around. If we act from a place of fear, we are either anxious, uncomfortable, filled with tension, sometimes overbearing or obnoxious, and most likely not very desirable to be around. A simple awareness tool when experiencing an undesirable emotion or situation is to ask ourselves, "Am I, or is the person I am encountering, coming from a place of fear or from a place of love?" Whether we are working to develop a deeper understanding of ourselves or trying to communicate with others, asking ourselves this one question will help to diffuse most stressful situations, and will save us a great deal of time and frustration.

If we discover we are coming from a place of fear, we need to stop and answer the questions, "What am I fearing?" and "What can I do to manage the fear in order to get back to a place of love?" If we decide the person we are encountering may be coming from a place a fear, we have two options in addressing the situation. If we have a close relationship with them, we can try to help them get to the root of the fear. If we do not feel comfortable asking them personal questions, just having the awareness will help us better understand their actions.

My husband, Rodney, and I have a saying we use if this kind of situation arises that helps us gain a clearer perspective and compassion toward the individual. This saying originated when Rodney and our good friend and master bass player, Michael Rhodes, were backstage at a music awards event. As anyone can imagine, egos are blaring and it is not out of the norm to have one artist explode emotionally during the evening. At this particular event, one artist was making everyone's life miserable. Rodney looked at Michael and asked him why this artist was acting out and ruining the joy of the evening for everyone else? Michael responded, "Oh Rodney, he's just rattlin' the love me cup across't the prison bars of life." This statement quickly worked its magic and they were able to enjoy their evening by gaining compassion for the artist. If we find ourselves in this form of uncomfortable situation, a quick reminder that the offending person is actually saying, "Please, please love me, I'm lovable," will not only defuse the frustration we feel, but if given the opportunity, we may be able to help them work through their fears. When we develop the ability to discern the difference between love and fear, we not only gain the skills to understand ourselves on a much deeper level, but our understanding of human nature and patience with others immediately increases tenfold.

LOVE

Man's two greatest needs are to love and to be loved...Love is the most powerful force in the universe...All we need is love...Love is the foundation of all great universal laws...True love can cure the soul, it can make it whole...Love is the glue...There's no greater love than to give one's life for a friend... Perfect love casts out fear...We are all born for love. It is the principle of existence...Love is the answer...

From basic psychology to Buddha, from the Beatles to Blaise Pascal, from Bob Dylan to Brian Billick, from the Bible to Benjamin Disraeli, our greatest and deepest need is to love and to be loved. This helps to explain why there have been more songs written on love than any other theme, and most of the highest grossing films in Hollywood or Bollywood (India) are primarily love story driven. Romance novels are one of the hottest selling genres of all books and in some years the top grossing books of all genres.

Love is not the easiest word or concept to define. Yet, we so freely use the word attaching it to trivial matters, matters of the heart, and great ideals all in the same breath. No wonder we may get confused when the word love is used is so many different contexts. We love our favorite foods, we love our pets, we love our sports teams, we love our homes or cars, we love our spouses, we love our children, etc. All these "loves" obviously carry different meanings within their context, but we can easily dilute the meaning of love and compromise its integrity by trivializing the word. According to linguistic experts, the English language is often very limited in its usage of words and because of this dilemma, words with powerful meanings sometimes lose their edge. So what is love?

Studying ancient languages such as the Greek language, considered one of the most colorful and descriptive of all languages, can offer us a deeper understanding behind the meaning of different words. There is wisdom in how the language breaks down concepts and uses a variety of words to describe the number of different meanings behind the concept. The word "love" is an excellent example. The Greeks have a number of words to describe love, but three very common ones; eros, phileo, and agape, illustrate different meanings to describe the depth of love we can experience.

Eros refers to sensual, physical, or romantic love. Eros is based on the physical and emotional aspects of our being. This includes infatuation or the "love at first sight" idea, which may evolve into a deeper love or fade away as quickly as a morning mist.

Phileo is best translated as "to like." Phileo is the strong natural affection we would feel for another person and is primarily based in the emotions and the intellect. Phileo is conditional in nature, because it is based on personal preferences and interests. However, it can serve as the spark to provide hope in attaining a higher form of love.

Agape is unconditional love and considered to be the highest form of love. Some of the characteristics of agape love include a sacrificial nature, generosity, a show of respect, a caring quality, perseverance, integrity, kindness, and a desire to choose wisely. Agape is primarily based in the will, the part of us where our choices lie. To love regardless! To perform a loving act or deed even if the loving feelings are not present.

A helpful compliment to the definition of agape love lies in the Pali language, a derivative of the ancient Sanskrit language. The Pali word "metta" is possibly the best word we have found to describe the love we all seek to experience and attain. Metta describes love as unconditional loving kindness toward another. It is an action word or verb because it is based in the will. Metta is to perform goodwill and loving actions toward others rather than merely thinking about doing them or reciting prayers about love. There are no acts of ill-will towards another human being in metta. Even if one harbors negative feelings toward another, they will still choose to perform acts of goodwill or compassion.

FEAR

Fear is a feeling of anxiousness, worry, alarm or panic, either imagined or genuine. A few of the most common fears include the fear of rejection, the fear of failure, the fear of being hurt, and the fear of being misunderstood. How we choose to respond to our fears will determine whether they become constructive or destructive for us. We can look at constructive fear in two ways:

1.) Facing our fear and making the choice to take our fear and our life in a positive direction regardless of the consequences or outcome.
2.) Paying attention to our fearful feelings that are warning us to choose either a fight or flight response to keep us from harm's way. The fight-or-flight survival instinct reminds us that fear should not always be seen as negative. For example, this constructive form of

fear provides appropriate nervousness, i.e., being leary approaching a dark or unknown alleyway, taking care of ourselves physically for fear of getting sick or being out of shape. Constructive fear can motivate us to prepare well beforehand in order to achieve a successful presentation or performance.

Fear is considered to be destructive when we choose to take the fear to a harmful place toward ourselves or toward others. The key to managing our fear is bringing it back into proper balance and perspective through first recognizing the fear, and then responding to the fear in a constructive, loving fashion.

In the film, *Monster's Ball*, every character, in their own way is, "Rattlin' their love me cup across't their prison bars of life." The principle character, Ray, played by Billy Bob Thornton, works as a prison guard on death row, following the career path of several generations of men in his family. Fear and racism runs rampant in Ray's home, but soon after his son, Sonny's (Heath Ledger) suicide, Ray makes the pivotal decision to begin taking baby steps towards choosing love over fear. He quits the job he hates, he bravely stands up to his hate-filled father, (Peter Boyle) and he reaches out in kindness to those he once hated and judged. Ray begins performing acts of kindness, helping out an African-American mother, Leticia, played by Halle Berry, by taking her critically wounded son, Tyrell (Coronji Calhoun) to the hospital. Sadly, Tyrell dies, but to Ray's surprise, he finds a soul connection with Leticia and eventually falls in love with her. Because he continuously chooses to make loving choices, Ray is able to open his heart, and find the joy and love he has never known. Ray was not perfect with his actions, but his intentions were honorable, sweet, and real. The fact that he stood up to years of destructive family tradition and a racist tyrant for a father, proved to Ray that through each baby step, he subtly moved toward a genuine loving heart. Ray chose fear for the first forty years of his life, which bread cynicism, anger, bitterness, loneliness, and hatred. When he chose love, his heart opened, his life possibilities began to flourish, and he finally found the love that had always been missing from his life.

When we choose to manage our fears as opposed to being controlled by them, we not only gain an open and loving heart, but we begin to find our lives progressively gaining growth and maturity. If we make the choice to be governed by fear whether consciously or unconsciously, we in effect resolve to make childish or immature choices thus promoting a stagnate or regressive life path. The impact of choosing love over fear is powerful.

The Grade "A" Plan For Fear

1. **Acknowlege:** *I acknowledge I am feeling fearful.*

2. **Analyze: Getting to the root of my fear**

A. "H.A.L.T." I am hungry _____ angry _____ lonely _____ tired _____
   What can I do to take care of myself? _____

B. The deeper emotions I am feeling about my fear are: I feel fearful, _____
   _____

C. The root cause of my fear is _____

3. **Action Plan: Tools to cultivate love**

A. Gain A Clear Perspective:
   1. What is out of my control and in my control regarding my fear?
   2. Ninety-seven percent of fears never come into fruition- the three percent that do are usually manageable.
   3. The anticipation of a fear is usually stronger than when facing the fear.
   4. Review what worked and what did not work for us personally in past dealings with fear.

B. Get MAD At The Fear:
   1. Make a difference (M.A.D) by volunteering a significant amount of time to a favorite charity.
   2. Get mad at the fear and do something constructive and fun to get out of a paralyzed state.
   3. Take the focus off ourselves and work to meet the needs of those around us.
   4. Perform random acts of kindness for strangers during an entire day.

C. Take A Risk:
   1. Take the risk of facing the fear head on especially if we have avoided resolving it in the past.
   2. Get involved in therapy or a support group to release feelings we may have never before risked sharing.

3. Live by our noble value system regardless of how hard it may be at times.

4. Risk exposing our insecurities by talking about our fears with another person.

4. Accountability: My plans to bridge the gap between my fears and love

1. _____
2. _____
3. _____

Emotional Attitude #2: FORGIVENESS - ANGER

Unless we are able to genuinely learn how to forgive, we will never be able to truly learn how to manage anger. Unmanaged anger can lead to resentment, bitterness, and revenge. Honey J. Rubin, a writer, poet, and motivational speaker who specializes in forgiveness says, "On the wings of forgiveness is carried all other wisdom." Almost all prominent therapeutic programs that have stood the test of time include forgiveness as one of the major themes to address before any serious progress is made. Of the many life skills taught in addictions recovery, forgiveness is the cornerstone virtue, which is emphasized. We have seen the magic of forgiveness affect our lives and other's lives in many powerful ways. We have witnessed artists and musicians who have gone through prolonged seasons of dryness because of unresolved anger, regain their passion and creativity when choosing to forgive. In counseling, clients who were dealing with stress related diseases or ailments, such as high blood pressure, were able to go off their medication with their doctors' approval after making the decision to forgive people in their lives. Dr. Lihua Sheng, of the Lotus Center in Nashville, Tennessee says, "I have seen many patients and colleagues cured of major health problems after releasing their anger and resentment."

Dave Ridgway, the Canadian Football League's most accurate field goal kicker, attributes his career success to forgiveness. In his first six seasons with the Saskatchewan Roughriders, Ridgway averaged sixty-eight percent on his field goal attempts. In his final eight seasons, he kicked at a record-breaking eighty-four percent accuracy rate. The difference between his sixth and seventh seasons is he worked through his anger issues with his father. Throughout his career, Ridgway felt he was playing football only to win over his father's approval. The fun or the joy in playing the game was gone for him, and the more he played and continued to struggle, the more his unresolved anger surfaced toward his father. Dave says:

"I flew halfway across the country to work through my anger with my dad. After sitting down and being honest with him about my feelings, I found out most of my anger was based around a misunderstanding of each other. I was able to shift my focus from trying to gain my father's approval to a better overall life perspective where perfection wasn't necessary. To my relief I realized my dad didn't care if I was perfect; he only cared if I was happy regardless of my performance on the field. Finding forgiveness with Dad not only turned my career around but I now consider my father my best friend."

FORGIVENESS

Forgiveness is oftentimes one of the most misunderstood words or concepts in all of human understanding. In order to comprehend the true definition of a word, sometimes it is helpful to first take a look at what a word does not mean before looking at what it does mean. Forgiveness does not necessarily mean that we will feel the emotion of pardon toward someone who has angered us or hurt us deeply. Forgiveness does not mean to flippantly let go of an offense just to ease the discomfort of a situation when no regret is being demonstrated by the person who has hurt us. Forgiveness does not mean that we should never pursue a healthy course of justice against someone who has hurt us. Forgiveness is not a synonym for pardon. These misconceptions of forgiveness are unhealthy and can be destructive for us, because we are not genuinely developing a forgiving spirit. We are actually compromising the personal growth of both ourselves and the ones who hurt us.

Forgiveness is volitional, or a choice of the will to love ourselves or to love others who have hurt us or made us angry, even when forgiveness seems to be a difficult or next to impossible task. Volitional forgiveness originates from the spirit, from the heart, or from the will. This is the part of us that makes choices. Therefore, in order for forgiveness to be genuine, it must come from the heart and involve a loving action in spite of angry or hurtful feelings. Otherwise, forgiveness will never be sincerely activated. When we truly desire to forgive from the heart or the will, true forgiveness can be one hundred percent activated whether loving, forgiving feelings toward the offender are present or not. In most cases, depending on the severity of the offense, as we choose to make loving choices in the light of forgiveness, our feelings will quite often evolve over time from anger and hurt to feelings of love and forgiveness. Ideally, the long term goal of forgiveness is to work through anger, bitterness, or resentment until it no longer carries painful feelings or a destructive emotional charge.

An example of volitional forgiveness comes from the story of my (Guy) cousin, Jeff, and his wife, Erin, regarding the forgiveness of the man who murdered Erin's mother, Faye, in June 1995. Faye, a principal in the small town of Spirit River, Alberta, Canada, was strangled by a school janitor who was eventually convicted of manslaughter and sentenced to serve fifteen years in prison with the possibility of parole in five years. Erin was kind enough to share her thoughts on forgiveness.

"Even though he received the maximum sentence, for me it meant absolutely nothing. My reaction was, no matter how many years he serves it will never bring my mom back, so what does it matter? It was just a hollow victory. I sat in our big armchair and cried for one whole afternoon, and then I decided that I didn't want to keep focusing on such a bottomless pit of despair. I did not want to give any more power to the man who had killed my mother. I didn't want him to have any place in my life, actually. The day after her death, we as a family, decided to gather together to say a prayer. I remember looking around at all of my family and them looking at me and all of us saying almost simultaneously, 'We're going to be okay.' I had never experienced such a supernatural sense of peace like I experienced at that moment. We all just knew we would be okay and for me that was really the starting point for forgiveness. It was like we all decided right there that we were going to choose to go on rather than let mom's death defeat us.

I was determined to use my time and talents as best as I could toward a path of positive living, rather than focusing on bitterness, anger, hatred, and all the other emotions that are typical when you lose someone unexpectedly. So where am I with all of this now? To be honest, I thought that time would help to fade the pain, but instead I am finding that with every new change or season of life that I go through (or that we go through as a family) there are new, fresh hurts that I must deal with and forgive. For example, when my children were born, I ached to have my mom to share in our joy, even more so when our latest addition to the family was a beautiful little girl with dark hair like my mom. We named her Faye after my mom, and there is joy in even calling her name, but there is also pain. When the waves of grief sneak in and I am right back at the fork in the road, I have the choice of going into a black hole of bitterness and anger, wallowing in what I am missing, hating the man who took her from me, or choosing the healing path of love and forgiveness. Whenever I find myself in this place of pain, I always continue to make the very conscious effort to choose forgiveness yet again."

ANGER

Anger is one of the most destructive emotions we will encounter due to its potential to inflict harm on ourselves or others if left unmanaged. Anger is an emotion, which is often caused by extreme hurt, disappointment, or injustice. Some of the emotions we can associate within the anger family include hatred, revenge, outrage, exasperation, and rage. What lies underneath these feelings are the emotions of sadness, grief, hurt, betrayal, disappointment, or unfulfilled expectations. One of the keys to moving destructive anger to a constructive place is to allow ourselves time to grieve over the hurt for a brief period of time and then work to regain our power in the situation by forgiving ourselves or others involved. Unmanaged anger can be one of our biggest roadblocks in developing our potential intellectually, spiritually, emotionally, and even physically. There has been a significant amount of research to confirm how anger can be likened to an addictive drug, because it causes a chemical reaction or emotional rush, which our bodies begin to crave over and over. When someone takes on an angry persona, they will often seek out unhealthy means to release their anger whether or not the party or parties involved are deserving of anger or if the situation calls for an appropriate level of anger. For example, these actions can range in extremes from as small as creating five minutes of angry chaos daily, to trying to slant a conversation into a harmful, angry, gossip session, or to eating, sleeping, and breathing anger all day long. Oftentimes coming to the awareness that we are functioning in a place of anger, can jumpstart us to make positive changes.

In the best selling book and hit film, *Seabiscuit*, jockey Red Pollard, played by Tobey Maguire, is living in a state of perpetual anger, which is proving detrimental to his racing career and his life. By living this way he is closing himself off to everyone around him. When his boss, race horse owner, Charles Howard, played by Jeff Bridges gently confronts him by asking, "Son, what are you so mad at?" it is as if Red has an awakening to finally realize how consumed he has become with anger. He immediately sets out to work through his anger, knowing its root cause is due to his parents leaving him with a virtual stranger at the age of fifteen. Red makes the decision to forgive his parents and to stop blaming them for the hard times he has endured over the years. Through his soul searching, he regains a clear perspective and he is inspired to take responsibility for his life. As he returns to the race track, we see a renewed Red who not only reassures himself but also his race horse, Seabiscuit, by telling him,"We're okay, we're okay boy, there's nothing to worry about." Together, Red and Seabiscuit go on to break records and win major races at a pace seldom seen before.

Not all anger is destructive. When anger is channeled in constructive ways, not only will it help serve to motivate us toward our own personal growth, but it can also motivate us toward making the world a better place. Martin Luther King, Nelson Mandela, and Ghandi are examples of leaders who chose to channel their anger towards creating momentous social change. When a sports team or participant experiences moments of anger during a game, these feelings can fuel their passion to win rather than simply giving up or trying to get even. After the terrorist attack at the World Trade Center towers on September 11, 2001, an example of constructive channeling of anger occurred throughout New York City. Rather than recoiling in fear and resorting to destructive, vengeful anger, New Yorkers used their anger to pull together as a community.

The Grade "A" Plan For Anger

1. **Acknowledge:** *I acknowledge I am feeling angry.*

2. **Analyze: Getting to the root of my anger**
A. "H.A.L.T." I am hungry _____ angry _____ lonely _____ tired _____
   What can I do to take care of myself?_____
   _____

B. The deeper emotions I am experiencing regarding my anger are...

I feel angry,_____

_____

C. The root cause of my anger is_____

3. Action Plan: Tools to cultivate forgiveness

A. Practical And Healthy Methods To Release Anger:

1. Take a bat and pillow and safely release anger by hitting the pillow and using our voice to vent until we have regained a functional or peaceful emotional place.

2. Make a venting call to a trusted friend or family member who is willing to just listen as we release our anger.

3. To change our mood we can create quiet time to journal, take a hot bath, listen to soft/loud music, read a satisfying book, meet with a support group, pray, or meditate.

4. Participate in a physical activity such as gardening, playing a musical instrument, or partake in a favorite sport.

5. Get involved in something fun, creative and joyful: go to a movie, to a comedy club, watch a sitcom, or engage in a hobby.

B. Make Amends:

1. According to Alcholics Anonymous ninety-nine percent of addicts who do not work or practice steps eight, nine, and ten of AA's 12 Step program will go back into using their substance of choice:

Step Eight: Make a list of all persons we have harmed, and become willing to make amends to them all.

Step Nine: Make direct amends to such people wherever possible, except when to do so would injure them or others.

Step Ten: Continue to take personal inventory and when we were wrong promptly admit it.

2. Letter writing exercises to release an offender, whether they are alive or have passed away. Once we have written these letters we can either save them, tear them up or burn them. Letter #1: Write a letter to an offender venting our anger.

Letter #2: Write a letter to ourselves as if we are the offender telling our side of the story.

Letter #3: Write a letter to the offender offering forgiveness.

C. Practical Tips to Remember:

1. Beneath anger lies sadness, beneath sadness, hurt or disappointment, beneath hurt, fear.

2. We live in an imperfect world. We cannot expect constant perfection from ourselves or others.

3. We may have a small amount of influence, but we cannot control one hundred percent of the choices of others.

4. Forgiveness is not a synonym for pardon. It is creating an attitude or willingness to pardon.

5. Justice is different than revenge. Justice is about seeking fairness and reconciliation. Revenge is seeking payback with no intent to reconcile.

6. Divine justice or retribution is a basic belief of all healthy orthodox religions.

7. As the Bible says, "Forgiveness means to forgive seventy times seven." And, "Do not let the sun go down while you are still angry."

4. **Accountability: My plans to bridge the gap between my anger and forgiveness**

1. _____

2. _____

3. _____

Emotional Attitude #3: CONFIDENCE - DISCOURAGEMENT

During the seventeen years I (Claudia) worked as a model, I was lucky enough to work in the fashion capital of the world, Paris, France. One of the highlights while working in Paris, was walking into the famed House of Chanel on Rue Cambon and finding out later in the day that I was hired for a week-long booking. Unfortunately, I was unable to do the job, because I soon found out I had already been hired for a job at Lanvin on the same days.

A few years later while working in Dallas, I overheard my runway booking agent, Kate talking about sending models to an interview for a huge Chanel fashion show occurring in town. I asked

Kate if I too could be sent on the interview. She said, "I would send you, but you do not fit the description of models requested, because they only wanted to see brunette models over 5'10." I tried to tell her I had met the woman in Paris who was conducting the auditions in Dallas, and that if I was just given a chance, maybe she would change her mind about the qualifications, and hire me once again. Kate continued to discourage me, because she had been given strict guidelines and did not want to come across as unprofessional.

While in Paris, this same woman had told me that Coco Chanel always loved using blondes when she was alive, and that they had been thinking of going back to using blondes in their ad campaigns, instead of brunettes. I just kept thinking that I could not miss my second chance to work for the House of Chanel. I had the inner confidence, because I knew they had chosen me before, so maybe they would choose me once again. Well, I just could not stand the angst inside me any longer, so I decided I had to crash the audition, even if it meant being dropped from my agency. I was a nervous wreck while awaiting either exciting or disappointing news from Kate.

On the day of the Chanel show, I proudly walked the catwalk as the only blonde model in the show, and I was surprised to find, I was the featured model in most of the press clippings. After taking this risk, I gained the confidence to do the same thing again soon after for a large Todd Oldham show, when I did not meet the audition requirements. I was hired for Todd's show as well. Thankfully, Kate did not drop me. In fact, she started sending me on more auditions.

Few things in life are as inspiring as watching someone's dreams come into fruition, especially when the path is laden with adversity. The film business counts on this fact to sustain their industry. Moviegoers are drawn back into theatres over and over again with the anticipation of watching a character overcome obstacles, and come out victorious in the end.

Discouragement is part of everyday life for all of us. Whether it is as emotionally devastating as someone telling us we do not have what it takes for a job, or we do not deserve a raise, or as simple as being told by a coffee shop worker that they are out of our favorite coffee. The key to managing discouragement is in seeking out helpful options to address the problem, and maintaining our confidence, rather than hiding away in shame. As the Tom Petty song so poignantly reminds us, *You Don't Have To Live Like a Refugee.*

CONFIDENCE

In the Marvel Cinematic Universe, character, Loki, is known for saying, "I am Loki of Asgard, and I am burdened with glorious purpose." What exceptional confidence. We should all be so lucky. Actor, Tom Hiddleston, who plays the character Loki in the *The Avengers* and *Thor* series, was staying at my (Claudia) home in the fall of 2014 while preparing with my husband, Rodney, for his role of Hank Williams in the film, *I Saw The Light*. We were discussing his intense preparation in creating characters, especially that of Loki. I said to him, "When your look came together and you were in your complete Loki costume, you must have felt so empowered." Tom said, "Oh, absolutely, I instantly felt like a badass. And, the weight of the costume really added to the feeling."

Confidence is a feeling of inner strength and the willingness to act with courage, regardless of whether one is feeling discouraged or fearful. Discouragement can cause us to want to give up and throw in the towel, but a person of confidence, has the fortitude to keep trying no matter what obstacles come their way. No one ever feels secure one hundred percent of the time; we all have moments when we experience a crisis of confidence. Most of us have to train ourselves to learn how to be confident, because confidence does not always come naturally. Valuable layers of confidence are built when we take small successful steps of courage.

If discouragement is not addressed, our confidence can get so beat down that we become lost in an abyss of pain, envy, jealousy, and an overall miserable life existance. And, as we all know, misery loves company. A discouraged person will seek out friends and family members who are in the same boat, only making matters worse. The choice is up to us whether we hold our heads high and take baby steps of courage to create faith in ourselves again and again, or risk cheating the world of our talents and presence.

Since 1994, I (Guy) have kept a well used photocopied magazine article in my wallet on CFL and NFL Hall of Fame coach, Marv Levy, to pull out and read whenever I feel discouraged and need a boost of confidence. The article tells how Levy, after suffering a third straight Super Bowl loss, was facing critics who wondered if the Bills should make major changes or if they had the resiliency to put together a strong enough team for a fourth straight attempt. On the flight back home to Buffalo, Levy, not wanting his players to end their third consecutive season on a bad note, pondered long and hard on what he could say to encourage his team the following day for their last team meeting. Having earned his PhD in English Literature, Levy is known for being able to quote famous people throughout history. The quote he believed would strike a cord with his players came not from his studies, but instead from his mother some sixty years earlier who had taught him the story of Sir Andrew, a fourteenth century Scottish warrior. He posted the quote on the white board of the dressing room door to the players' locker room, and proceeded to tell his team the story of how Sir Andrew had lost a major battle, but not the war. The quote read: "Fight on, my men... A little I am hurt, but not yet slain; I'll just lie down and bleed awhile; And then I'll rise and fight again."

The following year, Levy set an NFL record by leading the Buffalo Bills to a fourth consecutive Super Bowl appearance. They may not have won the game, but the fact that they were able to come back once again, proved to the critics it could be done. I have found many times in my life, I can always count on this quote and story to lift my spirits and confidence. On numerous occasions, I have even had friends ask me whenever they are going through tough times, "Where is your wallet?" or to say "Time to get out the wallet."

Sometimes all we need is a small ray of hope to get us back on track again with a reasonable amount of confidence. So often this infusion of hope comes through tangible symbols. Wearing tangible symbols or learning to "fake it until we make it" can be an inspiration for us to initiate steps of confidence. Whether it is through a quote on a piece of paper, a hero outfit, words of encouragement on a bracelet, or a game of pretend, each is just as effective as the last.

DISCOURAGEMENT

Discouragement has the potential to become one of the most damaging of all negative emotions for two reasons. First, discouragement can damage our self-esteem, and secondly, discouragement can have a negative impact on those around us. If we begin to buy into unrealistic thoughts we may have about ourselves, or to believe we are not competent or capable, due to opinions expressed by others, we may find ourselves living in a perpetual state of discouragement. This state has the potential to cause negative spiraling behaviors from total apathy on one end of the spectrum, to addictive behaviors on the other end of the spectrum. Our self-esteem may become so low that we begin taking out our frustrations on others and cheating ourselves from pursuing our life bliss.

Spiritual classics and cultural fables are filled with stories warning against associating intimately with people who have a discouraging aura, because of its contagious nature. There are far too many tragic stories in life where people were on the verge of great breakthroughs or accomplishments only to be thwarted by a core of discouraging people.

Within the word itself, "discouragement" has the connotation of someone living with a lack of courage. The opposite of courage is to be "dis-courage-d" or to possess a lack of confidence. If we become consumed with discouragement, we begin to give up, and buy into our fears and insecurities. Our self-talk becomes negative, we may feel overwhelmed, bitter, angry, paralyzed, or lethargic.

In the film, *A League of Their Own*, the star player of the team, Dottie Hinson, played by Gena Davis, quits right before the end of the baseball season and has the following conversation with her manager/coach Jimmy Dugan, played by Tom Hanks.

Jimmy: "*Taking a little day trip, Dottie?*"
Dottie: "*I'm driving home to Oregon.*"
Jimmy: "*Dottie, if you want to go home...Great. I'm in no position to tell anyone how to live. But sneaking out like this, quitting, you'll regret the rest of your life. Baseball is what gets inside you, it's what lights you up. You can't deny that.*"
Dottie: "*It just got too hard.*"
Jimmy: "*It's supposed to be hard. If it wasn't hard everyone would do it. The hard... is what makes it so great.*"

After leaving the team for six games, Dottie has a change of heart, regains a sense of perspective and confidence, and rejoins the team. Worthwhile endeavors in life are meant to be hard. Obstacles and discouraging days are a simple fact of life. If we are to effectively minimize and manage discouragement, we must be willing to find whatever means works for us to sustain a hopeful spirit and a clearer perspective. Civil Rights hero, Rosa Parks, understood this all too well when she said, "I have learned throughout my life that what really matters is not whether we have probelms but how we go through them."

The Grade "A" Plan For Discouragement

1. **Acknowledge:** *I acknowledge I am feeling discourage*d.

2. **Analyze: Getting to the root of my discouragement**
A. "H.A.L.T." I am hungry_____ angry_____ lonely_____ tired_____
   What can I do to take care of myself? _____
   _____

B. The deeper emotions I am experiencing with regards to my feelings are: I feel discouraged,
   _____
   _____

C. The root cause of my discouragement is _____
   _____

3. **Action Plan: Tools to cultivate confidence**
A. Regain A Sense Of Hope:
   1. Remind ourselves failure and discouragement are facts of life. We must brush ourselves off and try again.
   2. Count our blessings and realize how small our discouragement is in the grand picture. Review life accomplishments, our journals, or start a Hope Journal. Perform an act of kindness and reopen our hearts to make room for a sense of hope, and a clear perspective will return.
   3. Do not be so hard on ourselves. Set realistic goals versus perfectionistic expectations.
   4. Remember life can be three steps forward and two steps back.
   5. Take time to rest and relax. Take a solitude date or retreat.

B. Fake It Until We Make It:
1. Get a tangible symbolic item such as a bracelet, a clothing item, or a confidence building quote or story to keep in our pockets, purses, or wallets.
2. Take pride in our appearance and wear something that makes us feel better about ourselves.
3. Pretend we are already a scholar, a successful business person, a film star, or whatever we desire to be. Choose someone we admire, and imagine ourselves in their shoes for a day.
4. Do something that we know we are good at until we regain a sense of hope, power, and confidence.

C. Develop A Strong Support Team:
1. Find a mentor, real or fantasy. If choosing a mentor do as character Jess does in the film, *Bend It Like Beckham*. Hang a poster of our hero and pretend he/she gives us advice. Read books or articles on someone we admire.
2. Be cautious around or eliminate toxic people from our everyday lives. Surround ourselves with people who have positive attitudes.
3. Find a group of like-minded people, where we can vent our feelings without judgement and receive encouragement.
4. Maintain significant relationships.

4. **Accountability: My plans to bridge the gap between my discouragement and confidence**
1. _____
2. _____
3. _____

Emotional Attitude #4: ADULT - CHILD

> *One of the most prevalent problems in modern time is*
> *emotional immaturity. A surprising number of people act like*
> *little children walking around in grown-up bodies.*
>
> Elinor MacDonald

A person's biological age does not necessarily parallel a person's emotional maturity. Someone may be fifty years old, but have the emotional maturity of a person twenty, thirty, or even forty years younger. An emotional setback can quickly turn a fully functioning emotionally mature individual back into a child.

When relating to people, I (Claudia) learned a long time ago to suss out whether a person is coming from an adult or child state, guiding me in how I approach a conversation. If someone is in an adult state, I am more adult-like in conversation speaking of issues in the news, political opinions, etc. Recognizing when someone is in a child state, I take the conversation to a more loving and caring direction asking them about their personal lives and feelings. While in the child state, we are often more emotionally raw and can be hurt easily. Adult exchanges are the last thing we need. When in an adult state, we have a clearer perspective on life and are not wearing our hearts on our sleeves. We have the ability to endure more of life's challenges.

We are all going to waiver at times between adult and child states no matter our age, because we are emotional beings. But, if we find ourselves stuck in a child state, functioning in society will be difficult. We can go even deeper and break down the child state into two distinct categories. The healthy child-LIKE state, and the unhealthy child-ISH state. A childlike state is vital for our emotional health, and keeps us creative, full of life, and hopeful. A childish state is selfish, self-serving, angry, bullyish, uncomfortable to be around, and is detrimental to our emotional health. For us to gain emotional maturity, we must get to the root of our childishness; otherwise we may never be able to maintain significant relationships and live successfully as fully functioning adults.

ADULT

Emotional maturity begins to develop when a person, regardless of age, intentionally takes responsibility for their lives and choices, and has a growing awareness of others and their feelings. An adult functioning in a childish state of mind will act out behaviors ranging from a toddler throwing a temper tantrum, to a self-consumed young teenager who thinks primarily of their own needs and desires. If we fall into childish behaviors on occasion, our emotional buttons are more often than not being pushed by specific uncomfortable circumstances, or when we are around certain people. Studies have shown for most of us this type of behavior tends to be brought out by those we are close to, particularly co-workers and immediate family members. Nobody is immune, not even the Queen of England.

There was a television documentary back in the early 1990's on England's Royal Family. Watching the dynamics between Queen Elizabeth II and the Queen Mother was quite fascinating and humorous. Elizabeth was in her mid-sixties at the time, and her mum was well into her eighties. One of the scenes was at a racetrack with the Royal Family in the Royal Box cheering on one of their horses. Their horse lost a close race and Queen Elizabeth looked obviously sad over the result. The Queen Mother leaned over to her daughter and said, "You don't need to cry just because your horse lost." Elizabeth got quite defensive with her mother and said, "I'm not crying, I've just got something in my eye." The Queen Mother looked at her with a little smirk, got up, and walked away saying just loud enough for Elizabeth to hear, "Hmmmmmm." The Queen was perturbed by her mother's comments and trotted after her saying, "Mummy, I'm not crying....Mummy I really do have something in my eye."

In order to function as emotionally mature adults, we must first recognize when we are slipping into childish states. Our goal is to manage childishness and train ourselves to consistantly live in a place of power. Therefore, when we are tempted to act out in a childish manner, we have the skills to redirect ourselves back into an adult state before things get out of control. Allowing ourselves an outlet for childlike behavior is key. When we are able to release our fears, frustrations, and stresses through creative outlets, we will keep our childishness in check.

CHILD

A great example of childlike behavior can be found in the classic Tom Hank's film, *Big*. Hank's character, Josh, wakes one morning to find himself transformed from a twelve year old boy to a grown man after making the wish to be, "big" at a video arcade the night before. He lands a job working at a toy company in New York City while his best friend, Billy (Jared Ruston), helps him track down the arcade machine, so Josh can take his wish back. He quickly excels in the company, and is moved up to research and development. His co-workers, who have been at the company for years, become jealous of his rapid rise up the corporate ladder and decide to find out the secret to his success. Josh is oblivious to his co-workers dislike for him and innocently invites one of his suspicious co-workers, Susan (Elizabeth Perkins), to his home after a company Christmas party. To her surprise, she finds his apartment filled with a pinball machine, a trampoline, a vending machine, bunk beds, a train set, a basketball hoop, and many other childlike toys. As she gets to know Josh, she discovers his childlike manner is refreshing, innocent, sweet, and inspiring.

Susan soon teams up with him on a project at work, and begins to praise his childlike attitude and professionalism to her doubtful co-workers including, Paul (John Heard), a jealous ex-boyfriend. Paul misunderstands the definition of childlike and reacts in a childish manner bullying Susan to try and win her back. Instead, his actions backfire turning her off even more.

The film ends with Josh finding the arcade machine, making his wish, and happily leaving the grown-up world to become a twelve year old child once again. Josh tries to talk Susan into making a wish with him to also become twelve years old, but having discovered the beauty of embracing a childlike attitude, she decides to remain, "big."

For many the line between living in a childlike state versus a childish state is often a blurry line. Once we come to an understanding of the true essence of childlikeness, we can better appreciate its significance. The great paradox of childlikeness is we are more susceptible to deeper hurts, but at the same time, we are just as susceptible to deeper feelings of passion, idealism, and love. Therefore, if a person does not develop the coping skills to manage hurt and disappointment, he will often act more childish and less childlike the older he becomes. This accounts for why so many people, who once were in their power as adults, seem to act more childish the older they become. Their hurts, throughout the years, have not been dealt with effectively. If a person does not retain a childlike nature, they will shut down emotionally as an ineffective coping mechanism to prevent further hurt. By not allowing ourselves to nurture a childlike attitude, we risk losing our sense of creativity, our passion, and we can become old before our time.

The dynamic principle of fantasy is play, which belongs also to the child,
and as such it appears to be inconsistent with the principle of serious work.
But without this playing with fantasy, no creative work is ever yet come to
birth. The debt we owe to the play of the imagination is incalculable.

Carl Jung

The Grade "A" Plan For Childishness

1. Acknowledge: *I acknowledge I am in a childish place.*

2. Analyze: Getting to the root of my childishness

A. "H.A.L.T." I am hungry_____   angry_____   lonely_____   tired_____
What can I do to take care of myself? _____

_____

B. The deeper emotions I am experiencing in regards to my childishness are: I feel childish,

_____

_____

C. The root cause of my childishness is _____

_____

3. Action Plan: Tools to cultivate an adult state of mind

A. Take Responsibility For Ourselves:
   1. Practice an adult mindset without letting go of childlikeness. Apply the quote by St. Paul: "When I was a child, I talked like a child, I thought like a child, I reasoned like a child. When I became an adult, I put childish ways behind me."

2. Practice accountability: Make a list of things, yet to be accomplished, and start by taking steps to work down the list.

3. Take positive steps toward personal growth. Get into therapy or join a support group to talk through childhood issues. Read inspirational personal growth books.

4. Always take the high road with choices over the low road.

5. Be prepared. If we are about to encounter a situation that usually brings on childish behavior, choose to remain in an adult state of mind to prevent a full outbreak. An example would be family holidays.

B. Nurture Our Inner Child:

1. Take some time to allow the inner child to play and to release stress. Perform fun activities often only done as a child. Swing, run with a kite, play with other kids, or go for a bike ride.

2. Do something creative and fun. Develop or redevelop a favorite hobby or art project.

3. Hang out with friends or make new friends and do something that makes us laugh.

4. Take the time to dream without self-imposed boundaries.

C. Practice Unconditional Love:

1. Review relationships with family members and approach them with an unconditional loving attitude.

2. Make a goal to perform three unselfish acts right away or in the immediate future. Send a kind note or email to those who need encouragement, give to a charity, or physically volunteer to help someone who is lonely or in need of companionship.

3. Make a list of ways to heal in mind, body, spirit, and emotions. Begin applying them as soon as possible.

4. Resolve conflicts with others.

5. List any childish behaviors and challenge ourselves to get past them.

4. **Accountability: My plans to bridge the gap between my childishness and my adult state**

1. _____

2. _____

3. _____

Our emotions are the gateway into our souls. To be motivated to create positive change in our lives, we must feel an emotional charge or connection before we take the first step. Allowing ourselves to remain in destructive behaviors generally means we still prefer the emotional charge of something in that behavior. Developing emotional maturity or achieving emotional balance is key to discovering the masterpiece within. We need passion! We need emotion! As Benjamin Disraeli said, "Man only does great things when he acts from great passion."

CHAPTER 15

WORKBOOK CHALLENGES V

GET TO KNOW ME

1. What constructive emotions have had a positive affect on my life?_____
    _____

    What destructive emotions have had a negative affect on my life?_____
    _____

2. In what situation have I been recently that threw me into a fearful mindset?_____
    _____

    How could I have dealt with the situation better, out of love instead of fear?_____
    _____

3. What positive loving act can I do for someone that I have a hard time forgiving?_____
    _____

4. What one major event in my life could have been different had I chosen confidence instead of listening to other's discouragement?_____

5. What are my childlike qualities that have had a positive effect on my life?_____
    _____

What are my childish behaviors that have had a negative effect on my life?_____
_____

6. In past life situations that I have handled well emotionally, what lessons should I remember to apply in the future? _____

PRACTICAL POWER TOOLS

1. Create a "Personal Victories' Journal." The foundation for, *The Masterpiece Within* is based on learning that we have the power to make our lives negative or positive experiences. We are faced with events on a daily basis that can compromise our confidence. A Personal Victories Journal is a helpful companion to keep close by. Purchase a journal and divide the pages into the four sections we have identified.

    Section 1: Record personal accomplishments, breakthroughs, and good times where you overcame adverse events and built up your confidence.

    Section 2: Record the same kind of inspiring events relayed to you from close friends and mentors.

    Section 3: Record stories that inspire you from outside sources, readings, conferences, movies, music, etc. that will help build your confidence.

    Section 4: Make a list of things you love to do. Use this list to refer back to during tough times. It will bring you back into a place of love and security when you are sad, depressed, or having a tough time.

2. Develop personal release responses to prevent fear from eating you alive. These various techniques or personal symbolic gestures allow us to confront our fears and move on.

    a. Small Mannerism: Make small gestures to simulate not allowing fear to overcome you. Cross your fingers, scratch your chin, or brush the fear off your shoulder when fear presents itself. This technique can be done discretely in a room full of people or alone.

    b. Medium Mannerism: Simulate letting go by washing the fear off your hands with soap and watching it go down the drain, stating, "I release this unwelcomed fear." This can be performed in all circumstances, because bathroom privacy can be found everywhere.

    c.   Large Mannerism: Write out your fears and place them into a worry jar, make a worry release list, or perform a burning bowl ceremony and dispose of the ashes in a graveyard.

3. There is amazing healing power when enlisting the help of a trusted friend to verbalize your fears or anxieties. Try these two different styles.

    a.   Feedback: Practice with a friend ahead of time what you might say to another in a conflict or upcoming situation. Getting their feedback can aid in the effectiveness of getting through to another.

    b.   Venting: Find a friend that will be willing to simply listen. Ask them to give little or no advice, and let you vent your feelings. Reverse the roles if needed.

4. Make a list of any people you currently have conflicts with and plan out how you can best resolve these conflicts. This is an exercise that not only teaches us to free up our minds, but also helps to remind us no one is perfect. Consider first that you may have completely misunderstood their actions. When working to resolve the conflict in person, remember that you may not have a positive reaction from the other person. However, in most cases, the effort alone will be therapeutic for your emotional health.

5. Managing anger is a lifetime commitment. Here are some suggested proven power tools that have helped many along the way.

    a.   Deal with the anger quickly.

    b.   Choose your words carefully.

    c.   Release hostility before speaking. Try going on a drive, performing vigorous exercise, taking a bat and pounding a pillow to release anger into the pillow, instead of on the person, or try creating a time out between the encounter and any form of confrontation.

BRAIN MEDICINE

1. I choose to love myself and others
2. I practice forgiveness
3. I deal with my feelings before ending my day
4. I remain confident in all situations
5. I have the knowledge and power to stay in my adult self

PERSONAL BRAIN MEDICINE

1. _____
2. _____
3. _____
4. _____
5. _____

I've learned that people will forget what you said, people will forget what you did, but people will never forget how you made them feel.

Dr. Maya Angelou

CHAPTER 16

ESSENTIALS FOR SPIRITUAL GROWTH

If there is light in the soul, there is beauty in the person.
If there is beauty in the person, there is harmony in the house.
If there is harmony in the house, there is order in the nation.
If there is order in the nation, there will be peace in the world.

Chinese Proverb

In the summer of 1998, my (Claudia) youngest daughter Carrie, who was nine at the time, asked me if I could help her and her best friend, Eliza set up a lemonade stand at the end of our driveway. About half an hour into selling the lemonade, Carrie came running back into the house with tears streaming, because she and Eliza had had a fight and came to the conclusion they could no longer be friends. I could not imagine what they were fighting about, because they had been inseparable since they were four years old, and had never disagreed about anything. Carrie went on to explain that she and Eliza had discovered the one thing they did not have in common, their religious beliefs. Although both were raised in the Christian faith, they attended different Christian denominations. I reassured Carrie that there are many different faiths all around the world, and lots of people believe differently.

After calming down, she went back outside and found Eliza, who lived next door, still sitting at the lemonade stand. I watched from the window as they sheepishly worked out their differences and once again became best of friends. I asked Carrie later that evening, how they were able to work things out. She said, "I wrote, 'I'm sorry' on a leaf with a stick and so did Eliza. Then we agreed it was okay to disagree."

Wars upon wars have been fought for centuries in the name of religion and religious beliefs. If only we adults around the world could solve our differences as quickly and in such a loving manner as two nine year old girls in Tennessee. If we could all embrace the thought that individual beliefs are like snowflakes, "no two will ever be exactly alike," we would be given the opportunity to come to a place of love, understanding, and acceptance toward one another.

Ghandi taught, "A friendly study of the world's religions is a sacred duty." According to Rabbi Marc Gellman, Monsignor Thomas Hartman, and Thomas Acquinas there are five divine natural laws that govern all major religions. These five divine natural laws can be referred to as the "essentials" of a belief system. They include:

1. Respect for others
2. Respect for life
3. Practice charity
4. Forgive others
5. Create community

What most people argue over, including Carrie and Eliza, are the "nonessentials" or additional details of our beliefs, beyond the five divine natural laws. These nonessentials include:

1. Our own personal beliefs or preferences
2. Our traditions and ceremonies
3. Our particular religious rituals
4. Our own family and cultural upbringing practices

One of the oldest protestant denominations, The Moravians, first organized in the late 1300's by priest and reformer, Jan Hus, adopted the motto, "In essentials, unity; in non-essentials, liberty; in all things, love," which helps define the direction we should always strive to take.

This motto has since been embraced by numerous denominations, ministries, and mission societies worldwide.

SPIRIT - RELIGION - SPIRITUALITY

Plato, while engaging his students, said to them, "If you are going to converse with me, please define your terms." When it comes to defining the terms spirit, religion, and spirituality, we often find these three words can have a broad range of connotations for a variety of people. We developed their cumulative definitions from our research of mainstream and historical theological commentaries, and the general parallel definitions used by major world religions. For the purposes of *The Masterpiece Within,* we will be stressing the importance of gaining spiritual balance, and becoming a spiritual practitioner versus developing a particular religious belief.

SPIRIT

In theological terms, our spirit is referred to as our volition or our free will. In other words, spirit is the part of us that chooses, spirit is where our core values exist, and spirit is the true essence of our being. French philosopher and poet, Teilhard de Chardin, captured this truth when he said, "We are not human beings having a spiritual experience. We are spiritual beings having a human experience."

In the two major surveys we conducted for *The Masterpiece Within*, the results revealed that ninety-five percent of the respondents felt they still needed help in making wise choices, and ninety percent believed their spirituality was the most underdeveloped dimension of the four. The survey results demonstrate the connection between choice and spirit, and why most of us still need help making wise choices, because our choices are directly rooted in spirituality. This also sheds light on why the spiritual dimension tends to be the most underdeveloped, because it is also the most misunderstood dimension. This makes one wonder if, as the saying goes, "We only use ten percent of our brains," what percentage of our spirit do we use, even when we commit to being a spiritual practitioner?

Since we are born multi-dimensional beings, our spirit will always be highly influenced by our other three dimensions of emotion, intellect, and the physical. To be a truly mature spiritual person, we must learn to live our lives governed by our spiritual values rather than being governed by the other three dimensions. If we allow ourselves to be governed by our emotions, our intellect, or our physical dimensions, our lives will eventually take on negative or destructive patterns.

In the book, *The Hoffman Process*, author Tim Laurence, reminds us why it is so important to allow our spirit to guide the other three dimensions. Laurence says:

"*When negative patterns take over our lives, all aspects of our being are affected. Our spiritual selves are no longer our guiding voice. We are run instead by our emotional and intellectual selves, which is taking on all these negative patterns. While these two are battling it out, we will repeat our self-destructive cycles of behavior. Our bodies will suffer with headaches, back pain, and indigestion. The hardest part of all to bear is that we cannot hear the wise voice of our spiritual self. It is drowned out by the terrible racket these two make.*"

RELIGION

There are five major world religions, which make up ninety percent of the planet's population. This percentage includes practitioners and nonpractitioners of these five religions. The other ten percent is made up of tribal religions or those with no religious affiliation. Generally speaking, religion is a formalized belief system made up of rituals, beliefs, and morals, or ethical laws. Rituals, which are considered nonessentials, include customs, traditions, and practices. They were originally intended to aid the essentials, as well as a reminder or outward manifestation of particular religious teachings. All cultures have their own religious rituals, which are unique.

The core beliefs of a religion tend to center around the five divine natural laws. Nonessential beliefs, such as specific details of the afterlife, how much one should give financially, or how often one should pray are not necessarily less important, but they do not determine whether a person is a spiritual practioner. There are essential and nonessential moral and ethical laws in every religion.

In the Jewish faith, for example, the nonessential laws refer to ceremonial or manmade laws that were created to reinforce an essential law, but over time they may or may not translate culturally or hold the same significance. As we discussed earlier, the essentials, or five divine natural laws, do not vary much from religion to religion. In Sir John Templeton's book, *Wisdom From World Religion's*, Templeton reveals that all religions express the Golden Rule, or divine law #3, to practice charity. He also notes that, "Similar ideas of conduct are found in the writings of Aristotle, Plato, Seneca, as well as other great philosophers and teachers."

The Golden Rule As Expressed in World Religions

Bahai: *Blessed is he who preferreth his brother before himself.* - Bahaullah

Brahmanism: *This is the sum of duty: do naught unto others which would cause you pain if done unto you.*

Buddhism: *Hurt not others in ways that you yourself would find hurtful.* - Udnaa-Varga

Christianity: *So in everything, do to others what you would have them do to you.* - Matthew 7:12

Confucianism: *Do not unto others what you would not have them do unto you.* - Analects

Hindu: *This is the sum of duty: do naught unto others which would cause you pain if done to you.* - Mahabharata

Islam: *No one of you is a believer until he desires for his brother that which he desires for himself.* - Sunnah

Jainism: *In happiness and suffering, in joy and grief, we should regard all creatures as we regard our own self.* - Lord Mahavira, 24th Tirthankara

Judaism: *What is hateful to you, do not to your fellowman. That is the law, all the rest is commentary.* - Talmud

Native American: *Respect for all life is the foundation.* - The Great Law of Peace

Persia: *Do as you would be done by.*

Taoism: *Regard your neighbor's gain as your own gain and your neighbor's loss as your own loss.*

Sikhism: *Don't create enmity with anyone as God is within everyone.* - Guru Arjan Devji 259, Guru Granth Sahib

Zoroastraianism: *That nature only is good when it shall not do unto another whatever is not good for its own self.* - Dadistan-I-Dinik

SPIRITUALITY

Genuine spirituality is to consciously follow one's inner convictions and personal beliefs with integrity, and to make unconditional love the prime motivator of one's choices. The two conditions for entering a spiritual life as a practitioner are the commitment to being a practitioner and the commitment to humility. A spiritual practitioner is driven to maintain continuous growth or development of the soul, and is never satisfied with status quo. They also consistently strive to practice the deeper spiritual qualities of love, joy, peace, patience, kindness, goodness, faithfulness, gentleness, and self-control.

There is a wonderful quote by the former president of the World Fellowship of Religions, Kirpal Singh, which expresses the outcome one will experience when choosing the route of humility. Singh says, "When the light of humility dawns on the soul, the darkness of selfishness disappears and the soul no longer lives for itself, but for God." Gaining this perspective brings about a newfound respect and desire to align one's life by God's revealed will, or by how we have come to understand him. Humility is not about appearing meek, but instead, should be seen as taking a strong, powerful stand to come face to face with letting go of or not allowing the ego to rule our lives in a negative manner. As one commits to both humility and to being a spiritual practitioner, the evidence of growth manifests in two forms: we become more generous, loving people and we develop a growing desire to seek God. In other words, we seek to become the best person we can be. Our behaviors become more tolerant and compassionate toward others, and because our hearts have softened, generosity begins to permeate all aspects of our lives. We are motivated to create daily practices such as prayer, meditation, and study, due to the fact that a humble heart is a teachable heart.

HEALTHY SPIRITUALITY VERSUS TOXIC BELIEFS

One of the biggest challenges we face in developing healthy spirituality is the tendency to throw out the healthy aspects of religion along with the unhealthy aspects that have little or no relevance to genuine spiritual growth. The healthy aspects of a religion or the essentials, regardless of the tradition or practice, should always lead us to a deeper level of love. There are two extremes of toxic faith, which we should be cautious of or avoid at all costs. The first extreme can occur when we feel just entering a church or temple on a regular basis will guarantee us a glorious afterlife, because we are faithful in all the outward expressions, even if we are not truly a practitioner. Another closely related toxic mindset can occur, when we believe our point of view or faith is the only correct way to believe, and any others who do not believe exactly the same way risk God's disfavor and eternal damnation. In Christianity, for example, many have strong beliefs about the after-life, the existence of angels, the trinity, and the resurrection. Yet, strong beliefs do not always mean that a person is a spiritual practioner of the five divine natural laws.

> *There is a difference between knowing the path and walking the path.*
> Morphius to Neo, in the film, *The Matrix*

Religion then becomes unhealthy or toxic, because the morals, ethics, and traditions of a specific religion become the focal point and the spirit of these, which is love, is neglected. When this occurs, our spirit becomes very rigid, intolerant, and shallow.

Erwin McManus, originally from El Salvador, is an author and minister of a multi-cultural church in Los Angeles. In his book, *An Unstoppable Force*, he says, "The morals of the faith are the minimum standard for human behavior. God's call to us is much greater to love others, ourselves, and God unconditionally." McManus even refers to the Ten Commandments as the kindergarten aspect or minimum basics of one's faith. If we never push or challenge ourselves to grow beyond the infant stages or very basics of our religious or spiritual beliefs, we will never be able to truly gain healthy spiritual balance.

The second extreme of toxic faith occurs when we, for whatever reason, have decided that almost anything to do with religion or religious practices is a farce and extreme waste of time. If we are in this group, we may feel we are spiritual practitioners, because we have a strong belief in God and/or the supernatural. But, in our haste to throw out religious trappings, we have either minimized or completely thrown out the basics or five divine natural laws. This belief is toxic, whether we merely practice this belief alone or if we belong to a formalized spiritual community. The foundation we are building our beliefs upon is not based on solid divine universal truths, but primarily our own personal ideas and experiences. Regardless, we will rarely see significant spiritual growth and attain the soul satisfying life we are all meant to possess.

ACCESSING OUR SPIRITUALITY

We will all be given opportunities to discover and to develop our spirituality. When they present themselves, it is simply a matter of choosing when and how we respond to them. In the spiritual classic, *The Tibetan Book of Living and Dying*, author Sogyal Rinpoche reminds us:

"All we need to do to receive direct help is to ask. Didn't Christ also say: 'Ask and it shall be given you; seek and ye shall find; knock and it shall be opened unto you. Everyone that asketh receiveth; and he that seeketh findeth'? And yet asking is what we find hardest. Many of us, I feel, hardly know how to ask. Sometimes it is because we are arrogant, sometimes because we are unwilling to seek help, sometimes because we are lazy, sometimes our minds are so busy with questions, distractions, and confusion that the simplicity of asking does not occur to us."

Almost everyone waits to access these opportunities even after asking for them, because we still want to hold onto our destructive behaviors while at the same time we also want the change we desire. For some of us, it will take a deeply stirring moment of crisis before we are willing to finally make the mature decision to change.

I (Guy), witnessed this first hand while completing my internship for my social work degree at a drug and alcohol rehab center in Regina, Saskatchewan, Canada. During the six weeks of training, I participated in all the activities as if I had checked into the center as an addict myself. The other patients were made aware of my role. Part of the training included a daily one hour group therapy session, which focused on the 12 Steps. The day we were to address Step three, which emphasizes the importance of turning our lives and will over to God/our higher power as we understand him, the counselor threw in a twist saying, "I want everyone here to share one or two stories from your life where you felt God was making himself real to you and nudging you to turn your life and your will over to him." I honestly thought this would be a quick session and we would head over to the gym for extra time during our daily sports activities (everyone's favorite time of the day). Well, for the next four hours, we heard at least three to four stories from each person in the room.

Most of the stories shared were unbelievably moving and sensational in nature. They included miraculous physical healings, divine-like encounters with people whom had come along at just the right time with wisdom, encouragement or warnings. One man told a story of running out of gas while rushing his child to a hospital, but happened to find a gas can in a farmers yard with a note attached saying, "For anyone to use in case of an emergency." The counselor then asked us all, "After experiencing these 'miracles' or apparent miracles did you feel that God was telling you something in your hearts?" Every single person in the circle said the same thing in their own words that went something like this, "I felt God was saying, 'You need to honor me with your life, stop your destructive behavior, and give me your heart.'" I was blown away because nine of the twelve people said they knew they should follow God, but after each encounter, chose not to because they just did not want to give up their selfish and addictive behaviors. What I could not stop thinking was how often we are granted moments like these and how often we choose not to respond.

Every now and then we will all have experiences or encounters with the, "invisible supernatural realm" that we now like to call, "too odd not to be God" moments thanks to our good friend, Kathey Hurt, who introduced us to the phrase. In other words, these gifts are somewhat miraculous coincidences, occurances, opportunities, or invitations for us to walk into deeper spiritual growth; but it is only a matter of recognizing and acknowledging them. A select few will respond immediately, others will eventually respond while some may never respond. When we have these, "too odd not to be God" encounters, they can be likened to a bell ringing in our hearts when we know what we are experiencing is divine and true.

As a child the foundation to my (Claudia) spirituality was solidly established by my mother. She would often take me and my three siblings to various Christian churches throughout my childhood, whether we wanted to go or not. Around eight years of age, the focus of my attention suddenly turned from the fun Sunday School activities to wanting to hear more about the message of God's love. I quickly developed a relationship with my new best friend, God, along with an inner and sometimes verbally out loud prayer communication that still exists today. After a few months, it was as if a bell was ringing in my heart alerting me that it was time to publically profess my love and commitment to God. I promised God this public acknowledgement would take place at the next Sunday morning church service I attended. On the way to my public profession of faith and love, my mother announced that we were going to try out her friends' church instead of the one we had been attending. Being a shy child I instantly became terrified at the thought of speaking before strangers, but I had made my promise to God and I knew I had to keep it.

To my surprise, we walked into the largest church I had ever been to in my entire life. We arrived late so we sat in the back row of the very crowded service. My heart was racing the entire hour, partly out of sheer fear, and partly over the pride of my public profession. That day, even at such a young age, I knew I would always be proud of my own spiritual beliefs and my relationship with God no matter the consequences. To my family's surprise, their paralyzingly shy sister and daughter, got out of the pew and walked the length of the church toward the minister to let him know I loved God and it needed to be publicly acknowledged.

Working to develop my spiritual life has enriched my life and has helped me feel that I am never alone in the world no matter where I am or what I am going through. As my husband, Rodney Crowell's song, *Alone But Not Alone* says, "I'm alone but not alone, something inside me is trying to guide me on my long way back home, I'm alone but not alone."

When I (Guy) look back on my life and how I was lead into pursuing a relationship with God there were several, "too odd not to be God" moments convincing me that God was real. Even though I was brought up going to church every week I viewed religion as boring and with lots of rules. In spite of my misguided view of authentic spirituality I had a very strong belief in God, but a very weak desire to become religious. I was a lot like a soldier in an episode of the television series, M*A*S*H, who the character Father Francis Mulcahy was counseling. The soldier was trying to convince Mucahy he was a good Catholic boy, because he believed all the right stuff, but Mulcahy knew this young man was not even close to following his beliefs in a consistant way. He said to the soldier, "Young man you have a religion, but it is a religion of convenience, and a religion of convenience is a hollow faith."

Like the soldier, I picked and chose what I wanted to bring into my life in terms of the requirements of faith. One example was the Ten Commandments. I remember as a teenager agreeing with the logic of the commandments, but telling myself there were three or four of them that I considered optional if the circumstances of breaking them suited me in a self-serving way. My, "too odd not to be God" moment number one, was observing the power of changed lives when having a relationship with God. Pope John Paul II would often say, "God reaches people by what they are interested in or familiar with." As a teenager almost all my heroes were sports or music heroes. When I was around sixteen years old, I observed three lives that impacted me immensely. The spiritual conversion of Paul Henderson, Canada's hero of the famous 1972 hockey summit series vs. the Soviet Union; CFL star, Gary Lefebrve; and our high school band master and local hockey hero, Mr. Aurelle Bleau. These three people seemed to have so much contentment and peace without getting all weird after turning to God. I wanted what these three people had.

"Too odd not to be God" moment number two, came to me after discovering the book, *The Cross and the Switchblade,* written by David Wilkerson. It never dawned on me before reading the book that God would be willing to forgive me of my sins or perceived wrong-doings. I always felt that I was never good enough for God. Until then. After reading the book and hearing stories of lives changed through Wilkerson's ministry, I finally came to the understanding that God loves me as an individual.

My, "too odd not to be God" moment number three, was learning the difference between being religious and being spiritual. Through my search for God, I realized that most people with authentic faith did not like being called religious, because of the connotation of the man made rules and traditions that often do not make sense. What a relief it was for me to realize that I did not have to be religious, but I could be spiritual.

One of the most successful books ever published on spiritual growth was written by psychiatrist and author, Dr. M. Scott Peck. *The Road Less Traveled,* has been touted as being one of the most successful self-help books of the twentieth century, selling ten million copies and translated into twenty languages, remained on the New York Times Best Sellers List for ten years. In his book, Peck reminds us of the constant work it takes to sustain a balanced spiritual life.

"Again and again I have emphasized that the process of spiritual growth is an effortful and difficult one. This is because it is conducted against a natural resistence, against a natural inclination to keep things the way they were, to cling to the old maps and the old way of doing things, to take the easy path."

When we make the commitment to access our spirituality, some live under the assumption that by choosing this life direction, we will be sacrificing our "fun." Yet, when one truly commits to becoming a spiritual practitioner and consistently walks the road toward spiritual growth, a new inner joy that cannot be fictitiously manufactured begins to emerge. In the C. S. Lewis classic series, *The Narnia Tales,* Lewis refers to this inner joy as the "deeper magic." This "magic" will sustain us through difficult times and can manifest as pure happiness in the good times. Sometimes the deeper magic may feel distant, but nevertheless, one always has a sense that it is close by and will reemerge. Yes, developing spiritual balance will be hard, there is no denying this fact. But life will remain harder than it has to be the longer we delay the development of our spirituality.

BECOMING A SPIRITUAL PRACTITIONER

I (Guy) created a college level curriculum on how to grow spiritually, which I have taught in close to one hundred seminar settings, and which has been embraced in whole or in part by four Theological schools in Western Canada. These five essentials were taken from a study of the first Century Christian church, the principles of AA, and from studying churches all over the world that are making a difference. In my presentation, I use the acrostic P-O-W-E-R as my template to show the essentials of spiritual growth.

For our purposes in *The Masterpiece Within*, we have chosen to convert the P-O-W-E-R acrostic to the FIVE S's of solitude, service, study, support group, and sustaining growth to promote an even deeper understanding of the essentials for spiritual growth.

<u>P-O-W-E-R</u>	<u>THE FIVE S's</u>
<u>P</u> Prayer	Solitude
<u>O</u> Outreach	Service
<u>W</u> Wisdom	Study
<u>E</u> Encouragement	Support Group
<u>R</u> Renewal	Sustaining Growth

The one caution I always throw out for seminar attendees is that if we merely focus on solitude, study, support groups, and sustaining growth as means for progress and stop short of service, our spirituality will not attain its highest level of potential. We are simply making the means the end, which is never healthy. These five S's are designed for a greater end result than simply personal knowledge and growth. They are meant to open our hearts and inspire us to be of loving service to the world. Our goal in mastering solitude, study, support group, and sustaining growth is to imbed service so deep into our spiritual DNA that it becomes as natural as breathing.

Solitude + Study + Support Group + Sustaining Growth = Service

SPIRITUAL PRACTITIONER TOOLS

Spiritual Practitioner Tool #1: SOLITUDE

> *To know God and hear his voice, one must learn the discipline of*
> *solitude, because it is in the silence of the heart, that God speaks.*
>
> Mother Teresa

One of the most significant acts of self-love is establishing solitude time for ourselves. The time we spend alone is necessary and invaluable because our most substantial spiritual growth occurs in solitude. Creating consistent solitude time for ourselves also provides further opportunity to continue laying the foundation for discovering the masterpiece within. We can look at spending time in solitude from two very different perspectives, one from a positive viewpoint and the other from a negative. Positive solitude is intentionally spending time away from others in a quiet environment in order to nurture ourselves spiritually, emotionally, mentally, and physically. Negative solitude is intentionally or unintentionally spending time away from others and becomes unproductive and damaging, because it leads to extreme loneliness. There are many life circumstances, which create unintentional solitude: elderly shut-ins, victims of divorce, death of a loved one, a spouse who travels or works long hours, people who are disabled, or someone who is single. This form of isolation is usually not a conscious decision someone makes unless they intentionally choose to live in isolation as a coping mechanism, perhaps to heal from pain and suffering caused by prior relationships in an attempt to avoid further hurt and disappointment.

Loneliness can be exceptionally harmful unless we learn how to turn the situation around and make the time spent alone more constructive. Composer Ludwig van Beethoven is a prime example of someone who turned a potentially negative time of solitude into a positive and productive experience. At the age of twenty-nine, Beethoven became increasingly aware of his advancing deafness. Agonizing over the possible end to his successful musical career and becoming sentenced to a silent chamber of isolation, he contemplated committing suicide, but instead he chose to view this life obstacle as a fresh start. Amazingly enough, the quality of his work increased and many of his greatest masterpieces including one of his most famous pieces, *Ode To Joy,* were composed after he became deaf. Solitude is a state of mind. Instead of seeing this time as negative or lonely, it is important to view it as an opportunity to take better care of ourselves and learn to adopt a more positive mindset toward spending time alone. Negative solitude is rooted in fear and can set off a steady downward spiral of loneliness, isolation, and depression. Positive solitude is based in love and is most often productive because it provides time for self-awareness, personal growth, increased self-worth, and much needed life balance. When we choose to make a sincere effort to improve ourselves, we begin to feel more secure within. This type of security can be very attractive. As a result, we may find others are more drawn to us than ever before because we have become more comfortable in our own skin.

> *The worst loneliness is not to be comfortable with yourself.*
>
> Mark Twain

For centuries monks throughout the world have been renowned for their solitude time spent in prayer and silence. Significant influential history makers throughout time have also demonstrated and praised the benefits of taking time for solitude. They believed solitude was a necessary component for their personal development whether spending time in prayer, study, journaling, resting, walking or by whatever means necessary. These history makers valued solitude as much as a formal education, putting in long hours at work, perfecting their crafts or performing their civic duties. In Michael J. Gelb's book, *Discovering Your Genius*, he refers to a study conducted by Catherine Cox at Stanford University in 1926, on three hundred of history's greatest minds. She found that no matter what their field of expertise, these high achievers had many common characteristics. One of the most common was using notebooks or letters to express emotions, record personal ideas and deepest thoughts. Through additional research we found, aside from journaling, walking was also a major form of solitude. Danish Philosopher and Theologian, Soren Kierkegaard stated, "Above all do not lose your desire to walk. Everyday I walk myself into a state of well-being. I have walked myself into my best thoughts, and I know of no thought so burdensome that one cannot walk away from it." We have compiled a list of personalities and how they have chosen to practice solitude in order to achieve the greatest benefits for themselves.

1. Winston Churchill- Painting and two hour baths
2. Teddy Roosevelt/Henry David Thoreau- Bird watching
3. Gandhi/ Beethoven/Thomas Jefferson/Sitting Bull/Jimmy Carter- Walks in nature
4. Charles Dickens- Walking around the streets of London alone following dinner
5. Francis Ford Coppola/Michelangelo- Horseback riding
6. Christopher Columbus/Leonardo da Vinci/Plato- Writing and journaling
7. Ernest Hemingway/Zane Grey- Fishing
8. Carlos Santana/Elvis/Dolly Parton- Built a chapel near their homes

9.   Steven Spielberg/Bill Russell- Long drives

10. Renee Russo/Phil Jackson/Mother Teresa- First hour of every day spent in study and prayer

With the influx of stress brought on by everyday living, taking time for ourselves is increasingly necessary in order to properly function in our world today. Scheduling solitude time into our daily or weekly calendars may be necessary to hold ourselves accountable for taking this time. At first, making solitude time a habit may also be difficult because we are relational beings by nature and solitude may not feel natural. However, neglecting a regular time of solitude causes our lives to be counter productive over an extended period of time. We begin to wear down in health, we feel mentally drained, we lose our grip on managing stress, and we regress spiritually. The key benefits we receive from spending time in solitude include personal reflection and contemplation, rest and renewal, heightened spiritual awareness and compassion, self-discovery and cultivation of our inner voice, and inspiration to carry out our genuine life bliss. Once we get used to taking this time for ourselves, we may wonder how we ever made it through a week without solitude time due to the tremendous benefits, which quickly begin to manifest. The irony is, we need more selfish time to become less selfish because taking the time to properly care for ourselves is the essence of true self-love.

> *The best thinking has been done in solitude.*
> *The worst has been done in turmoil.*
>
> Thomas Edison

The Irish Celtic mystics placed great value on solitude time. They considered solitude as one of the main gifts of grace from God to connect our human spirit to His spirit. Realizing we live in a tangible 3-D body, which prevents us from seeing into the invisible spiritual realm, the Celtics created the concept of "thick walls and thin walls." They were referring to the barriers or thick walls we encounter as spiritual beings living in a physical form, which can prevent us from making an authentic spiritual connection. The thicker the walls the further away we feel from God, diminishing our ability to make wise choices. The thinner the walls the closer we feel to God enhancing our ability to make wise choices. The Celtics believed spending daily time in solitude was one of the best means for breaking down these thick walls. They also acknowledged there are other experiences, practices, and disciplines such as a birth, death, nature, music, humanitarianism, and living a life of integrity, which can make these walls thinner. For example, someone may not have developed their spirituality at all, but once they experience the birth of their own child or the death of a loved one, this undeveloped dimension is challenged leaving them more open than ever before to making a spiritual connection. Oftentimes, it takes a crisis to wake up the desire to pursue the spiritual dimension, but sometimes even a normal everyday activity or encounter can strike us as an "aha" or thin wall moment. Like the Celtics, learning to value the discipline of solitude and making it a priority will allow us to receive its benefits throughout our lives.

Practicing Solitude

How often do we awake to a noisy alarm, turn on the television as we get ready for work, listen to the radio or music to and from work, get home and turn the television back on until bedtime, and start the entire process over again the next morning? Remaining in this state of habitual distraction makes time for inner reflection virtually impossible. Developing meaningful times of solitude can also be quite difficult because we are so used to the distracting noise. Once we do make the choice to turn off the noise, it can be very hard getting used to slowing everything down, quieting our minds and being comfortable in the silence. We can expect our minds to be cluttered in the first few minutes of solitude, but we can speed up the process by allowing time for the clutter to pass and for a sense of calm to move in. There are a number of helpful practices and principles, which can enhance our solitude time in a balanced fashion if we learn how to implement them on a regular basis. We have included twelve of the most significant ones in the following list.

1. Prayer: Prayer involves speaking to God either verbally or internally. We can approach prayer as formal or informal. Formal prayer involves reciting written verses or memorized phrases. Informal prayer is a free-flowing release of frustrations, fears, and feelings, asking for guidance, asking for personal needs to be met, prayers for others, along with thankfulness and adoration of God's blessings. By making prayer a habit we gain divine wisdom, life direction, inner strength, a deeper awareness of God's presence in our lives, and a sense that we are never alone.

2. Meditation: Meditation is primarily centered around listening and receiving divine wisdom from God, and sharpening our inner voice. There are two main forms of meditation. One is sitting still in a quiet environment with the goal of stilling the negative, toxic mind clutter. Another form, is taking an inspirational truth or phrase and thinking it through in quiet contemplation until we gain a full understanding of it. The goal of meditation is replacing harmful or selfish thoughts with positive or affirming thoughts and messages.

3. Inspirational Study: We have more access to sacred texts and inspirational resources than at any other time in human history via libraries, the Internet, through instructional CD's, downloads, webinars, audiobooks, or DVD's. The key to inspirational study is to approach it with the intent to gain and apply spiritual knowledge. Authentic spiritual wisdom and growth will accelerate in direct proportion to how quickly and consistently we put into practice what we are studying.

4. Nature: Connecting with nature provides healing and rejuvenating therapeutic qualities. Intuitively we all feel the inspirational aspects of getting out of the house and spending time with nature whether it involves watching a sunset, a walk in the woods or around the neighborhood, breathing in cool air on top of a mountain, or enjoying the warm waves of an ocean. Anytime we take the opportunity to connect with nature, we are able to view stressful life situations from a more realistic perspective. In doing so, we are able to reignite our life passion because we have allowed ourselves time to refocus our minds on the important aspects of life rather than being consumed by negative or petty issues.

5. Journaling: Taking the time to write down our thoughts on a page gives us the chance to express our deepest feelings and to vent paralyzing emotions such as fear, anger, resentment, and jealousy. Through this exercise we release stress, gain clarity, allow creativity to flow, and we are better able to reevaluate goals. Journaling connects us to our true essence, and is one of life's most useful tools in breaking down the barriers to our creativity.

6. Affirmations: As first discussed when introducing *Brain Medicine*, we are reminded here once again of the benefits positive affirmations bring to our lives. Affirmations can serve as a powerful tool to make our solitude time more productive because they build confidence and faith, they minimize doubt, and they open the possibilities for positive events to occur.

7. Sacred Space: In order to maximize our solitude time we must create or find a location that feels comfortable. This sacred space could be by a stream in the woods, in our car, a chapel, a park, or a room in our home, which can be filled with candles, our favorite books, music, or photos. It can be anywhere that creates a safe as well as inspirational atmosphere to take care of ourselves mentally, emotionally, physically, and most importantly of all, spiritually.

8. Scheduling In Time: Today's busy schedules can get so overwhelming that often we must schedule in solitude time for ourselves whether for five minutes, fifteen minutes, or half an hour. Finding small windows for solitude will help us get through our day much easier. Practicing solitude at specific times during the day helps create a much needed habit for developing our spiritual life as well as maintaining good emotional and mental health. Ideally, if we begin our day in solitude, we establish a loving pattern of self-care and set the tone for this pattern to continue throughout the day.

9. Setting Boundaries: Sometimes our commitments are so stretched that we barely have time to breathe, let alone the time to take care of ourselves mentally, physically, emotionally, or spiritually. Learning to set boundaries with family members and friends in order to have solitude time is a great way to begin taking care of ourselves. When we teach others how to treat us, they also learn respect for us at the same time. Others may not fully understand the importance of our solitude time in the beginning, but when they see for themselves the many benefits in our lives, particularly helping us treat others with more love, they may be encouraged to create their own solitude time.

10. Ceremonial Practices: Throughout history people have used structured or traditional practices: performing ceremonies, reading from prayer books, or the use of symbols during their solitude time to enhance their personal growth. These practices and the previously explained vow ceremony can be extremely rewarding to our lives. Additional methods such as a burning bowl ceremony, fasting, visualizations, and a vow of silence can also be beneficial because they are intentionally practiced to deepen our spirituality.

11. Play: For some, creating a regular routine of solitude time can seem like a lot of extra hard work and unneeded pressure. Because of this misconception, we may see fun as something usually done as a reward after all the hard work is complete. Our solitude time is meant to be enjoyable and is only truly effective if elements of fun are included. Continually reminding ourselves that our inner child is the guardian of our passion, dreams, and creativity is vital. To nurture this childlike attitude we must have a steady dose of play time or fun. This could involve listening to our favorite music, going to see a film or art exhibit, painting a picture, participating in any form of physical exercise, or whatever childlike fun that takes us to a place of renewal and teachableness. When play is practiced on a regular basis, we find we are able to think outside the box, relieve stress, and gain a fresher perspective on life.

12. Solitude Date: A set amount of daily solitude time is ideal, but we can also schedule once a week dates with ourselves. This time should be a one to three hour window to allow ourselves the time for proper rejuvenation. Completing weekly solitude dates allows us a greater appreciation of life, loved ones, humanity, and brings a sense of calm to our lives. Scheduled play time grants us the opportunity to revitalize all four dimensions.

> *I don't like to be idle; in fact I often feel somewhat guilty unless there*
> *is some purpose to what I am doing. But spending a few hours or a few*
> *days in the woods, swamps, or alongside a stream has never seemed to*
> *me a waste of time. I derive special benefit from a period of solitude.*
>
> Jimmy Carter, 2002 Nobel Peace
> Prize recipient and 39th US President

The time we spend in solitude is our own private time to use as we choose giving us a great deal of freedom and limitless possibilities. Seeing this time alone as a positive and joyful opportunity allows us to continue discovering the masterpiece within, become more conscious of making wise choices, become the hero of our own life story, cultivate our genuine life bliss, live a balanced life emotionally, spiritually, mentally, and physically and be inspired to make a difference in the world. The amount of self-love we receive is priceless, but most important of all, we are able to create thinner and thinner walls between God and us.

Spiritual Practitioner Tool #2: STUDY

> *Spirituality is about retaining the wonder of childhood*
> *while cultivating the wisdom of age.*

Timothy Freke

Our goal for spiritual study is not only to study but to integrate knowledge into our lives. In the Psalms of David there is a short passage that speaks of the importance of applying what we study. *"Oh, how I love your law. I meditate on it all day long. Your commands make me wiser than my enemies, for they are forever with me. I have more insight than all my teachers, for I meditate on your statutes. I have more understanding than the elders, for I apply your precepts."*

We could all have towers of spiritual books sitting next to us that we have read, but without application all the knowledge in the world will not help create spiritual depth. We can achieve spiritual depth by applying what we like to call, *The Spiritual Wisdom Triad,* which is to research, ponder, and personalize.

The Spiritual Wisdom Triad

1. Research: Read spiritual classics. Research and study inspirational materials that lead to a better understanding of the five divine natural laws. If we are not huge readers, we can always listen to audiobooks, or find a trusted spiritual mentor to educate us on the five divine natural laws along with additional valid spiritual teachings.

2. Ponder: Take an indepth look at the material we are studying. Ask ourselves what the knowledge means for our lives and how we can apply the lessons learned.

3. Personalize: Incorporate spiritual lessons into daily life. Memorize truths and be open to self-examination while thinking of ways to integrate and apply.

Reasons To Study

Apart from increasing knowledge in general and the application of spiritual truths into our lives, there are other valid and beneficial reasons to study inspirational resources.

1. Solidifies and/or clarifies our own beliefs
2. Increases open-mindedness and religious tolerance
3. Helps us better understand others
4. Gives us more confidence and validity in social situations
5. Helps us see each person as a soul-being that lives breathes as we do
6. Grants us comfort and peace of mind
7. Helps us sustain a teachable heart and allows our soul to evolve
8. Reminds us love is the most important virtue
9. Gives us clarity in thinking
10. Draws us closer to God

Methods Of Study

When looking for methods of study, there is no right way or wrong way to study spiritual truths. Whatever works best for each of us is the correct path to take. One person may enjoy reading a book while another may prefer listening to an audiobook. One person may enjoy discussion groups while another may enjoy attending a seminar and just listening. It is important to remember that up until the invention of the printing press, less than ten percent of the world's population could even read, yet education and study was a high priority in all cultures. There are informal and formal methods of studying: attending workshops or seminars, taking college courses, going on overnight personal retreats, forming small study groups, researching at libraries, seeking out and developing relationships with deeply spiritual individuals, speaking with friends about their beliefs, reading or listening to audiobooks, as well as watching films or documentaries. Most of the spiritual greats throughout time have been open to studying or had a working knowledge of all the major religions. Mahatma Ghandi once said, "I consider myself a Hindu, Christian, Muslim, Jew, Buddhist, and Confucian."

One of my (Claudia) favorite methods of spiritual study is to gather a small bag of books, a notebook and pen, and head to Radnor Lake in Nashville. There is a private spot I discovered on one of the walking trails with a bench where I like to pray, study, take notes, journal, and meditate while drinking in the beauty of nature. For some reason as of late, I am better able to access a genuine spiritual connection when in nature, more so than when I am in a traditional religious church setting. When the mood strikes and I feel like listening to a speaker or minister, I seek out a formal church setting. In 2012, my husband, Rodney, and I built a home and in the planning we created a prayer garden right outside our master bedroom. After moving in, the prayer garden quickly became a preferred spot. I love going there in the morning and at dusk for a five or ten minute repose.

I (Guy) have a fairly regular routine of personal study. After going through my divorce, I had a hard time going to church on Sunday mornings, yet I still knew I needed a weekly pick me up, so I developed what I call, "Java Church." I would go to a coffee shop for a couple of hours each Sunday with the intent of studying the Bible, reading inspirational books, and journaling. Sometimes a friend or two would join me and we would have some terrific discussions around spirituality and life issues and oftentimes people sitting close by would inquire and even join the discussion. My spiritual and personal growth over the next fews years continued on a positive path. I still attend a church setting on special occasions or if someone invites me, but my prime growth times have occurred during Java Church.

I like to have three books on the go at all times. I love to read my Bible daily, have another Christian book to supplement my convictions and an inspirational book that could vary from leadership to a biography or nuggets from other religions. I always have a notebook, an exacto-knife, pen, and yellow highlighter handy to clip out and record what I am learning. To mix things up at times I will listen to an inspirational CD, watch a movie or a documentary. I supplement my personal study times with church related events, seminars, coffee chats, and workshops.

Any one of us can benefit from developing a consistent discipline of spiritual study. The Saskatchewan Roughriders of the CFL are often referred to as Canada's team for their national following. In 1999, the team hired on an entirely new coaching staff that stayed together for almost seven seasons. One of my (Guy) former neighbors, Gail Mund has worked in the administration office for over twenty years. Gail really enjoyed working alongside this coaching staff and told me, "They are so nice yet have that burning intensity to succeed. They have a high level of integrity, have created a warm family atmosphere, and are such good community and family guys. Can you believe that six or seven of them all come to the office about an hour or two earlier than they have to every day, to study their Bibles or other inspirational readings before they start their day? I have never seen this before. And, they are not showy or preachy men at all." Richie Hall, defensive co-ordinator for the Riders, has been a family friend ever since he arrived in Canada from Colorado State in the late 1980's. He elaborated for us what goes on behind these closed doors so early in the morning;

"It just kind of happened that so many of us are doing this. This is certainly not a requirement from the top brass, it's hardly ever talked about, and none of us go to the same churches in Regina, but all of us are committed to grow as spiritual people. Some of us journal and take notes during our spiritual study time, pray, listen to inspirational CD's, or even watch spiritual DVD's during this time. Everyone seems to connect with God with whatever works for them. I mean it varies a lot. Are we better coaches as a result? I don't know but I think we are better equipped to make wiser choices in life and to manage whatever life, not just football, is thrown our way."

Spiritual Practitioner Tool #3: SUPPORT SYSTEM

In everyone's life, at some time, our inner fire goes out. It is then
burst into flame by an encounter with another human being. We should
all be thankful for those people who rekindle that inner spirit.

Albert Schweitzer

The goal of a support system should be to focus on a loving, safe, and supportive environment, a support system that promotes learning and growing in the spiritual sense to feel refreshed, to feel heard, to get understanding from others, and to hear encouraging words. A healthy support system should not only be encouraging but challenging. We should be held accountable while finding inspiration to blossom as individuals. The groups work best when kept small in size. If the group gets too big, it should be broken into smaller groups. The fruit of a healthy group will be hope, inspiration, and the desire to give to others in service in some manner. A group becomes unhealthy when gossip or negativity becomes the main focus. When this occurs, we will no longer feel recharged or encouraged. Beware of small group leaders or factions within the group who become controlling, judgemental, promote false guilt, or violate basic principles such as confidentiality and equality.

These groups can take on many different forms. We can find many support groups in formal settings such as churches, synagogues, temples, mosques, AA meetings, and large scale seminars. Informal group settings can be found through postings in libraries, universities and colleges, coffee shops, community centers, local newspapers, the Internet, or church bulletins. They can range from ask an elder or wise soul to common interest small groups that meet monthly or weekly to casual workshops and seminars.

Suggestions for Support Groups

1. Keep the group small. Use AA meetings as a model. When their meetings reach a certain size a new group is created to make sure everyone's needs are being met.
2. Use topics, books or movies for discussions or study.
3. Meet on a regular basis and make attending a priority.
4. Keep integrity in the group. Make sure the meetings are based on love and acceptance, and that everyone feels understood, encouraged, and hopeful. Keep an open mind about bringing in new members.
5. Make sure everyone gets air time to vent, speak, or ask for needed help.
6. Must be thought of as a safe haven. Everyone must keep details confidential.
7. Keep equality a priority. One person may organize the meetings in the beginning but there needs to be shared leadership without one particular leader.
8. Make the gathering place a neutral meeting ground not one particular home at all times. Meet in creative places such as art galleries or paint your own pottery shops.
9. Resolve differences before parting. Agree to disagree on topics of discussion. Remember no one thinks or believes exactly alike.
10. Plan ways to make a difference in our local community.

When I (Guy) first moved to Calgary, I saw an advertisement on the side of a bus which read, "Life is hard…join a support group." I remember thinking there was a lot of truth in that statement because most of my significant spiritual growth and encouragement had occurred in support groups. Being a minister for most of my life, I have participated in and lead many styles of support groups, which range from prayer meetings to biblical life skill classes to gender specific groups. Still to this day, the best support group I have ever been a part of occurred between 1986 and 1988. The group consisted of six spiritual men who all worked in different vocations. Our time together was based on our spiritual struggles and how we could best incorporate our faith into our daily lives. In each meeting, we shared our struggles, what we were learning, and prayed for each other. I have never grown so much, and so quickly as during my time with these friends. We practiced accountability, confidentiality, brutal honesty, and yet I never felt so safe and loved in my life. For almost two full years, this was the highlight of my week, and that is saying a lot for I am not a morning person we met at 6 a.m. every Saturday.

I (Claudia) have always been a, "people person." I love meeting new people and learning about their lives and listening to their life stories. Oftentimes for me meeting a new friend leads to a lifetime friendship. I am always amazed at how often I will think of someone that I have not spoken to in a while and I will get a call, email or text from them just as I am about to reach out to them. Checking in with others can be very therapeutic for both parties, whether we need to vent our troubles or speak about all the good things in our lives.

In the fall of 2005, my friend, Lisa Seals, and I formed a support group we called, *The Artist's Wives Club*, which met bi-weekly for two years. Our group of women were all married to music artists and entertainers who frequently traveled for work, while their wives were home the majority of time working on their own careers as well as taking care of the home and children. When we got together we made sure each woman was given the opportunity to check in and discuss their lives.

Cheers, one of the most successful television series of all time (1982 to 1993), had a memorable and well-crafted theme song titled, *Where Everybody Knows Your Name,* written by Gary Portnoy and Judy Hart Angelo. The song represents the essence of what an ideal support group should possess.

Spiritual Practitioner Tool #4: SUSTAINING GROWTH

> *You must be prepared to endure the hardships involved in a genuine spiritual*
> *pursuit and be determined to sustain your effort and will... and understand*
> *that the key to a successful practice is never to lose your determination.*
>
> Dalai Lama

We must constantly challenge ourselves to grow spiritually. With the busy schedules each of us have it is often easier to just go home, put on comfortable clothes, numb out, and channel surf all night rather than to make any extra effort after a long day's work. Of course having time to relax is necessary, but in order to sustain a significant level of spiritual growth a strong level of commitment is required. In the long run the work we have put in for our efforts may seen small in comparison when weighed against the rewards we receive.

My (Guy) father, Herb Scholz was a John Deere farm equipment dealer back home in Saskatchewan throughout my childhood. I learned from a very young age that there are five stages for preparing a harvest, and that each stage requires specific machinery to help foster a healthy crop. We can liken each stage and the tools required to fostering a healthy spiritual harvest.

Cultivating: Cultivating the dormant hard soil can be likened to spiritual study. In order to unlock our hearts to the learning process, we must be willing to study. Remaining open and commited to the process keeps our hearts tender and amenable to spiritual awakenings. Julia Martin was known thoughout Northern Alberta for almost five decades as the trucker's wife with the nickname "Mother Teresa," because she continuously opened her home to anyone in need. One of the secrets to her compassion came from her daily habit of studying inspirational books. Half of her kitchen table remained covered with well-used study books, and half was reserved for a home cooked meal, which she prepared for anyone in need.

Planting: Planting the seeds for the crop can easily be coupled with solitude. The image of the lonely farmer spending long days planting his seeds can be seen the same as spending time alone developing our quiet time of inspiration and rejuvenation, through prayer and thanksgiving.

Weeding: Weeding a potential crop is the same as keeping short accounts in the spiritual realm. Removing the weeds or overgrowth helps keep the crop strong and vital. Sustaining a strong spiritual life requires constant vigilance to keep distractions and unresolved conflicts to a minimum. Floyd McClung, a missionary and author who established two highly successful missions in Afghanistan and Amsterdam, taught that dealing with unresolved conflicts is foundational to creating spiritual depth. He emphasizes this discipline is often the hardest to practice but possibly the most important.

Watering: A potential crop needs outside resources in addition to counting on rain such as watering equipment or irrigation to help grow a bountiful harvest. Watering our spiritual life through private time with God is vital, but our growth can be accelerated even further in a support group setting.

Harvesting: Harvesting a crop can be likened to service, love, and generosity. A crop is harvested, brought to market, and sold to feed people around the world. In the same manner, our spiritual growth provides a bounty of love and generosity to be shared with the world. Bruce Doerksen is a respected Canadian gospel singer/songwriter who travels the world training church worship leaders in his lectures. Doerksen is known for advising leaders to "feed the poor" or to unselfishly look for ways to give outside the safe confines of their spiritual community. As my (Guy) father taught me years ago, successful farmers pay constant attention to servicing their required machinery, and consistently committing to the work necessary in each of the five stages of growing a healthy crop. If the farmer is faithful in doing his part during the process, more often than not the harvest will be a success.

Attitudes And Behaviors That Hinder Growth

So often the elimination of clearly selfish choices is all it takes for us to sustain a high level of spiritual growth. Having the courage to make loving choices can open our hearts to divine aid and strengthen our spiritual life when unrealistic or unnecessary fear, guilt, or shame is screaming at us to take the low road. Buddha, Mohammed, Moses, and Jesus all taught that elimation of certain negative attitudes and destructive behaviors is vital for spiritual growth.

We can easily adopt these negative traits because of our environment or circumstances, but if they become a major inner force in our lives, we must learn how to neutralize them or else they can lead to even more destructive behaviors.

The theological term all four major religious leaders used to describe destructive behaviors rooted in our choices was "sin." For many, sin is a controversial word, yet it has never been able to be eliminated in our cultural lexicons. The overall acceptance of the word "sin" seems to move in cycles of what is in vogue and not in vogue. So what is sin? Jesus describes sin as a person building a house on a sandy or weak foundation, which will crumble when one does not consistently make choices based in unconditional love. Buddah once used the metaphor of a swift current that leads to a dangerous rocky destination to describe the result of sin.

In both cases, the sin they were speaking about refers to choices that were clearly unloving and selfish in orientation. Maybe Hollywood got the definition of sin as accurately as any religion ever has and the importance of eliminating it in the film, *Bruce Almighty*. The main character, Bruce, played by Jim Carrey, is a television reporter who is temporarily given divine powers from God portrayed by Morgan Freeman. Early in the film he makes the declaration, "I am Bruce Almighty, my will be done!" As Bruce begins to abuse his power, his life spirals down a dark and empty path. The more his choices become self-serving, the more he drives away those closest to him. His life eventually loses meaning and everything becomes a mess. God allows him to learn these lessons on his own and then intervenes by teaching Bruce that everything is going wrong for him because his choices are based in selfishness. In order to, "play God" his choices must be made from a place of unconditional love. He is finally able to turn everything around when he goes from "Bruce Almighty, my will be done" to practicing "God Almighty, your loving will be done."

Keys To Ongoing Spiritual Renewal

If we feel unsettled or if we find our lives are not giving back to us all that we need, or if something just does not seem quite right, the first question we should ask ourselves is, "What is the present state of my spiritual life?" Most likely giving our spiritual life attention will turn things around in a positive direction. Remembering at all times we are spiritual beings on a human journey, and focusing on the core of who we are will more often than not reboot our inner joy. Holding ourselves accountable to practicing the five S's is key to sustaining renewal, and should be addressed as a high priority throughout our lives. To sustain our spiritual growth we have listed a few additional key points to keep in mind:

1. Make choices from a loving place versus a selfish place
2. Continually take the high road with all things in life
3. Discover and develop life purpose and meaning
4. Practice forgiveness of self and others
5. Incorporate study, solitude time, and support groups into our schedules
6. Resolve conflicts as quickly as possible
7. Practice love of ourselves and others
8. Consciously choose to have hope and faith
9. Get priorities aligned
10. Find charities or ways to help others on a continual basis

Guy's top three sustaining growth practices:

1. Daily quiet time of study and prayer.
2. 1/3 - 2/3 rule! A reminder to keep making a difference at the forefront. So often in life we build relationships with like-minded people, and forget about shining our light with others outside those relationships. 2/3's of my relational contacts are with like-minded people but I try and consciously build 1/3 of my relationships with those outside my comfort zone.
3. Daily adding and/or reviewing my pocket-sized notebooks. I journal, record thoughts, cut out newspaper articles, record my study notes, add quotes I find, write out film or television stories and quotes.

Claudia's top three sustaining growth practices:

1. Read books, watch films/documentaries, listen to speakers or meet with those I know will teach me new insights and challenge me to think deeper.

2. Once a week solitude dates to renew myself.
3. Pray, meditate, and journal often holding myself accountable to the current state of my spiritual path.

Spiritual Practitioner Tool #5: SERVICE

Neither a lofty degree of intelligence nor imagination nor both together
go to the making of genius. Love, love, love, that is the soul of genius.

Wolfgang Amadeus Mozart

Developing the four S's of solitude, study, support system, and sustaining growth will most assuredly propel our overall personal growth, but if we merely focus on these with only self development in mind, our hearts can actually grow colder and more aloof from the needs of others around us. We can become selfish in orientation, intolerant and impatient of others who are less fortunate than ourselves, and begin to focus more on being right rather than being loving. When we make the heartfelt commitment to serve others, we open our hearts to love and growth, and in turn our lives take on a much deeper meaning. When one studies or meets deeply spiritual people in the league of Mother Teresa, Ghandhi, Sitting Bull, Billy Graham, Vaclav Havel, or the Dalai Lama, one will find they all exude a generosity of spirit. As Aesop said in *The Lion and the Mouse*, "No act of kindness, no matter how small is ever wasted." Maturity in spirit is in direct proportion to growth in service. We feel so strongly about the importance of service that we have devoted an entire section of the book to *Making a Difference*.

When all five S's are a high priority and are worked in unison, there is an energy and excitement fueled within, a genuine spiritual awakening occurs, and we shine in the world as an authentic ray of hope. Considered a classic of American business and popular culture, the book, *A Message to Garcia*, had more than eighty million copies in worldwide circulation in 1936, has been translated into thirty-seven languages and is considered to be one of the top ten best selling books of all time. The fifteen hundred word essay was written by Elbert Hubbard in 1899 for *Philistine* magazine, but due to the massive response it was quickly printed as a pamplet, and soon after as a book. The essay tells the inspirational story of American officer Andrew

Summers Rowan, a West Point graduate whom President McKinley dispatched to accomplish the daunting feat of delivering a letter to Cuban Insurgent leader, Calixto Iniguez Garcia in the treacherous mountains of Cuba. Without asking questions, making no objections or excuses as to how hard the task would be and with no requests for help, Rowan set out on his arduous mission.

The questions addressed in *The Message to Garcia* included, "How many of us would do the same as Rowan? How many would make excuses? How many would try to pawn off the work to someone else?" Hubbard writes:

"Slipshod assistance, foolish attention, dowdy indifference, and half-hearted work seem the rule; and no man succeeds, unless by hook or crook or threat he forces or bribes other men to assist him; or mayhap, God in His goodness performs a miracle, and sends him an Angel of Light for an assistant. Civilization is one long anxious search for just such individuals (as Rowan). He is wanted in every city, town, and village – in every office, shop, store, and factory. The world cries out for such: he is needed and needed badly – the man who can 'Carry a Message to Garcia.'"

For years, this story was known to military men and women, business leaders, factory workers, and memorized by school children around the world. If we could only embrace the same initiative as Rowan, apply the lessons in this fifteen hundred word essay and dedicate ourselves to the five S's, what a living work of art our lives would become.

CHAPTER 17

WORKBOOK CHALLENGES VI

GET TO KNOW ME

1. Reflecting on taking care of myself spiritually, where do I fall on a scale of 1-10? _____
   a. What holds me back from developing my spirituality most?
      Fear _____   Lack of knowledge _____   Laziness _____   Turned off by religion _____
      Bad time management _____   Other _____
   b. What step can I take to begin accessing my spirituality?
      Read a book _____   Seek out a support group _____
      Make an appointment with a spiritual advisor _____
      Spend time in solitude or go on retreat _____
      Seek out materials referenced in this chapter _____   Other _____

2. What beliefs would I like to better understand or study in depth to deepen my spiritual connection or answer questions I struggle with most?_____
   _____

3. The three people I admire most spiritually are?
   1. _____   2. _____   3. _____
   a. What qualities do they possess that I admire and would like to incorporate into my own life?
   1. _____   2. _____   3. _____

4. I am currently practicing a beneficial discipline of solitude?

    Yes_____ No _____ Sometimes _____

    a. When I practice solitude what accelerates my spiritual growth the most?

    _____

    b. If I am not currently taking time in solitude how can I work it into my schedule?

    _____

5. My most recent act of kindness was?_____

    a. It made me feel? _____

    b. What act of kindness could I take part in on an ongoing basis? _____

PRACTICAL POWER TOOLS

1. Brainstorm times in your life that were, *Too Odd Not To Be God* moments. How did these moments affect your life at the time? How do they affect you now that you have been made aware or reminded of them? Keep them on hand to remind yourself to remain hopeful when going through times of struggle.

2. Plan out and complete a thirty day, "Spiritual Development Challenge." Journal throughout the month to record your progress. Upon completion, review and record how you feel, how the challenge changed your life, and how you plan on incorportating spiritual development into your life.

3. Think outside the box. Dream up creative and fun methods of studying to replace the traditional means of reading a book. Plan an evening with friends by renting a message driven film and then open the room up for discussion afterwards. Some film suggestions, which are clearly inspirational include, *It's a Wonderful Life, Chariots of Fire, Bruce Almighty,* and *Ghandi.* Also consider films which compliment spiritual principles, *The Matrix* series, *About Schmidt, Chronicles of Narnia, Shadowlands,* or *Schindler's List.* Buy audiobooks or rent them from the library. Seek out seminars, workshops, and spiritual services to attend.

4. Schedule in a week of taking care of yourself with quality solitude time. Each day map out at least ten to fifteen minutes of your time to read, pray, meditate, sing, close your eyes, relax, or rest, and see what a diference this practice can make. How did you feel at the end of the week? What were the benefits? How can you incorporate this time into your schedule on a consistent basis?

5. Take a day and perform random acts of kindness. Be gracious, open doors for people, or even choose a total stranger whom you will never see again and do a nice deed for them. Volunteer at a soup kitchen, mission, or social service agency. At the end of the day review the lessons learned and how just one day of making a difference can make you feel. Tell others about your day and maybe they will be inspired to do the same.

BRAIN MEDICINE

1. I am loved by God
2. I am never alone in the world
3. I embrace constructive behaviors
4. My solitude time builds a strong foundation
5. I make time to learn and grow spiritually

PERSONAL BRAIN MEDICINE

1. _____
2. _____
3. _____
4. _____
5. _____

Only a life lived for others is a life worthwhile.

Albert Einstein

CHAPTER 18

FUNDAMENTALS TO A PEACEFUL MIND

All that we are is the result of what we have thought. The
mind is everything. What we think we become.

Buddah

P EACE. Just hearing the word can provide a sense of comfort. If we found ourselves in a
room full of people and the phrase, "peace of mind" was thrown out for discussion, the
majority, if not all of us, would express a very strong desire for gaining peace of mind. And most
would reveal their willingness to pay top dollar during certain periods in their lives just to gain
a few moments of mental relief from everyday life pressures. This desire is not new to mankind.
Greek philosophers Plato, Aristotle, and Socrates all pondered the state of being mentally at ease.
The term, "eudaimonia," which translates as happiness in our mental state, can be found in all
three of these Greek philosophers' writings. There have been great debates over time about the
exact definition of eudaimonia, but it appears Aristotle's definition found in his Nicomachean
Ethics writings is considered by most as the correct and often referred to translation. Aristotle
defines eudaimonism as, "Flourishing happiness that must be rooted in virtue extending over
a complete lifetime." He believed, "All correct actions lead to a greater well being." Thus, the
correlation between virtue and happiness. Most likely he was referring to the four cardinal
virtues of wisdom, bravery, temperance, and justice. All translations agree getting to a place of
flourishing happiness is the ultimate goal of all humanity. If we are to reach this ideal mental

state of being we must once again address our choices in life and how they affect our life path in a negative or positive manner. First century Judean Theologian, Hillel Hazaken maps out the power of thought in this manner:

"Watch your thoughts; they become your words. Watch your words; they become your actions. Watch your actions; they become your habits. Watch your habits; they become your character. Watch your character for it will become your destiny."

St. Bernard of Clairvaux was a deeply spiritual French monk who lived around 1000 A.D. He strongly believed what we allow our minds to focus upon will influence who we become and the degree of inner peace we will experience. This philosophy is also very similar to German reformer, Martin Luther, who taught some five hundred years later that we cannot always control what goes into our minds but we can take control of what takes up permanent residence.

Learning to create a healthy mind-set and keeping unhealthy negative thoughts to a minimum is to become conscious of the thoughts we bring into our heads and allow to swim around. Gaining habitual, long-term peace of mind begins when we learn to recognize negative or destructive thoughts when they first creep in, and then learn to manage the floodgates before too much damage is done. Developing this state of eudaimonia is a bit ironic in the sense that we must learn to be mentally strong and to take our thoughts captive in order to get to a place of inner peace.

Baseball is often referred to as sports' best metaphor for life, because of its marathon nature, constant mental challenges, and its realistic view of imperfection. Consider that the most successful baseball team of all time, the New York Yankees, won only sixty percent of their games in their twenty-seven championship seasons. Yet, the Yankees are considered sports overall standard for champions in North America's four major sports of hockey, football, basketball, and baseball. A wise baseball manager/coach would not advise his players to expect perfection from themselves over the course of a long season. Instead, he would advise the team to strive for consistency, allowing them a greater shot at earning a spot in the World Series. The same holds true in gaining peace of mind. There will be missteps and mistakes along the way, but as long as we remain on a virtuous path toward achieving flourishing happiness, we will find ourselves more often than not in a peaceful mental state.

Buddy Bell, a future Hall of Famer, successful manager, and the third generation of a rare four generation Major League Baseball family, wrote about the keys to developing mental equilibrium in his book, *Smart Baseball:*

"Fear of failure is big in baseball. It is so easy to lapse into negative thinking, and be afraid to make a mistake or make an out. So many bad things happen if you make an out. Ball players must learn how to shift their attention from the negative to the positive. That's what mental toughness is all about. Those who are mentally tough have disciplined their minds to the point that they do not allow negative thoughts to creep in. They block out all the fear, all the anxiety. In the face of adversity they are able to keep their minds on the positive."

Kevin Costner may be the most well-known film star for choosing roles in which his characters are baseball players: *Bull Durham, Field of Dreams, For Love of The Game,* and *The Upside of Anger.* In the film, *Bull Durham,* Costner plays a wily veteran catcher, Crash Davis, who is sent down to a lower level of the minors to mentor and groom an up and coming star pitcher, Nuke LaLoosh (Tim Robbins), for the big leagues. Much of what he teaches Nuke is on mental strength. One scene early in the film captures Crash's level of mental maturity when he faces an opposing pitcher for one of his own at bats. The viewing audience hears Crash's self talk as he reminds himself not to let his mind get in the way of his performance. He tells himself: "You ain't getting that cheese by me, Meat. Look for the fastball, he's got to come with the cheese, relax, relax, quick bat, pop the club head, open the hips, relax. You're thinking too much, get out of your freakin' head Crash, get on top of the ball, quick bat, don't let him in your kitchen."

Crash swings and misses the first pitch. His mind then wonders to Annie, the sultry part time English professor played by Susan Sarandon, whom he met the previous night. The pitcher is about to throw his next ball when Crash calls a time out because he cannot clear his mind. He gets himself settled, but as he returns to bat his self-talk begins to ramble once more: "Annie, Annie, Annie-who is this Annie? Geez get out of the box you idiot where's your head? Get the woman out of your head. Time out!"

Even though he strikes out, Crash gives a look to the opposing pitcher as if to say, "I'll get you next time." After clearing the technical clutter and potential romance, he goes back to concentrating on the task at hand and is able to hit a home run later in the game.

How many of us can relate to this scene or mental state of being in everyday life? There is so much clutter going on in our minds throughout our day it is a wonder we get anything of significance accomplished. Alex Pattakos, PhD, founder of the Center for Personal Meaning in Santa Fe, New Mexico, bases his life work on the principles set up by Viktor Frankl. In Pattakos's book, *Prisoners of Our Thoughts* he writes on how we create metaphorical prisons for ourselves:

"In effect, we create pathways in our minds in much the same way that a path is beaten through a grass field from repeated use. And, because these patterns are automatic, we may believe these habitual ways of thinking and behaving to be 'beyond our control.' Life, it seems, just happens to us. Not only do we rationalize our responses to life but we also fall prey to forces that work to limit our potential as human beings. By viewing ourselves as relatively powerless and driven by our instincts, the possibility that we create, or at least co-create, our own reality becomes difficult to grasp. Instead, we lock ourselves inside our own mental prisons. We lose sight of our own natural potential, as well as that of others."

Developing peace of mind, or eudaimonia, is learning the discipline of taking our thoughts captive, and then performing the tasks necessary to clear our minds of negative destructive thinking. An eudaimon practitioner trains himself to consciously choose to be courageous, not ruled by fears, distractions, or discouragements and is able to consistently make wise decisions regardless of the circumstances. To live successfully in the twenty-first century, we believe there are five fundamentals critical to gaining peace of mind.

Fundamental #1: STRESS MANAGEMENT

Being the stepmother to four extremely outspoken young women, I (Claudia) knew at some point in my relationship with each of them I would find they were none too pleased with me. One of the tensest moments came nine years into my relationship with my oldest daughter,

Hannah. The day we were to resolve our conflict, I remember thinking I would remain a strong adult while I allowed her to freely vent her feelings. We would then discuss the problems, work through them, and move forward in our relationship. To my astonishment, I was quickly reduced to five-year-old status without the skills to properly respond as her tsunami of anger was hurled towards me. After she left, my chest hurt to such an extreme that I could hardly catch my breath. I came very close to calling 9-1-1. After all, I am not one to complain when I am sick, and I do have a heart murmur and a family history of heart disease. I talked myself into taking a hot bath and tried other relaxation techniques.

After a few days, I could no longer take the heart palpitations and tight chest feeling so, I finally made the call to get a full heart checkup. Looking through the test results the doctor assured me I was in excellent shape. He then proceeded to educate me on the perils of stress. I learned that even though someone may have an extremely healthy heart, they still run the risk of having a heart attack in highly stressful situations. Hannah and I learned to work through our issues in a timely manner and I am proud to say in April 2006, she named her first child, Adeline Claudia.

Hans Sleeve, a Slovakian born endocrinologist, was one of the first medical specialists to study the effects stress has on the body in 1926 at the University of Montreal during his second year in medical school. The term "stress," which Sleeve coined, made its first appearance in a medical article he wrote in 1936. Nominated for ten Nobel prizes for his pioneer work on stress, Sleeve concluded that high levels of stress play a role in the development of every disease.

Princess Caroline of Monaco suffered from "alopecia areata," or the loss of her hair in the mid-nineties following a series of stressful events surrounding the death of her husband from a boating accident. Oscar winner, Anthony Hopkins has commented on the stress and depression he sometimes goes through for months following certain intense roles he has undertaken. He finally realized a common thread to why this occurred. Hopkins was only playing a role, faking it, acting as if, but his body did not know the difference.

In the book, *YOU: The Owners Manual*, Dr. Michael Roizen, M.D. and Dr. Mehmet Oz report that for the first thirty days following the attacks on September 11, 2001, heart attacks increased threefold in New York City, Washington, D.C., Chicago, Kansas City, and Alabama. According to numerous sources job stress costs US businesses three hundred billion dollars annually and over $250,000,000 prescriptions are filled annually for tranquilizers.

Not all stress is negative stress. Some stress is actually healthy or motivational. Dr. Donald Tubesing, author of the book, *Kicking Your Stress Habits* likens stress to the tension of violin strings. The strings need enough tension to make music, but too much tension and the strings will snap. According to the National Center for Health and Wellness, there are four types of stress. The first three have negative implications: hyperstress, hypostress, and distress. The fourth type of stress, eustress, is positive and fulfilling in nature.

Hyperstress

Someone who is under hyperstress feels pushed beyond their limits. This can occur when someone is overly tired, overworked, or loaded down with too many responsibilities without the aid of others. When someone is functioning in this state of stress, little things that would not normally bother a person can bring a strong emotional charge and reaction. A person who has a hard time saying no could easily experience hyperstress. They may erupt following a build up of stress or when too many deadlines approach them at one time.

Hypostress

The polar opposite of hyperstress is hypostress. The underlying cause of hypostress is most often boredom. Someone may be unchallenged in school, on their job, in their relationships, or by anything and everything in life. They have lost all inspiration and motivation and are paralyzed in their apathetic routine.

Distress

We humans like to have a certain amount of routine or familiarity in our lives. When our comfort zone is disrupted by abrupt change, we experience feelings of discomfort. There are two forms of distress: acute and chronic. Acute distress is a fierce form of stress that comes on rather quickly and usually fades away. This could be the death of a loved one where normal grieving time will allow a person to begin functioning at normal levels. Chronic or static stress is a form of underlying stress that can last for weeks, months, or years. This describes someone who is overwhelmed with constant stress hanging over them, such as never being able to get out of serious financial debt.

One of the most severe forms of chronic distress is post-traumatic stress disorder (PTSD). Johns Hopkins University describes PTSD as:

"A collection of psychological, emotional, and behavioral symptoms occurring when a person has experienced bodily injury, has been threatened with death or bodily injury, or has witnessed the death or injury of someone else. Some common PTSD stressors include: serious motor vehicle accidents, plane crashes and boating accidents; industrial accidents; natural disasters (tornadoes, hurricanes, volcanic eruptions); robberies, muggings and shootings; military combat (initially diagnosed in soldiers, PTSD was known as 'shell shock' or combat neurosis); rape, incest and child abuse; hostage situations and kidnappings; political torture; imprisonment in a concentration camp; being forced to flee as a refugee; and surviving a potentially terminal illness. Symptoms include flashbacks, nightmares, intrusive thoughts, severe anxiety, avoiding places and persons that trigger memories of the event, avoiding discussions of the trauma, feeling emotionally 'numb,' and showing signs of increased arousal or vigilance, as if expecting danger."

I (Guy) was at a good friend's wedding a few years after the tragic 9/11 terrorist attacks on the twin towers in New York City. The bride's sister and brother-in-law, Risa and Larry Hall, were sitting at our table. About halfway through the festivities, Larry revealed his office was in one of the twin towers the day of the attack. He explained to me how he had helped evacuate his company's office and got everyone out before the towers came crumbling down. Larry said he was so full of adrenaline that day as well as a few days afterwards that the full impact of the events had not really hit him.

A few months later, he found he was having trouble sleeping as thoughts of how he and his colleagues had almost died while he was surrounded by so much suffering and death. His company had offered to provide free counseling to anyone who was at work that fateful day so he decided to seek help. Larry was diagnosed with Post Traumatic Stress Disorder. The counselor explained to him that the stress he was under was similar to what many soldiers go through after returning home from a war zone. He was surprised how hard the events hit him so many months after 9/11. He got to the point where his work was suffering, and he was almost terrified to cross the bridge from New Jersey into New York City.

He and Risa decided it was best to move out of the New York City area to a smaller community for awhile, because so many everyday big city sights and sounds triggered his PTSD, and caused him to suffer with unrealistic fears. Loud noises, the sound of an airplane in the sky, the sight of landing jets, fires in the distance, and the sound of police cars and fire trucks would set him off. I discreetly asked his wife if I should change the subject, but she quietly reassured me talking about that fateful day was part of his healing process and they really appreciated my genuine interest.

So often we would like to eliminate the negative effects of stress from our lives. Maybe we would be better served to eliminate the word "eliminate" from our lexicon concerning stress and replace it with the word, "manage." None of us will ever live the perfect ideal stress-free life we hope to gain. Life WILL injure us.

In the film, *The Upside of Anger*, Kevin Costner plays ex-baseball player, Denny Davis. Denny develops romantic feelings for family friend, Terry, played by Joan Allen. Terry is playing the relationship cautiously, because she has recently experienced the traumatic breakup of her marriage. Terry says to Denny, "It's not the kind of wound that heals." He responds with these words of wisdom, "Yeah it does. It heals. It just heals funny. You know, you more or less walk with a limp." My (Claudia) husband, Rodney echoes these sentiments in a song he wrote for our good friends, Burt and Sanna Stein, who lost their nineteen-year-old son, Adam, to an undiscovered heart condition. *Adam's Song* contains this potent line. "We're learning how to live with a lifelong broken heart."

Eustress

Eustress comes from the Greek word "eu," which means good. This form of "good stress" involves feelings of excitement, joy, accomplishment, fulfillment, and happiness. Eustress can bring health to our bodies by triggering endorphins, which in turn can benefit our immune system to ward off diseases, and provide us with the emotional energy to face challenges. Eustress can range from the strings on a musical instrument, to the thrill of downhill skiing, to working towards accomplishing a dream, to the delivery of a baby. Eustress is motivated by hope while distress is motivated by fear.

The key to balancing stress is finding ways to manage distress while also finding ways to cultivate eustress. Tony La Russa, Baseball Hall of Famer and three time World Series winning manager with both the Oakland A's and the St. Louis Cardinals, described his stress before each game in the book, *3 Nights in August,* as an excited nervousness mixed with the fear of failure: "I'm as nauseous as I've ever been. I have a terrible headache. My head is pounding. I feel like throwing up and I'm having trouble swallowing. And, the beauty of it is you want to feel like this every day."

When we feel the same as La Russa, our thoughts are not necessarily dominated by the fear of failure. Although the emotion of fear may be present, they are dominated by a nervous excitement and a desire to accomplish something of significance. When we are in a eustress state, our concentration levels are increased, we are more alert, we are more creative, and we are more focused on the process of what will help us become successful rather than worrying about the end result. For La Russa, when a game is taking place or when we are nervously anticipating an event, there is often a huge inner rush of satisfaction that gets our endorphins flowing. These moments in life are what make us feel alive, and give us hope to face future challenges or obstacles.

Stress Management Tools

According to Dr. Sleeve, "Stress is a fact of life," and, "Its only escape is death." Therefore, learning to manage stress is key in gaining peace of mind/eudaimonia and discovering the masterpiece within. Unmanaged stress causes us to lose hope, to feel powerless, and to close our hearts. To regain our sense of hope and power, and to reopen our hearts again, we must have an arsenal of tools to help us get back on the path. We must remember each and every individual is different. One tool or technique may prove miraculous for one person while for another it may prove to be even more stressful. We have to find what works for each of us and remind ourselves to incorporate these tools into our daily lives. Tobacco, alcohol, and drug use, excessive shopping, or even food binges may provide us temporary relief from stress, but each of these will eventually lead us down an even deeper path of distress and may cause long term injury or harm. Prescription drugs used for stress management may prove helpful for a short period of time, but the ideal goal is to do the work necessary to divulge and heal the root cause of the stress. Always consult a physician before taking or stopping any medication. In severe cases of stress, seek professional help. In researching the best methods to manage stress, we identified and placed techniques into five different categories.

1. Physical and verbal releases

Slow deep breaths, take a walk, laugh, cry, run, eat something crunchy, take a hot bath, clean, organize, dance, relax in candlelight, get a massage or facial, garden, practice yoga, participate in sports, cook, rest, socialize, sing, delegate responsibility, exercise, yell, bat a pillow, or go to a batter's cage.

2. Solitude

Spend time alone, see a film, create quiet time, pray, meditate, clear our minds of clutter, read a book, journal, go on a retreat or mini vacation, close our eyes and relax, spend time in nature, take a walk, play video games, be kind to ourselves, listen to music, play with pets, practice positive visualization, find a hobby or go to card store, and read funny and sentimental cards to reopen our hearts.

3. Generosity

Perform an act of kindness, donate money, volunteer, write kind letters, write thank you notes, practice road driving kindness, hold a door open for someone, practice intentional courtesy, verbally thank others, and ask what we can do for friends or family members to lighten their load.

4. Create healthy boundaries

Learn to say no, take short breaks, examine self-talk, practice patience, release negative thought patterns, stop people pleasing, simplify busy schedules, release expectations of perfection, examine toxic relationships, focus on the positives, practice good time management, establish a healthy eating routine, release unhealthy habits, take a time out from heated arguments to stop those from harming us mentally, emotionally, physically, and spiritually.

5. Relationships

Get a hug from friend or family member, do something unselfish or kind for a friend to release feelings of rejection, phone a friend, gain a clearer perspective from a friend or family member, go on a vacation with someone fun or at least like-minded, seek a counselor for professional help, maintain healthy relationships, and resolve differences with others. Become a team player in all aspects to feel the support of others, whether by being a good one on one partner, or by feeling the support of a group, such as a sports league or a creative hobby group.

Fundamental #2: THE ART OF COMMUNICATION

Paul Newman portrays Lucas, *Luke* Jackson in the highly acclaimed film, *Cool Hand Luke.* The film became one of the top cult films coming out of the turbulent Sixties, and the phrase used often in the film, "What we've got here is a failure to communicate," captured the total essence of a culture at its time and the breakdown of relationships in almost all facets of life. So many of life's problems could be solved if we were all natural experts in communication. Even though many of us are natural born, "talkers," no one is a natural born, "communicator." Think about how many conflicts could be reduced to nearly nothing of consequence if we developed the skills to communicate!

The art of good communication is a struggle to master. It can be a lifelong process because learning to communicate effectively never ceases due to life changes, life circumstances and human nature. Miscommunication is a fact of life. We come from different walks of life, cultures, traditions, family backgrounds, age groups, life experiences, and not to forget gender differences, which makes us even more susceptible to being misunderstood. These are all valid reasons why communication breakdown can occur, but these differences should never give us permission to hurt or harm another. We would be wise to always keep in mind that words have the power to be as destructive as a raging fire, and can literally harm another for their entire lifetime. Yet, words can be the most powerful instrument known to mankind when used in loving and inspirational means, allowing for a tremendous amount of growth and healing to take place.

One of our most beneficial lessons in writing this book occurred, as we were learning the art of co-writing; especially considering we began writing a month after meeting. Blending our male/female perspectives and our life philosophies, proved to be a much easier task than we ever imagined. The biggest roadblocks occurred in making sure our thoughts were communicated clearly and understood correctly. Luckily, we were able to solve the problem by creating our own co-writing language. To our surprise, this language proved highly successful not only in writing, but also in our professional and private lives as well. By co-mingling our language with additional research, we have come up with the following tools. We have shared these tools often in workshops, the counseling room, with friends and family, and extensively with Guy's sports psychology writing and consulting.

Communication Tools

1. Care Level

This communication technique can be highly effective in all sorts of situations ranging from trivial matters to intensely heated arguments. For example, a family of four may be casually deciding what type of food they will have for dinner. Each person shares his or her own care level on a scale of one to ten. The person with the highest care level gets to choose the restaurant. This same format can also work when getting nowhere in a heated argument. We may be acting as if we are dug into our opinion about which direction to take, but when asked for our care level, we may realize we are only at a three or four. Upon this realization, we then have the awareness to back down and reach an agreement in an easier manner.

2. Dirty Talking

The first year, I (Claudia), attended the Nashville Screenwriting Conference, I learned the meaning of, "writing a dirty script" from a panel of veteran screenwriters. They revealed that most would-be writers never take the first step to write a screenplay, because they hold onto the belief that the words have to come out in perfect form right off the bat. They taught that if a, "dirty draft" is written, at least the story gets out of our heads and onto paper. After the entire first draft is completed, the editing can begin and the words go from dirty to clean. Having the freedom to speak raw thoughts can be just as clarifying and healing. Venting or talking things through instead of worrying about filtering what we say can help us come to a better end result. Of course having respect for the other person is vital and should never be seen as an opportunity to be cruel. For example, the discussion may be, "Where should we go on a family vacation this year?" Everyone in the room is given permission to freely brainstorm and to throw out ideas without anyone else getting in personal stabs or without holding them hostage to the first place mentioned. The key lies in each party feeling as though their opinions are valuable and heard before arriving at an agreed upon end result.

3. Keeping Short Accounts

There is an old Hebrew proverb that says, "Do not let the sun go down on your anger." In other words, if we are in an unresolved conflict with another, we must learn to become determined not to end our day with the conflict unresolved. I (Guy) was having a coffee with a former neighbor, Fred Kulak, after a wedding rehearsal I had performed for his daughter and future son-in-law. Someone asked Fred and his wife, Louise, who were in a fifty plus year marriage if they had any advice on how to maintain a long-term relationship. Fred revealed:

"Louise and I determined a long time ago never to ever go to bed with anger in our hearts towards one another. I can honestly say we have practiced this idea our entire lives. Sometimes we came to an impasse and would just say to each other 'let's agree to disagree and try again in the morning.' And you know what? In most cases, after a good night's sleep, the issue we were fighting over seemed awfully small or only took a few minutes to resolve."

4. Filtering

Filtering is learning the fine art of listening to a person's heart intent. Far too often we listen to another person's words only to misinterpret their intention or attitude. If we could only edit in life the way a writer gets to edit their work until the words are right, or how a film director gets to edit a project until it is ready for the big screen. But as we all know, in the heat of the moment, we do not always get second chances, let alone twenty or thirty. Learning to filter our communication involves a couple of dynamics. Instead of responding quickly with our words, sometimes we are better off stopping for even an instant and asking ourselves why this person is responding as they are. Probing a person as to how their day has gone, or remembering triggers from their past and how they may respond in certain situations when life pressure gets out of hand, is another effective filtering practice. These two exercises can be useful in seeing a person's heart intent more clearly. Asking ourselves whether they are coming from a place of love or a place of fear, or if they are acting from an adult state or from a child state as mentioned in Chapter 14, can also speed up the filtering process.

5. Listening

Be quick to listen, slow to speak and slow to become angry.

Hebrew Proverb

One of the most profound bits of wisdom my (Claudia) younger brother, Kevin, has taught me about life concerns the art of listening. One day, we were discussing the key factors to thriving in the workplace. Having worked for two very large corporations, Kevin interacts with a great deal of people around the world on a daily basis. He attributes two main factors to his success: being a good listener and reminding himself that people are their own favorite subject. Engaging others in conversation by asking them numerous questions about themselves and listening more than speaking will always put them more at ease. I have tried this technique more times than I can count, and it works like a charm every time. And, I find I learn so much more by listening than speaking.

This concept became even clearer for me when I was placed on vocal rest by the doctors at the Vanderbilt Voice Clinic for a week, in the middle of recording my first CD. Not speaking taught me a great deal about people that I may not have learned otherwise. For the entire week I observed how people are very similar: we all want to feel important, and we all want to feel heard. Tom Peters, whom *Fortune and Economist* magazine called, "The uberguru of management," said, "Every person is the star of their own movie. If you always remember that the other party is the epicenter of their world, you'll be a lot better off. Let their star shine, they'll love you for it."

6. Container

My (Claudia) husband and I made the decision before getting married that we would do everything in our power to proceed wisely into marriage. So, we enrolled in a pre-marriage couple's group with respected Nashville therapist, Bedford Combs, for two years. One of the key benefits to being in the group, was learning a communication technique called, "A Container." Bedford combined his own ideas along with the guidelines in the book, *Getting The Love You Want* conceived by marriage and family counselor, Dr. Harville Hendrix. We have since taught the technique to our friends, our daughters, their boyfriends, and their spouses. Over time and practice, we have created our own terms and added twists to make, the container even more effective for us. Our daughter Chelsea, one day while discussing "doing a container" came up with the term, "doing a Tupperware," and we have used the nickname ever since.

The need for a container/Tupperware arises when one person is angry with another and wants a safe and mature outlet to resolve issues with them, or when two people feel misunderstood and are locked in a communication struggle. Requesting a specific time and private place with the other party to work things out is the best way to begin. For example, person #1 may say, "I'd like to schedule a container today at 4p.m. in the living room. Would you be agreeable to that?" Once agreed upon, the container is best carried out while sitting on the floor. Using a square as a model, person #2 sits inside the square the entire time while person #1 moves around into metaphorical chairs in north, east, south, and west positions.

The container participants face one another at all times, trying best to look into each other's eyes. Person #2 sits in the middle of the square; the "listening chair" while person #1 sits in the north position called, the "feelings chair." Person #1 begins by expressing their feelings such as, "I am feeling sad, angry, hurt, and misunderstood. Person #2 is only allowed to repeat or "mirror" what they hear. "I hear you saying, you are sad, angry, hurt, and misunderstood." This exchange is repeated until person #1 is finished expressing their feelings and ready to move on to the east position in the square called, the "judgment chair." Physically moving to the next position symbolizes moving on to a higher understanding.

Once in the judgment chair, person #1 would begin by saying things such as, "My judgment is you have been insensitive and cruel when you..." Person #2 would mirror the statements back. "I hear you saying you feel I have been insensitive and cruel when I..." When person #1 is finished releasing all their judgments and feels understood and heard they are ready to move on to the south position or "wisdom chair." Person #1 would say something like, "My wisdom in this situation is that I have been under a lot of stress and I have been taking it out on you. I realize now that you have also been under a lot of stress and I have interpreted your quietness as not caring about me..." Person #2 then mirrors back these statements until person #1 is finished. "It is your wisdom that you have been under a lot of stress..." The west position or the "king and queen chair" comes next. This is the power chair and begins with person #1 saying what they want and what they are willing to do. Such as, "I want to have a once a week date night to have time alone with you. I am willing to make our relationship a priority versus making work a priority, etc." After person #2 has mirrored all of person #1's king/queen statements, it is time to repeat the container by switching places if the need is there. This technique is repeated until each party feels heard and understood.

Hendrix explained the three ground rules for performing a container:

1. Neither partner is allowed to leave the room until the exercise is completed.
2. Neither partner can damage any property or touch the other partner in a hostile manner.
3. The angry person must limit all remarks to a description of behavior, not a description of character. In other words, the angry person can say, "I am furious at you for not coming home last night," but not "You are a despicable person for staying out all night."

7. The Emotional Languages Of Love

One of the major tools I (Guy) use in my pre-marital counseling sessions when teaching effective communication, is determining what emotional language each person gravitates toward. When a couple is in love and trying to communicate their hearts intent, they do not always connect as well as they hope. This often occurs because they are communicating from different perceptions or emotional languages of how to give and receive love. In all relationships, if we take the time to discover the other person's emotional language, we improve our communication, we teach others how we feel loved, and we come to understand one another on a much more advanced level.

The emotional language we understand and the emotional language another person understands may be as different as Slovakian and English. No matter how hard we try and communicate in Slovakian, if the other person only understands English, we may never truly understand one another. Deciphering these languages takes conscious thought and effort from both parties. Utilizing this communication tool helps to prevent misunderstanding with family, friends, and coworkers and has been known to save many marriages. Depending on the researcher, six to eight emotional languages have been identified. As we begin to identify our emotional language, a primary one will come to the forefront, but we will find we have minor or secondary emotional languages we also relate to on a smaller scale. Remember, we teach people how to love us.

Emotional Languages

A. Meeting Material Needs

This person feels loved when receiving something thoughtful from another that means a great deal to them regardless of monetary value. Since they are among the most generous of souls, they will in turn show love towards others by displaying acts of thoughtful generosity.

B. Helping

A helper gives love through helping another person shine or helping a person in need. This expression of communication can manifest in ways as simple as taking out the trash, to as complex as helping another fulfill a goal or dream. They feel loved when someone shows appreciation for their help and gives help back to them in return.

C. Spending Time Together

This person operates best when they feel connected to people by spending time with them. The best way we can show this person we care is either by taking the time to meet with them, or just touching base when life gets too hectic.

D. Meeting Emotional Needs

This person has a real desire to empathize with others. Getting past a superficial level is important for them to feel as if a relationship has meaning. They feel close to those who take the time to understand their deepest joys and sorrows.

E. Saying It With Words

Our words can bring both healing and encouragement or unbelievable destruction. This person is a verbalizer who tends to take their words and the words of others very seriously. They like to process their heart and their relationships by talking things through, and they appreciate when others do the same for them.

F. Saying It With Touch

This is easily the most misunderstood of the eight emotional languages, because our society tends to associate touch with something sensual or being overly needy, which is not always the case. In order to feel connected to others, this person desires physical contact or close physical proximity to another. They may be big on giving hugs, a quick pat on the back, or any other form of physical touch as a loving reassurance from others.

G. Being On The Same Side

The word "supportive" best describes this person's emotional language. These people are the consummate team players rooting for and extracting the best in those around them. They take equal pleasure in another's success as they would their own. Due to their supportive and disarming nature, they can get to an emotional level with those they come into contact with at a rather quick pace.

H. Bringing Out The Best

This person loves to encourage, teach, or coach others to live up to their highest potential. They in turn flourish when the same is done for them. These encouragers are very practical in their thinking and could be referred to as "how to" people. They have the ability to get others from point A to point B in order to reach desired end results.

8. Walk With The Wise

There is a Hebrew proverb that says, "He who walks with the wise becomes wise." This proverb can apply to almost every area of life and discipline. Like most life skills, one can learn best from someone else who is already skilled in that area. A classroom education can only take us so far.

As a new father, my (Guy) children's pediatrician advised us to find a mother whose children were already grown so we could consult with them on children's issues from health to communication. Many doctors believe finding a mother with twenty to thirty years of experience raising children, is like going to someone with an advanced PhD. We were lucky we found two such women who had over twenty children between them. Almost any issue one could think of, from the death of a child, to eating disorders, to trying to potty train a toddler was covered. We both found as parents, their wisdom was as good as any textbook, if not better.

9. Major in the Majors - Minor in the Minors

Billy Graham, his wife Ruth, and their children have been interviewed countless times about their family life. In a series of interviews a few years before Ruth passed away, she was asked about her philosophy towards parenting her six children. She explained her parenting came out of the principle of, "majoring in the majors and minoring in the minors." Major practices like discipline and communicating life principles to her children were strictly nonnegotiable. Universal truisms such as the Ten Commandments and the Golden Rule were her guide. Their son, Franklin, said his parents never seemed to worry about what they called minor issues or individual preferences. He and his siblings were encouraged to follow their interests and passions, not somebody else's idea of what they should or should not be. Growing up through the Sixties when long hair and music was an issue for many families; these were considered minor issues in the Graham household. But treating a date inappropriately, was immediately confronted, stealing or cheating would never be tolerated, gaining an education was a high priority, and honoring one's commitments were part of the nonnegotiable rules. Franklin found applying this communication tool helped him immensely in his vocation and in raising his own family.

When majoring on a major issue, unnecessary conflicts are kept to a minimum and minor issues are kept in their proper context. If a major conflict does occur, identifying the root issue at hand is much easier, because personal attacks such as hair length or music preferences are either nonexistent or a rare occurrence. People are much less defensive because everyone's dignity has been kept intact.

10. Third Party - Intervention/Therapy

If we find we cannot solve our communication problems on our own through the previous nine techniques, getting help from a third party may be our most productive next step. Asking for help from an unbiased trusted friend could be a starting point. If we still cannot resolve the problem, find a respected therapist through our health insurance provider or primary care physician, through friends, our minister, or even respected Internet health sites.

Fundamental #3: OVERCOME ADVERSITY

A few years into our marriage, my (Claudia) husband Rodney and I, decided it would be fun to take scuba diving lessons. Little did I know that after taking the initial lessons in a pool, and then completing our open water certification in the Cayman Islands, I would open myself up to debilitating panic attacks. I found working with a different kind of breathing apparatus in the ocean than the one I was used to using in the pool back home made me feel as if I was not getting enough oxygen, so I began to panic believing I would suffocate and die. Of course breathing under water is certainly not a natural occurrence, so looking up through 110 feet of water can be quite scary even with a full oxygen tank. I chose to challenge myself and continue pushing through the panic. Thankfully, I was able to receive my certification with the help of a master diver. I managed to work my way through my attack by diverting my mind away from destructive thoughts and breathing in for a count of five and breathing out for a count of seven, to prevent further panic and hyperventilation. On the rare occasion when I feel a panic attack coming on, I still use the technique I learned at 110 feet to avoid a full-blown attack.

Most of us are familiar with the saying; "There are two guarantees in life - death and taxes." We could easily insert a third: adversity. Quite often we are made to believe success means getting to a stage in life where we can avoid or eliminate adversity. That will never happen. Speed bumps, glitches, crises, and opposition will always find us along our life's path when seeking personal growth or success in our vocations. As we have covered throughout the book, setbacks and adversity can be devastating, but when seen as an opportunity to learn and grow, they will not be viewed as quite so crippling.

Adversity Tools

1. Re-Establish A Clear Perspective

Missouri native, Samuel Langhorne Clemens, better known as Mark Twain, is commonly thought to be one of the most accomplished literary giants in American history. Ernest Hemingway called Twain's book, *The Adventures of Huckleberry Finn,* "The best book we've ever had in America." What is not commonly revealed, is the numerous bouts Twain endured with reoccurring heartaches, adversities, and life setbacks. From an early age, he witnessed his father's heartache over financial failures. Twain was an eleven-year-old boy when his father suddenly passed away. With mouths to feed in the house, he began a series of jobs after school. In the summer months, they included errand boy, grocery clerk, and blacksmith's apprentice. At fourteen, he left school to work full time. At seventeen, he set out into the world to make his mark and to send home much-needed money. Twain's dream was to one day become more successful than his father and to never fail as his father had failed. Much to his dismay, he made and lost fortunes many times over. Moving from job to job, he found himself to be a printer's apprentice, riverboat pilot, Confederate militiaman, silver miner, newspaper reporter, and lecturer before landing a successful career in writing.

While living in San Francisco, Twain's career as a writer started out with a bang. He was praised for his work and often invited to social gatherings until a much-chided article he wrote for a local paper caused him to hideout in a hotel room for weeks on end. Adding to his misery was his constant pain of feeling responsible for his brother Henry's death in a riverboat explosion years earlier. Twain came extremely close to committing suicide by putting a revolver to his head. Instead, he quietly snuck out of town in the night. Soon after, he decided to begin using various pseudonyms for writing. He eventually took on the pen name, Mark Twain, taken from his riverboat pilot days. The name originated from the practice of bringing a riverboat into harbor. A pilot needs a safe depth of water to dock his boat: a quarter-twain measurement is good, a half-twain measurement is better, but a mark-twain measurement meaning two fathoms or twelve feet of safe water is ideal.

A natural born storyteller, Twain became a self-taught literary genius. He pulled himself out of emotional, mental, and financial ruin many times over when he focused on his skills and talents, such as writing books or making a living traveling around the world as a humorist. During these live performances, he would read aloud from his works and make commentaries on life. Two of his favorite sayings were, "Troubles are only mental; it is the mind that manufactures them, and the mind can gorge them, banish them, abolish them." And, "Against the assault of laughter, nothing can stand."

2. Remain Focused On What Can Be Controlled

Much of what consumes our thoughts in times of adversity or setbacks is focusing on too many situations that are out of our control. If we allow these circumstances to dominate our minds, the mental anguish can become quite damaging, affecting all parts of our lives to the point of physical exhaustion, disease, emotional breakdown, or spiritual cynicism. Learning to keep our focus on what we can control while letting go of what we cannot control, will help minimize mental stress. When we are battling this mind space, it may be good to look yet again to the farmer for a bit of life wisdom.

A farmer's goal is to yearly harvest a bumper crop. But, there is a process to farming a healthy crop. The farmer plows the land in early spring, seeds the field, and trusts nature to provide the right amount of sunshine and rain. The growing process can take four to six months before the harvesting begins. The veteran farmer knows it is pointless to worry about the threat of natural disasters such as drought, frost, hail, or tornados during this time. He focuses on elements he can control, such as weed killing and irrigation. Yet, he knows much of the process is trusting in nature, which is totally out of his control. More times than not, the crop is sufficient to bring in the resources to provide for his livelihood.

NFL Hall of Fame coach, Bill Parcells, was interviewed during his first year as head coach for the Dallas Cowboys on how much a coach can actually control the outcome of a football game. He shared this little nugget, which is apropos to certain life situations: *"At the best we can control about seventy-five percent of the final outcome of a game if we do almost everything right in our preparation. We have to always keep in mind that there is an opposition who cares about the outcome as much as we do, weather/elements, unforced errors, and flukes because of human nature. Maybe seventy-five percent period!"*

3. Develop A Tender Heart

There is nothing more important in life than love and relationships. In times of great adversity or setbacks, it is so easy to become overwhelmed with fear that we sometimes forget other people even exist. So, how do we reconcile this dilemma and steer clear of becoming hard and cynical? We make every attempt to prevent our hearts from closing down. Only love and action can prevent this infection from taking over.

Throughout the years, I (Claudia) have used various tools to re-open my heart when I feel it closing down due to times of adversity. First and foremost, I challenge myself to stop operating primarily from my head and to once again include my heart. I find spending time with my grandchildren, or nieces and nephew; bringing lunch, dinner, or groceries to an elderly or sick friend; or making a list of cards I need in the future and going to the closest Hallmark store to read funny and sentimental cards works like a charm every time.

There are a handful of tools that work for me (Guy): my Hope Journal, volunteering at a shelter, attending inspiring events, and trying to keep my eyes focused on the big picture. For some reason, going to sporting or musical event with hundreds or thousands of people, flying on a jet and pondering life down below, or having a meal on top of a large building overlooking a city keeps my heart tender. It is very similar to Julie Gold's song, *From A Distance*, which Bette Midler made famous. When I consider life and circumstances from a distance, I realize that many of these petty issues, which can lead one down the path to cynicism, are just that – petty.

One of the most inspiring events I have attended happened at the Canmore Folk Festival near Calgary, Alberta, in the summer of 2007. Peter Yarrow, of *Peter, Paul, and Mary* fame, was a featured performer and workshop leader. During his concert, he encouraged the audience to keep their hearts tender when endeavoring to bring about social change, because seeking to create change can be difficult and draining on our spirits. One of the most profound statements he made that I will always remember occurred when he said, *"It takes more than technology, or money. It takes heart, persistence, determination, dedication, kindness, gentleness, vulnerability, sweetness, and the refusal to give up one's center (values), it takes magic!"* The implication was we must challenge ourselves to develop a tender and loving heart in order to stay strong in adverse situations. He went on to say his greatest desire as a performer is to offer hope, healing, and the opportunity for us "change agents" to recommit frequently to great causes so we never grow stale and cynical.

4. Seek Support

Seventeenth-century English poet clergyman, John Donne, is famous for his quote, "No man is an island, entire of itself." His quote can easily be adapted to emphasize the importance of having a community of supportive friends in our lives. When attending a sporting event, the theatre, or a concert, for instance, it is much more enjoyable if we bring a friend along. Why is it that almost every successful weight loss program from Weight Watchers, to Curves, to Jenny Craig suggests the easiest method to get in shape or lose weight is to tackle the challenge with a friend or with a group of friends? For more than fifty years, the Weight Watchers Program has taught that group meetings provide a motivational environment. Jenny Craig gives one-on-one support from an assigned personal consultant. Curves furnish an environment that includes laughter, conversation, and a sense of support. One of their mottoes from over the years is, "Will power can be borrowed from a friend."

Regardless of life circumstances in aiming to achieve peace of mind, our goals are much easier to accomplish when we have physical, emotional, and spiritual support we can count on. We find adversity more manageable and major changes in our lives easier, when we can rely on a support group or friend. They provide a built-in cheerleading squad as well as the accountability to honor our commitments.

An article in the American Airlines bi-weekly magazine, *American Way*, former tennis superstar Andre Agassi revealed, the 2006 US Open ranks as the most treasured moment of his career. That is no small statement. After all, Agassi won eight Grand Slam tournaments and an Olympic Gold Medal. Yet for Agassi, despite his third round exit in a seven round tournament, he says, *"That was the best tournament. That last tournament was everything to me. That moment out there in New York was worth every bit of work for twenty-one years. It was worth every… single… day for twenty-one years."*

We live in a world that tends to look at finished results and finished works of success, but we do not give as much airtime to the process of what it takes to get to those destinations, which are always filled with set-backs and adversities. In most cases, it takes weeks, months, and sometimes years before arriving at our desired destination if we ever arrive at all. And once we do achieve our desired goals, we so often forget that life continues on. Andre Agassi is a good case study of a person who had a very lengthy career with sustained success, but endured much adversity along the way. He rose to become the number one tennis player in the world, maintained his stardom for many years, and then dropped to #141 in the rankings. He reinvented himself and again rose to number one status, staying in the top ten for almost the remainder of his career. For a man with so many tangible successes it is ironic that his most cherished memory on the court was his very last major tournament where he finished in the middle of the pack. This tournament provided him the opportunity to reflect back over his career and to acknowledge the lasting lessons the tennis community had given him by supporting his career.

Agassi gave one of the finest public farewell speeches of anyone in any profession who was able to retire without regret or bitterness. His heartfelt speech captures the attitude we would all be wise to adopt when looking back over a journey that lead us to positive results and to lessons learned, whether we met our perceived expectations or not.

"The scoreboard said I lost today but what the scoreboard doesn't say is what it is I have found. And over the last twenty-one years, I have found loyalty. You have pulled for me on the court and also in life. I've found inspiration. You have willed me to succeed sometimes even in my lowest moments. And I've found generosity. You have given me your shoulders to stand on to reach for my dreams,

dreams I never could have reached without you. Over the last 21 years I have found you. And I will take you and the memory of you with me for the rest of my life. Thank you."

5. Develop Mental Toughness

I (Guy) have interviewed over two hundred National, World, and Olympic caliber athletes while researching for magazine articles and writing for my first three books. The one commonality I continue to discover is the mental toughness each athlete possesses. Their temperaments and personalities may all vary, but each one learned to become mentally strong by overcoming seemingly impossible odds. One of the most mentally tough athletes I interviewed was the late Sandra Schmirler of Regina, Saskatchewan. My first book, *Gold On Ice,* told the story of Team Schmirler, the first gold medal women's curling team in Nagano, Japan, at the 1998 Olympics. A few months before the team qualified for their right to represent Canada at the Olympic games, Schmirler, the team's skip, had her worst melt down during the expanse of her career. Coming off a series of games where she was playing well below her standards, Schmirler revealed:

"I felt like a lost puppy out on the ice. A couple of days before leaving for an Olympic qualifying tournament, I pulled my car over and just started to weep. I had zero confidence and out of desperation suggested to my teammates they replace me with an alternate so as not to blow our chances. They wouldn't hear of it even though I did my best selling job possible. I literally had to suck it up and find a way to trust in my ability. I kept telling myself, 'Just do the best you can.' I also chose to shift my focus from my negative feelings and worrying about possible negative end results to the process of what helped me as a player. When I got to the event, I was still terrified inside but after I made my first couple of shots I knew I was back. We won the event and qualified for the Olympic trials."

Pope John Paul II has often said something to this effect, "The divine likes to speak to our hearts through what we love and are familiar with." One of the main tools we have both used for years are stories and quotes from people we have met or admire from a distance who encourage us to develop mental toughness. We have saved and filed dozens of these quotes and keep them at close proximity at all times.

Guy's Favorite Quotes

"Nobody is gonna hit you as hard as life. But it ain't how hard you hit; it's about how hard you can get hit, and keep moving forward. How much can you take, and keep moving forward. That's how winning is done."

Sylvester Stallone as Rocky Balboa

"When nothing seems to help, I go and look at a stonecutter hammering away at his rock perhaps a hundred times without so much as a crack showing in it. Yet at that hundred and first blow it will spilt in two, and I know it was not that blow that did it – but all that had gone before… Some defeats are only installments of victory."

Jacob Riis

"It's tough to win, tough to win a championship. So we didn't get there the first few times, but I think we really got to show what we're all about, how mentally tough we are. I think that's the message – that you're going to be disappointed. That's what sport and life teaches you. But the real test of a person and the test of a champion is, can you continue to fight when things don't go your way?"

Tony Dungy

Claudia's Favorite Quotes

"If I had to break it down, I'd say about 99 percent of the people in my life were telling me I wasn't going to make it. All that adversity and lack of faith ended up just strengthening my own convictions. All that negativity really helped me in the end, because there's no better inspiration for doing something than having somebody say that you can't do it."

Willie Nelson

"Don't say you don't have enough time. You have exactly the same
number of hours per day that were given to Helen Keller, Louis Pasteur,
Michelangelo, Mother Teresa, Leonardo da Vinci, and Albert Einstein."

Anonymous

"If people knew how hard I had to work to gain my
mastery, it wouldn't seem wonderful at all."

Michelangelo

"You build on failure. You use it as a stepping stone. Close the door on the
past. You don't try to forget the mistakes, but you don't dwell on it. You don't
let it have any of your energy, or any of your time, or any of your space."

Johnny Cash

Fundamental #4: CONTROL DESTRUCTIVE BEHAVIORS

Gaining peace of mind also involves addressing the side of us that is prone to destructive behaviors. None of us are immune to developing certain destructive behaviors. We all have the potential to allow our dark side to dominate our thinking and actions. There are many factors involved as to how great a degree and as to why we may go down this dark path. Minimizing or eliminating these behaviors comes down once again to how often our choices are dominated by fear or how often our choices are dominated by love.

In the process of discovering the masterpiece within, we may encounter one of many degrees of destructive behaviors over which we feel powerless. According to the founder of the Haight-Ashbury free clinic in San Francisco, CA., David Smith, MD, defines addictions as, "The compulsive use with loss of control and continued use in spite of adverse consequences." These damaging behaviors can come in the most severe life-threatening forms of alcohol, drugs (prescription and illegal), or eating disorders, but they can also include sex, gambling, tobacco, and over spending on down to what could be seen as bad habits: lying, gossiping, fits of anger, and negative talk. The best means to become enlightened to our own negative behaviors is to ask ourselves two insightful questions, "What am I doing in my life that I feel powerless over?"

and "What do I do compulsively over and over again despite continued negative outcomes?" The path to healing takes sustained hard work, but the peace of mind we receive from getting help is well worth the effort. Breaking the pattern of self-destruction is about making the conscious choice to love ourselves on a daily basis. Regardless of how our destructive behaviors are exhibited, if we do not learn to control these behaviors, they will hinder us from gaining peace of mind and becoming a living work of art.

Having witnessed a family member go through the perils of destructive behaviors in the form of a drug and alcohol addiction problem for nearly two decades, has forever changed my (Claudia) life and the way I view those with addictions, the process of addiction recovery, and the damage caused to everyone around the addict. Before being exposed to the world of addictions recovery, I naively held the belief that those who drank heavily or used drugs could quit cold turkey at any time with no problem if they just exercised stronger will power. How wrong I found myself to be. One of the rehabilitation facilities where I attended almost daily meetings with and without my family member over a forty-five day period was Las Encinas Hospital in Pasadena, California. The medical director of the department of chemical dependency services was well known addictionologist, Dr. Drew Penski. In one of Dr. Penski's many family sessions I attended, I learned that addicts become powerless over their drugs or alcohol especially those people who are genetically predisposed to chemical dependency. Some are able to work through their issues and recover. The most severe users will push their use to the limits returning to one rehab after another, relapsing over and over, until death occurs. My family member describes her destructive, addictive behaviors as:

"Always a choice. I have to daily remind myself why I'm a good person and why I should take care of myself and hold myself accountable. Staying away from destructive behaviors is different for everyone. For me it's spiritual. No one can force you to love yourself. I have to make that choice. When I get into a bad place, I tell myself to get out of my head and reach out for support. I find a meeting, speak to my sponsor or therapist, go surfing, take drum lessons, go to my job that I love, remind myself that these things are so much better than damaging behaviors, and that practice makes perfect. I work toward my recovery one day at a time."

Of all the philosophies we share in *The Masterpiece Within*, we find that we have based the largest majority of principles for life transformation on the lessons we have learned from 12 Step recovery programs. In our experiences with people from all walks of life over the years, we have found recovering addicts to be some of the most authentically loving and gracious people on the planet. In learning to control destructive behaviors, we have compiled the following tools foundational to addictions' recovery programs, because they are appropriate for overcoming any destructive behavior.

Recovery Tools

1. H.A.R.D. Work

The four most common words used in addictions counseling are: Honesty, Accountability, Responsibility, and Desperation. If a person stands the chance to overcome a destructive behavior and walk the road to recovery, it is critical for them to embrace the necessary H.A.R.D. work.

Honesty: The first step towards recovery is admitting we have a problem. Unfortunately, this well-known first step has become a trite cliché for some people who believe admission alone is equal to recovery. Admitting to a problem is crucial and shows signs of honesty, but the level of honesty needed to turn a life around is admission combined with a commitment to the process of change.

Accountability: One of the main attitudes in overcoming destructive behaviors is blame shifting or making excuses for our deliberate choices, which have caused hurt to other people and destruction to ourselves. We may have all the external resources in the world available to us to rid ourselves of destructive behaviors, but the key lies in our will. Unless we choose to remain honest with ourselves as well as others, and commit to making wise life choices, we will never be able to master destructive behaviors.

Responsibility: Making the commitment to seek help and to follow the principles of recovery is the only way we can overcome a destructive behavior. Ultimately, we are the only ones who can choose to incorporate the principles we are given. By taking responsibility for our actions, we assert control over what can be accomplished.

Desperation: There is another truism in addictions that teaches an addict will only be able to succeed if they first hit rock bottom, which is true for any destructive behavior. But what is rock bottom? This does not necessarily mean that a person will have an emotional epiphany although for some this happens. Rock bottom is simply coming to the awareness or understanding that, "My life is on a destructive path and I need help to deal with my negative behavior." Another concept in addictions' recovery is learning to raise the addicts' bottom so they will see they are living at or very near rock bottom. This means caring friends are intervening in such a way as to help us understand the serious state we are in.

2. Detox

When we find ourselves in the out-of-control whirlwind of a destructive behavior, we become a natural magnate for additional destructive behaviors to be drawn to us. Instead of continuing down this path, we must seek means to put a stop to this behavior before any more harm comes to our lives or the lives around us. More often than not, the only way to get control of these destructive behaviors is to remove or detox ourselves from the stimulant or the influences for a period of time before we can begin to think clearly again. Detoxing can be as severe as checking ourselves into an alcohol or drug treatment facility or as mild as fasting from over-spending, or giving up negative speaking for a designated length of time. In the world of addictions' recovery, detoxification occurs when the addict goes to a rehab center and is monitored by trained professionals over a period of days. The addict has absolutely no access to alcohol or drugs in order to clean out their systems before the educational portion of treatment can begin. This painful process is commonly referred to as, "going cold turkey."

Consider that every major religion encourages the discipline of fasting in order to deepen his or her spirituality and address behaviors each individual believes is taking him or her away from spiritual growth. For example, the well-known Catholic practice of Lent is a form of detox when taken seriously. During the six-week period, we sacrifice something we love or take the time to address a negative behavior. The end result is, we gain clarity of mind to view our lives objectively and begin the process of eliminating destructive behaviors.

3. Act As If

"Act as if" is the inspirational phrase for AA's famous, "Fake it till you make it" motto. The Rev. Samuel Shoemaker, who was Bill Wilson's mentor in the early days of forming AA, first coined the phrase for a feature he wrote about the organization in the magazine, *The Christian Herald*. In 1954, Reader's Digest reprinted the article. It became their most requested piece and still ranks as one of the most requested articles in their history of publication. The idea behind this concept is that if we want to attain a certain habit or attitude, we must start acting as if we already possess the quality. Many actors who have portrayed roles as superheroes in films, often say just putting on their costumes gave them a feeling of empowerment. The importance of maintaining a childlike spirit throughout our lives comes into play here. How often do we see children pretending they are someone they admire, be it a cartoon hero or character from their favorite film or television show? When children take on the noble values of their heroes, their negative behaviors are often altered for the long haul, because these positive attributes have been incorporated into their actions.

While Rodney and I (Claudia) were visiting our friends, Steve and Genia Winwood, in the Cotswolds area of England, their daughter Lily, who was six years old at the time, almost never changed out of her Jessie Cowgirl outfit from the film, *Toy Story*. She made quite an impression on everyone, acting out Jessie's free-spirited and adventurous personality. Seeing that I had a camera one morning, Lily asked me if I would go outside with her. Once outside, she insisted I take photos of her posing next to the horses and that I was only allowed to call her Jessie. I have thought of this moment many times in my life especially when adult responsibilities or negative thoughts attempt to sneak in. Revisiting Lily's humorous photos serves as an apropos reminder that childlike pretending or acting "as if" will usually lead me down a more mature, wise, and self-loving path.

4. Work The AA Program

The most successful tool for walking the road toward addiction recovery is the renowned Alcoholics Anonymous program. The vast majority of respected counselors and rehabilitation facilities around the world use the AA model for treatment and if they do not, the principles they do use usually mirror the program in some indirect nature. As we stated earlier, for over seventy-five years the AA program, which includes attending meetings, finding a sponsor, and working the 12 Steps, has proven to effectively change millions of lives. We can easily use this same blueprint to work our way through destructive behaviors. Dr. Mavor Eagle, a psychologist and family-counseling specialist in Calgary, Alberta, who believes in the power of the AA principles, had this to say:

"Working the program is the key. And there are other good programs and principles out there that can also help us overcome the behaviors we want to change. The key is in finding the right program, and that is the one, which best works for each individual. So many of these principles are the same because they work; we just tend to get caught up in unnecessary semantics."

There are many varieties of support groups available: Alcoholics Anonymous, Narcotics Anonymous, additional 12 Step Groups, Spiritual or Religious Services, Weight Loss Programs, Senior Groups, Children's Groups, Abuse Support, Grief Support, New Mothers Support, and the list goes on. No matter the circumstances we find ourselves facing, creating a strong support system such as finding a friend or sponsor to speak to in times of trouble before acting out, attending daily meetings, seeking one on one therapy and working the 12 Steps will draw us closer to a healthy outcome. Remember one of AA's most popular slogans, "It works if you work it."

THE 12 STEPS:

Step 1. *We admitted we were powerless over our addiction (the destructive behavior) – that our lives had become unmanageable.*

Step 2. *Came to believe that a Power greater than ourselves could restore us to sanity.*

Step 3. *Made a decision to turn our will and our lives over to the care of God, as we understood God.*

Step 4. *Made a searching and fearless moral inventory of ourselves.*

Step 5. *Admitted to God, to ourselves and to another human being the exact nature of our wrongs.*

Step 6. *Were entirely ready to have God remove all these defects of character.*

Step 7. *Humbly asked God to remove our shortcomings.*

Step 8. *Made a list of all persons we had harmed, and became willing to make amends to them all.*

Step 9. *Made direct amends to such people whenever possible, except when to do so would injure them or others.*

Step 10. *Continued to take personal inventory and, when we were wrong, promptly admitted it.*

Step 11. *Sought through prayer and meditation to improve our conscious contact with God, as we understood God, praying only for knowledge of God's will for us and the power to carry that out.*

Step 12. *Having had a spiritual awakening as the result of these steps, we tried to carry this message to other addicts, and to practice these principles in all our affairs.*

5. Develop Spiritual Values

Developing spiritual values is the one facet in overcoming destructive behaviors that can be so easily misunderstood. French philosopher Voltaire's advice may be helpful here, "If you wish to converse with me first define your terms." The concept of bringing in spiritual values into one's life for some is a scary proposition. For many the words, "religion" or "spirituality" brings preconceived notions of empty religion and religious rituals such as lighting candles, saying formal liturgical prayers, singing songs with little meaning, going to lethargic church services, feeling shame, guilt and fear due to the pressure of being perfect, having to learn church-speak, etc.

There are some working the 12 Steps who will say they struggle with Step 3, which says, "God, as we understood God," because the God they were taught to understand is either unloving, judgmental, not tangible or they believe has not been there for them in the past. For recovery programs such as AA they make a clear-cut distinction between religion and spirituality as to not scare people in need away. Counselors in recovery programs emphasize that practicing spiritual values regardless of whether they partake in religious rituals or not help people accelerate the process in overcoming destructive behaviors. These recovery programs promote universal loving values, which include love, kindness, decency, fairness, respect, forgiveness, and healthy relationships.

6. Substitution

One of the keys to conquering an addiction or destructive behavior is replacing it with a positive habit. In rock legend Alice Cooper's autobiography, *Alice Cooper, Golf Monster: A Rock 'n' Roller's Life and 12 Steps to Becoming a Golf Addict*, Cooper writes how golf has replaced his former drug and alcohol addiction. Cooper who has been clean or substance free for over thirty years attributes his sobriety to the 12 Step program, his relationship with God and finding a healthy obsession (golf) that reinforces the same principles the most effective recovery programs promote. For him, competitive golf taught honesty, discipline, practice, fairness, and the importance of having a healthy alternative to take his mind off the everyday struggles and demands of life.

The Bible, Jewish commentaries, and Buddhist writings reinforce this idea of positive substitution while addressing destructive behaviors. If negative behaviors such as stealing, gossip, or greed rear their ugly heads, spiritual masters would recommend reacting in the opposite spirit. When trying to break the habit of stealing, one would perform generous acts of service. When struggling with gossip or slander, one would purposely look for the positive in others and find ways to encourage people. The AA program calls this, "changing our gaze" or taking an unhealthy focus and replacing it with a healthy focus. For Alice Copper, his gaze is golf, for others it may be taking art classes or returning to a passion from long ago.

> *If one is master of one thing and understands one thing well, one has at the same time, insight into and understanding of many things.*
>
> Vincent van Gogh

This is the message in the film, *The Legend of Bagger Vance*. A former Georgia State amateur golf champion, Rannulph Junuh, played by Matt Damon, returns home after WWI and is asked to be the local golf celebrity in a special tournament with two PGA pros, Walter Hagan and Bobby Jones. Junuh has not been able to pick up a club since returning home, because of the inner pain in his heart from fighting on the front lines in Germany. Unfortunately, Junuh has become an unemployed drunk. Bagger Vance, played by Will Smith, seemingly appears out of nowhere to become his caddy teaching him valuable life lessons from the game he once loved and played with great passion. As Junuh spends more time with Bagger Vance, his "authentic swing" returns, he becomes healed of his inner demons, he deals with his drinking problem, and his mental health is restored. When Junuh began to apply the lessons he learned on the golf course (trust, integrity, practice, focus, and forgiving oneself) to his personal life, his life reversed from a destructive path to a constructive path.

Fundamental #5: GOAL MAPPING

> *Our goals can only be reached through a vehicle of a plan, in*
> *which we must fervently believe, and upon which we must*
> *vigorously act. There is no other route to success.*
>
> Vincent van Gogh

Along our journey toward becoming a living work of art, mapping out life goals is critical to the process. Functioning without specific goals in mind leaves us wide open to live as Thoreau describes, "...lives of quiet desperation, and going to the grave with the song still in us." Seeking to achieve our goals should never be viewed as a neat and tidy checklist, but as a grand adventure filled with passion and purpose, especially when our goals are of noble nature. The alternative to not setting goals is as Herb Brooks, coach for the 1980 US Olympic Gold Hockey Team challenges, "When there are no goals, neither will there be significant accomplishments, only existence. Do you want to just exist?"

Living a goal-oriented life is a dance of flexibility and persistence alongside celebrations of achievement. Life circumstances will throw wrenches upon our path so learning to adapt and adjust while keeping our eyes upon our goals should be a welcome challenge. As prominent Calgary, Alberta, heart surgeon Dr. Alex Bayes says, "Even if one doesn't achieve their goals as expected, it is better than never trying. You learn so many things about life and yourself in the pursuit. And, who knows what new doors may open up along the way that you'd never expect and may be more meaningful than your original goals." We are all unique individuals with different likes and dislikes so each person's goal map will take on a different appearance with no two ever looking exactly the same. One person may have the desire to become a CEO of a major company with an extensive list of steps to get there while another's goal mapping may not have any vocational items on it at all. Instead, the map may be filled with community service ideas, art projects, or simply being a great parent. The point being, as Zig Ziglar reminds us, "What you get by achieving your goals is not as important as what you become by achieving your goals." We have found the following goal mapping tools to be incredibly helpful in the on-going process of discovering the masterpiece within.

Goal Mapping Tools

1. Reality Check

Swedish industrialist, Alfred Nobel, invented dynamite at the age of thirty-three, an invention that netted him a vast fortune. According to the website nobelprize.org, a French newspaper mistakenly published Alfred's obituary in 1888 instead of his brother's, which said, "The merchant of death is dead." Nobel was devastated to learn that instead of being remembered for his life's work, he would only be remembered for his most recent invention; dynamite. And not for the positive aspects of the invention, but the fact that dynamite was responsible for killing people. He had an awakening of sorts. Not wanting to be remembered in such a negative manner, he set out to find a means to serve humanity. In writing his will, he laid the groundwork to develop an annual financial prize honoring those for outstanding achievements in peace, literature, medicine, chemistry, and physics. Upon his death in 1896, the bulk of his estate went towards establishing the Nobel Foundation, which by today's standards amounts to well over one hundred million dollars. The first prize was awarded in 1901. Throughout the world, today the Nobel Prize is regarded as the most highly respected and sought after life achievement award an individual can receive.

When setting goals, we would be wise to stop and take a moment to have our own "life reality check" by asking ourselves if our current life path is leading us toward our preferred or desired outcome. Using Nobel's awakening example, we could ask ourselves if our own obituary showed up in today's paper would we be proud, disappointed, happy, or ashamed of its content? If we are not one hundred percent satisfied, therein lies the answer. There is no time like the present to make necessary changes, to take control of our life course, and to create a life worth remembering.

2. Write Down Goals

The simple act of writing down our goals and referring back to them on a consistent basis reinvigorates priorities and serves to remind us what is most important in our lives. Taking the time to sit down and map out our lives can serve as a supplement to jumpstart our goal setting path. Very vivid and specific details are key, because as we have stressed previously, "We achieve what we emphasize in our lives." Begin by mapping out long-term goals first. Create short-term goal sub-lists under each so that goal achieving motivational markers are set up ahead of time to encourage us to celebrate significant destinations along the journey.

Dr. Martin Luther King, Jr. understood this principle well in his quest for equality in the civil rights movement when he spoke on the subject of achieving goals, "Take the first step in faith. You don't have to see the whole staircase, just take the first step." Recording short-term goals and celebrating them throughout the process, provides healthy ego strokes preparing us to better face the tougher goals ahead. Be advised that if we fall into the trap of thinking the act of writing down goals is equal to achieving goals; no real progress will ever be made. Writing our goals down on paper and seeing the words in front of us is meant to hold us accountable to goal progress, while in turn, we also manifest the goals at a much quicker pace.

There will be inevitable goal-achieving roadblocks along the way so anticipating them ahead of time will contribute to maintaining peace of mind. Having pre-determined Plan B, C, or even D goal-achieving methods waiting in the wings will help manage the unexpected roadblocks more effectively. Reviewing the other goal mapping tools is a good kick-start to pull ourselves back into goal achieving progress, as well as engaging our own time tested methods. Remember, obstacles are simply an occupational hazard we all have to face, and they will either open new and better doors for us, or they will serve to make our character stronger. So press on, and do not give up.

3. Time Management

Teddy Roosevelt was not only one of the most colorful Presidents in American history, but he was also considered one of the best time management practitioners. Roosevelt said, "Nine-tenths of wisdom consists in being wise with our time." Nobody ever accused him of not doing his duties and sloughing off, yet he would often have all his daily presidential tasks finished by lunchtime to free himself up for his family and other outside interests for which he was so famous. He was a big believer in minimizing minutiae and focusing on the tasks that really needed attention. Roosevelt often said that we get bogged down with tasks that do not need as much attention to fill our time and can fool us into feeling we are working really hard. On the flipside, he believed we do not focus enough on tasks that need our attention. Roosevelt felt it was not so much how many hours we put in that matters, what matters is how effectively we are working with the time we are allotted. How are we spending our waking hours? Are we working hard toward a blissful outcome? Are we working hard toward a frustrating dead end road? If we continually find our hard work feels as if we have become a guinea pig on a wheel, going, going, going without forward progress, mapping out good time management could be one of the answers we are seeking.

The first sign for me that I (Claudia) am in bad time management mode comes when I discover I have actually walked into a stall of the men's bathroom rather than into a stall of the women's bathroom. Oh, yes it is true. Not only have these embarrassing moments shocked me into slowing down long enough to take a good long look at my frenzied schedule, but some of the conversations I have overheard between men as I wait until the coast is clear have been quite entertaining.

Creating good time management begins with the awareness that we have faulty time management. The next step is to record for a minimum of three days to a maximum of seven days how our days unfold from the time we wake up until the time we go to sleep. Try this exercise in our usual daily manner rather than any altered version to establish accuracy. After our specified time period is up, make two columns, one for achieving what we wanted to achieve and one for things we wanted to achieve but did not. Analyze our routine paying close attention to how much time is wasted throughout our day. Now create three separate columns divided into work, home, and play. Write down what is required of us for our work in the work column, what is required in the home for the home column, and what we would like to do for ourselves during our down time in the play column. If we do not have a day planner, now is a good time to get one. Create a well-balanced schedule and practice good time management one day at a time, giving ourselves a minimum of three days straight in order to feel the benefits. Allow those around us to be included in our plan and ask them to hold us accountable. Family and friends will love participating along not only because they will see more of us, but also because they will get a less stressed version of us. And who knows, our good time management skills may rub off on them. If we tend to do everything ourselves, there is no time like the present to start learning the art of delegating tasks or asking for help from others. If we slip into bad time management, simply start fresh right on the spot or the morning of the following day.

4. The Law Of Attraction

The concept of the law of attraction was brought back into mainstream culture with the release of the highly successful book, *The Secret.* The book reminds us that this law was first recorded in stone in 3000 B.C.E. and has long been used by the most famous of poets, musicians, artists, thinkers, leaders, and religions. The law, also known as "universal truth," states that like attracts like, or as we think, so shall we become. By now, at this point in the book, after having gone through six different sets of brain medicine, the concept and effectiveness of positive affirmations has become very familiar. To understand the concept on a more guttural level, try out the difference between how these two statements resonate. "I am a loser and never accomplish any of my goals." And then, "I am a winner and everything good I want for my life happens." Try repeating the negative statement over and over again for a few moments on up to an entire day. Then try on the positive statement, noticing the difference in our body language, our facial expressions, what occurs around us, and how people respond to us when repeating positive versus negative statements. What we visualize, imagine, or verbalize is what we draw near to us. Negative brings negative, positive brings positive.

In the book, *You Can Heal Your Life* Louise L. Hay writes, *"What we think about ourselves becomes the truth for us. I believe that everyone, myself included, is responsible for everything in our lives, the best and the worst. Every thought we think is creating our future. Each one of us creates our experiences by our thoughts and our feelings. The thoughts we think and the words we speak create our experiences."*

In the film, *Last Holiday*, Georgia Byrd, played by Queen Latifah, creates a scrapbook of goals and dreams she calls her, *Book of Possibilities*. The pages are filled with visuals such as magazine cutouts, articles and photos of places in which she dreams of traveling, alongside life, career, and romantic goals. Georgia looks through her scrapbook often, but never attempts any of her goals and dreams until she is given dire health news from her doctor that she only has three weeks to live. Setting out on her first adventure, she lives out her dreams of meeting her hero, an accomplished French chef, and winds up cooking alongside him. The man she has always dreamed of having a relationship with, Sean, played by L.L. Cool J, discovers her feelings when he happens upon his photo in Georgia's, Book of Possibilities. Sean goes on his own first adventure, not only to profess his love for her, but to also share the good news from her doctor that she was misdiagnosed and in fact, she is very healthy. The film comes to a close as Georgia opens her own restaurant and reflects back by saying, "I wasted too much of my life being quiet. I was afraid I guess. You know how it is, you keep your head down, and you hustle and you hustle, and you look up one day and wonder how did I even get here?"

All of us, at one particular time or another, have hung our heads low feeling as if we do not deserve or do not have the right to go after our dreams. Oftentimes, a major crisis is the only thing that will shake our minds free from our mental prison. Reading this book shows that there is a belief somewhere inside us that breaking free is possible. When we find ourselves "jogging in place," we must challenge ourselves to believe all things are possible, and make the necessary changes toward a more productive path if we are to gain peace of mind. Creating visual imagery as in Georgia's Book of Possibilities is a great start.

I (Claudia) have used this practice since I was a teenager, and it works like a charm. From time to time, I create a new vision board using poster board paper to tape goal lists, alongside magazine cutouts, photos, etc. I place it on the inside of my closet door, so as I get dressed I see daily reminders of my goals. I also place a piece of paper next to these visuals and record all my progress, which inspires me to keep moving forward.

5. Planning

In 1992, when going through my (Claudia) divorce, I found myself in serious financial debt. No longer having anyone to financially support, except for myself, I decided to take control of my finances putting a stop to financial bingeing and all unnecessary spending. After all, my mother is the queen of stretching a dollar, so I kicked in what I learned from her over my three decades as well as my own newly brainstormed ideas. I outlined a strict bare bones plan to take responsibility for my debt, and work my way out of financial turmoil as fast as humanly possible. I started by making a list of my debt and attacked credit cards with the highest interest rate first. My extremely frugal budget allowed only for the bare necessities in life: toothbrush and toothpaste; shampoo, conditioner, and soap; rent and utilities; car payments and gas. I used less electricity by turning out lights, watching less television, reading more, and washing and drying clothes during the times I learned were the cheapest rates for electricity usage. Rarely eating out, I clipped coupons and planned meals around weekly grocery store sale ads. The creativity involved in finding ways to make extra income and cutting corners added to the joy, relief, and satisfaction of seeing my debt reduced. This challenge not only helped me gain a deeper strength and self-confidence in myself, it also taught me how very little I could comfortably live on. All the while, I found myself developing discipline in other areas rather than just financial. Operating my personal life as a well-structured business, I was able to work my way out of thirty thousand dollars of debt in less than two years.

Many of us are intimidated when it comes to paying off debt, or in addressing the embarrassment of our debt when talking to credit card company employees. I found that calling the company in which the debt is owed and being honest with them up front is the best method all around. Establish a good relationship with one employee and ask for them specifically each time we call. Share with them the financial plan and stay in touch with the employee when sending out payments, making sure they receive them. This act shows integrity and the employee will write positive notes on the account. Avoiding phone calls or contact with the company gives them no choice but to believe the debt will not be paid. Never raise our voice during the phone call. If the employee we first speak to is in a bad mood, excuse ourselves and call at another time until we get someone that is easier to work with throughout our process. Ask the employee nicely if they will reduce the interest rate on the current debt and close the account to ensure that no additional debt is accrued.

Some credit card companies increase the interest rate for each late payment to as much as thirty percent over a short period of time without alerting the debtor. If a company tries to settle the debt with a lesser payment than the debt owed, which would result in the company taking a loss, try to avoid paying the lower amount to get rid of the debt, because this action will go on our credit rating as negative. Tell them we want to be responsible for the debt owed. If they have added late fees, ask if they will remove these fees. Take notes during all phone calls, recording what is said, whom we are speaking with, and the date and time of the call. Check our credit rating at least twice a year. If there is any incorrect information, call each company involved immediately to make the corrections. Remember kindness goes a very long way. Send thank you notes to the employee for their help, and ask for the manager to praise the employee's work. And most of all, try to buy only what we can afford to pay for immediately or within thirty days.

Business and financial manager, Gary Haber, of The Haber Corporation, had offices in Los Angeles, Nashville, and Paris with four decades of experience in the financial sector before his passing in April 2014. Gary was my (Claudia) husband's business manager since he opened his company in 1978, and he became mine in 1994. Gary so kindly offered his advice on how to maintain good financial practices.

A. Live within our financial means: *"Create a budget and stick to it. Do not have unrealistic expectations of our family or ourselves. Re-examine the budget every six months to a year and fine-tune it. Avoid impulse purchases. Sleep on large purchases. If we still want to buy the item 24 hours later, then only purchase the item if we can afford it. Avoid sales techniques that force us to buy something on the spot or the opportunity is lost, cars for example. Put credit cards in a safe. Think* *about purchases. Keep track of spending. When using credit cards day after day, we do not really have an accurate internal calculator. If we need to dig out of bad credit, see a credit card counselor or consider filing Chapter 13 Bankruptcy, which means the cards will stop accruing interest while the payment is minimal. This way we still take responsibility for our debt, but remember we will have to cut up credit cards. Pay bills on time. Good credit is like having money in the bank. Pay credit card bills in full otherwise interest can mount up before we know it. Do not buy what we cannot afford to pay for when the bill comes unless it is an emergency situation. When choosing a credit card company, consider those with additional benefits such as air mile awards especially if we travel or plan to travel. Try not to have more than two credit cards otherwise spending can be more tempting."*

B. If something sounds too good to be true then it is: *"Graduated mortgages are an especially bad option, because the payments keep going up and up. When purchasing a home, buy something in which the payment is not a burden. This will help us to avoid the crisis of losing a home from the very start. Do not put ourselves in the position of owning a home four times what we can afford. Avoid any and all get rich quick schemes. They rarely, if ever, pan out in a positive manner."*

C. Plan for the future: *"Have a monthly savings account, even if it is small. Do not tap into our savings or retirement plan because we will need the extra money later in life. Everyone will need additional forms of financial support because Social Security alone will not meet the financial needs of most households. Financial planning takes discipline. The earlier we start planning, the better. If we begin early, we will not feel the pain of saving money like we would later on when every dime is spoken for. If we wait, we will have to put away larger amounts to have anything of significance."*

D. Find a job we love doing: *"We will be doing our jobs for a very long time. Waking up everyday miserable is not worth the money we are making. Those with jobs they love heal so much faster when sick if they are motivated to get back to their job. I experienced this first hand when battling cancer."*

E. Give back to others: *"I have always given financially to charities, even when I had very little. Not only is giving a good tax deduction, but the practice is good for the soul and we will always benefit in more ways than one. I still find it astounding whenever I hear of a wealthy person who has never given a dime to any charity, and they do exist. It makes no sense to me."*

6. Ongoing Knowledge

In France, St. Bernard of Clairvaux was known for his social conscience and was a big proponent of seeking knowledge in order to create spiritual, social, or political change. St. Bernard was a man who set lofty goals and understood the knowledge he personally gained was one of the strongest weapons in his arsenal. He steadfastly believed the attainment of knowledge for the sake of knowledge alone was cheating those around us.

"There are many who seek knowledge for the sake of knowledge: that is curiosity. There are others who desire to know in order that they may be known: that is vanity. Others seek knowledge in order to sell it: that is dishonored. But there are some who seek knowledge in order to edify others: that is love."

Most of us have goals of one form or another, but not everyone has the knowledge to implement them. Intentional goal setters tend to be teachable and are always looking to educate themselves in ways to achieve their goals. They surround themselves with those who are goal achievers and take joy in helping others realize their goals as well. They instinctively understand two ancient Jewish proverbs, "Those who walk with the wise become wise," and "Those who water will be watered."

An inspiring example of the benefits of seeking knowledge is Joe Juneau. Juneau is quickly becoming a Canadian folk hero, not for his outstanding thirteen-year NHL career and Olympic Silver Medal in 1992, but for his willingness to be part of the change he believes needs to happen in northern Quebec. His passion to help Inuit children in the Nunavik region of Northern Quebec is garnering international attention. In a 2008 *Sports Illustrated* article, *A Northern Light*, by Michael Farber, Juneau said; "I always put my degree from Rensselaer Polytechnic Institute (Aeronautical Engineering) ahead of what I did in the NHL. I think this program here in Nunavik is the biggest accomplishment in my life."

Juneau, his wife, Elsa Moreau, and their family made the decision to move to the remote northern region to create a community of social work programs by using hockey as the carrot for the children, both male and female. Elsa said; "If he were to open a business or something, I would have said no. But he's investing in a mission, something bigger than himself. This is a

Grand Project Humain." A brilliant athlete who could have cared less about the party scene and perks an athletic career can provide was known for reading books and watching educational television while on the road. Most of what he read challenged his mind and spirit in how he could make a difference with his life. Juneau was drawn to help the Inuit community address the high suicide rate, to avoid the high level of addictions, and to overcome an abuse rate dramatically above the national average.

There are three conditions to be part of his program, in which the Inuit community and parents have embraced. The children must be in school consistently, they must meet a certain level of behavioral standards, and they must show effort in their studies. In only a few short years the community social service agencies noticed a dramatic drop off in substance abuse and the school grade-point average went up significantly. By being a powerful mentor, Juneau inspired an entire community to value gaining knowledge on an on-going basis as a key link to developing and pursuing life goals. Juneau is very clear that this is not a hockey program, but a social service program primarily to build up children's emotional, social, and mental capabilities. What began as a pilot program, it now has the momentum to continue on indefinitely. Because of Juneau's desire to keep on learning and edifying others, he has not struggled with life after a lengthy athletic career, and claims he is even more fulfilled now than at the peak of his hockey career.

Dr. Mehmet Oz and Dr. Michael Roizen speak often about the health benefits of continuing to pursue knowledge and exercising our brain throughout our entire lifetime. In their on-going research and study, they are convinced, "Seventy percent of how we age is based on our lifestyle, and not our genes." And they share, "Aging is not about avoiding diseases but living with vitality." In the best selling book, *You: Staying Young,* Doctors Oz and Roizen say:

"When you increase your learning during life, you decrease the risk of developing memory-related problems. That means your brain has a fighting chance if you keep it active and engaged. If you keep challenging it with new lessons, if you learn a new game, or new hobby or new vocation. You have to challenge your mind - even making it a little uncomfortable. Doing tough tasks reinforces the neural connections that are important to persevering memory. Like a clutch athlete your mind has a way of rising to the occasion. Challenge it and it will reward you."

7. Enjoy The Journey

Act on it! Execute! Just do it! We will be surprised at the resources, that will come to our aid from unexpected places to keep us on the journey, whether they are financial, the influence of key people, or internal motivation. In order for these resources to appear, there must be movement toward the goal. Too often we can be fooled into thinking our primary goals will simply happen or fall into place if we have a worthy dream and a good heart. When we choose to follow the promptings of our hearts and live in our bliss, God takes great delight in honoring us whether we are aware of it or not. Great thinkers from the past, such as Augustine and Marcus Aurelius, to current world influence-makers, such as Nelson Mandela and the Dalai Lama, believe we are honoring God as we choose to live this way.

German philosopher, Johann Wolfgang von Goethe said, "The moment one commits, providence acts." W. H. Murray built his life philosophy around this Goethe statement and saw the results in many tangible ways as he endeavored to follow through on achieving his goals. Murray was a WWII P.O.W. and famous Scottish mountain climber who many say was the greatest mountaineer in Scottish history. Murray co-led a Scottish Himalayan Expedition in 1951. In his book, *The Story of Everest* the following passage is written:

"We had definitely committed ourselves and were halfway out of our ruts. We had put down our passage money – booked a sailing ship to Bombay. This may sound simple, but it is great in consequence. Until one is committed, there is hesitancy, the chance to draw back, always ineffectiveness. Concerning all acts of initiative (and creation), there is one elementary truth the ignorance of which kills countless ideas and splendid plans: that the moment one commits oneself, then providence moves too. A whole stream of events issues from the decision, rising in one's favor all manner of unforeseen incidents, meetings and material assistance, which no man could have dreamt would have come his way. I learned a deep respect for another one of Johann Wolfgang von Goethe's couplets: Whatever you can do or dream you can, begin it. Boldness has genius, power and magic in it!"

If there is one mantra world-class athletes follow to the tee in my (Guy) numerous interviews it is: "Focus on the process not the end result. Take the time to celebrate or at least acknowledge the secondary goals, which are met along the journey, because these are critical achievements."

As Richie Hall, the long-time defensive co-coordinator of the CFL's Saskatchewan Roughriders says:

"Every coach worth his salt constantly teaches fundamentals, which are the equivalent of secondary goals. Yes, we all want to win a championship, but it will never happen unless we commit to the journey and what is necessary to achieve along the way. As an example, a football team cannot hope to win a championship unless they are committed to mastering basic fundamentals such as tackling, blocking, mastering coverage techniques, catching consistently, and having a quarterback who makes good decisions. When a team consistently masters these fundamentals, they need to be rewarded for the attainment and encouraged to keep on — keeping on because if these secondary goals aren't achieved at a certain minimum level, all the talent in the world will never take them to a championship level."

8. Stay In Our Power

Day to day life will present us with challenges, especially as we interact with one another. One day we may be feeling strong and steady, and the next we may feel knocked down and defeated. Rudyard Kipling said, "Words are, of course, the most powerful drug used by mankind." In order for us to remain on the path toward our goals when negative words or behaviors attempt to knock us off our strong footing, we must learn techniques to remain strong in mind, body, spirit, and emotion as well as in our hopes and dreams. First and foremost, if our ego is bruised or challenged, staying in our power will be a monumental task. Eckhart Tolle addresses this issue in his book, *A New Earth*. He says;

"At times you may have to take practical steps to protect yourself from deeply unconscious people. This you can do without making them into your enemies. Your greatest protection is being conscious. Somebody becomes an enemy if you personalize the unconsciousness that is the ego. Nonreaction is not weakness but strength. Another word for nonreaction is forgiveness. To forgive is to overlook, or rather to look through. You look through the ego to the sanity in every human being as his or her essence."

When we challenge ourselves not to react to others from our ego, we are able to stay focused on the movie we are making of our own lives. We may not be able to control the words or actions of those around us, but we can change how we react to them. When we choose not to respond to their negative behavior with negative behavior, such as an angry reaction, they will have no other choice but to back down.

Another roadblock we may come up against is the one within ourselves; our self-talk, our sudden disbelief in our own abilities. The best way to get past this state of mind is to be gentle with ourselves, trusting that this too shall pass. Most likely a good night's rest will hold a clearer and more self-loving perspective toward others and ourselves. Some goals may take longer to achieve than we anticipate and some sooner. Trust that whatever occurs on our journey, the lesson is necessary for us to become a living masterpiece. Reading back through our own goal lists and life mapping, along with working the self-empowering techniques and tools placed throughout this book will also help us to rediscover our inner strength.

Staying in our power is almost like a dance in the sense that we need to learn to navigate around a tremendous amount of adversity and opposition while maintaining our focus to achieve our goals. In other words, it is freakin' hard!

Joan Boaz embraces the expression, "Bash on regardless" when life seems discouraging. She learned the phrase in England, while doing a series of concerts, which involved lobbying for social change. The people organizing the shows were a group of dedicated goal-oriented social workers. Boaz wondered how they kept up the faith and persevered in spite of severe odds? Their mantra, "Bash on regardless." They elaborated that major social changes do not occur overnight but in small increments. Sometimes things do change for the better. Learning to bash on regardless or staying in our power is a critical component in goal-setting, but the payoffs may astound us as encouragement and help will eventually come our way and often from unexpected sources.

In the book, *Pursuit of Happyness* and the film of the same name in which Will Smith received an Oscar nomination for his portrayal of struggling father, Chris Gardner, we are shown the emotionally thought-provoking and moving evolution of one man's life story. Following a string of unfortunate events, Gardner finds himself living on the streets with his son, Chris Jr. Having grown up in a home of little means and suffering extreme trauma in his childhood from a string of abusive stepfathers, he became determined to "break the cycle of child abandonment in his family." The moment of relief came for Gardner when a flash of bright sunlight reflected off a red convertible Ferrari 308 catching his attention. The man driving the car looked, "As cool as the musicians I used to idolize." He continued, "In that instant, the car symbolized everything I lacked while growing up- freedom, escape, options." He struck up a friendly conversation with the Ferrari owner, finding out how he was able to gain financial success in life. The man replied, "I'm a stockbroker." Gardner set his path in motion to do the same. Without a college degree or any former experience on Wall Street, he tackled a road laced with heartache and sheer determination turning his life around in what could be considered as one of the most inspirational rags to riches stories to come along in years. Gardner says about his path:

"As long as I kept my mental focus on destinations that were ahead, destinations that I had the audacity to dream might hold a red Ferrari of my own, I protected myself from despair. The future was uncertain, absolutely, and there were many hurdles, twists, and turns to come, but as long as I kept moving forward, one foot in front of the other, the voices of fear and shame, the messages from those who wanted me to believe I wasn't good enough, would be stilled."

Gardner also attributes his successful path to the help of his friend and mentor, Reverend Cecil Williams, who was known in Oakland for, "feeding, housing, and repairing souls." Williams consistently preached the theme, "walking the walk," not just "talking the talk." He stressed the importance of moving forward, counting the baby steps along the way because they are equally important. Today, Gardner says he is not most proud of owning his own company, his fame or his fortune but that he is a good father.

While walking our journey in life, we must consistently remind ourselves there is help, hope, and mental relief available to us no matter the circumstances we find ourselves. Peace of mind is at our constant disposal when we focus our attention on making wise-loving choices rather than choices based in unrealistic fear. Love-based choices are rooted in logical reality while fear-based choices are rooted in illogical, "what if" questioning that forces our human nature to focus purely on worst-case scenario outcomes. Remember we are the director of our own life story. When chaos and disorder arises, we have the power to pull in the reins and direct our life into a more positive and productive direction.

If we choose to give into unrealistic fear, we step onto an unhealthy ego-based decision-making path fooling ourselves into thinking our choices are wiser than they are in reality. When this occurs, we are choosing to operate from an illogical mental place that serves as a Petri dish for unrealistic fear and anguish to multiply. This destructive path will stifle our masterpiece potential and motivation to live out our full talents, gifts, hopes, and dreams. When we find ourselves in a place of mental anguish and fear, reminding ourselves to get out of our heads and to move into our hearts instead, will provide us with the self-nurturing to operate from a place of love and acceptance.

CHAPTER 19

WORKBOOK CHALLENGES VII

GET TO KNOW ME

1. What clutters my mind and consumes my time in a negative way? _____
   _____

2. What causes the most stress in my life?_____
   _____

3. Who do I feel most comfortable communicating with?_____
   Why?_____
   Who do I feel most uncomfortable communicating with?_____
   Why?_____

4. In stressful situations what do I do or crave for relief? _____
   _____

5. In the last year what beneficial life knowledge have I gained?_____
   _____

6. Do I have a current short-term life plan? yes_____   no_____
   Do I have a current long-term life plan? yes_____   no_____
   How can I improve my life plan?_____

7. Am I happy with my current financial situation? yes_____ no_____

   Am I happy with my long-term financial situation? yes_____ no_____

   How can I improve my financial situation?_____

PRACTICAL POWER TOOLS

1. Pick your favorite tools for managing stress. Try them out for a week or longer and record the impact it makes on your stress levels.

2. Choose a positive experience you have had in communicating effectively. Examine why it went well for you. Now think of a negative experience and examine why it did not go well for you.

3. Am I An Addict?

   a. Have you ever decided to stop drinking for a week or so, but only lasted for a couple of days?

   b. Do you wish people would mind their own business about your drinking and stop telling you what to do?

   c. Have you ever switched from one kind of drink to another in the hope that this would keep you from getting drunk?

   d. Have you ever had to have an eye-opener upon awakening during the past year?

   e. Do you envy people who can drink without getting into trouble?

   f. Have you had problems connected with drinking during the past year?

   g. Has your drinking caused you trouble at home?

   h. Do you ever try to get extra drinks at a party because you do not get enough?

   i. Do you tell yourself you can stop drinking any time you want to, even though you keep getting drunk when you don't mean to?

   j. Have you missed days of work or school because of drinking?

   k. Do you have blackouts?

   l. Have you ever felt that your life would be better if you did not drink?

Did you answer YES four or more times? If so, you are probably in trouble. Only you can decide.

4. What have you always wanted to research and gain knowledge about? Over the next month, take your subject and explore it as deeply as you can. Check out library books, buy books, rent movies, take classes, etc. Keep a notebook. Choose a different subject when you feel inspired and create a file system, collecting your findings. You may be surprised where it will lead you.

5. Reverse learning: Many CEO's and leaders say one of the quickest ways to learn is to observe a person in a leadership position who is not qualified to lead. It often reveals a stark contrast to what the intended end result should be, forcing one to think and research more effective ways to accomplish the task.

BRAIN MEDICINE

1. I have all the tools I need to manage stress
2. I am a great listener and communicator
3. I have a clear perspective
4. I am open to learning, growing, and attaining wisdom
5. My goals are reachable

PERSONAL BRAIN MEDICINE

1. _____
2. _____
3. _____
4. _____
5. _____

By every inch we grow in intellectual height our love strikes down
its roots deeper, and spreads out its arms wider.

Olive Schreiner

CHAPTER 20

COMPONENTS TO A
HEALTHY BODY

The body is the soul's house. Shouldn't we take care
of our house that it doesn't fall into ruin?

Philo Judaeus

The human body is an amazing machine. According to *The Mayo Clinic Family Health Book*, the human brain is eighty percent water. Although constituting just two percent of our total weight, our brain uses over a fifth of our body's energy. Our heart beats about 2,500,000 times over our lifespan. The liver carries out over five hundred functions such as breaking down fats and removing bacteria from our blood stream. The inner wall of the stomach contains five million glands that secrete gastric juices for digestion. We are made up of approximately one hundred trillion cells. Our entire body is rejuvenated every seven years. These statistics may be considered useless trivia to some while amazing facts to others. Whichever category we fall into, there is no denying our bodies are amazing machines.

Shakespeare had it right when he said, "Our bodies are our gardens, to which our wills are gardeners." We face a tough crossroads as we progress into the twenty-first-century in managing the battle of wills within ourselves, considering what we put our physical selves through during our lifetimes. According to modern medical experts, our emotions reek havoc on our bodies causing strokes and diseases such as cancer and diabetes. Our unmanaged mental stress damages our bodies in the form of clogged arteries, heart attacks, and whole body deterioration. Throughout the ages as our species has evolved on planet earth, our life expectancy has steadily increased. In Ancient Greece, life expectancy was twenty years. When the US Constitution was signed in 1776, twenty-three years. At the turn of the twentieth century, forty-seven years and currently in North America, seventy-nine years. Medical advances, better hygiene, education, and lack of wars have contributed to this increase over the years, but health experts and scientists are warning us that children of today may be the first generation in history to live shorter life spans than their parents. The #1 cause... LIFESTYLE. In essence, our modern day lifestyle practices have finally caught up with us. If we are to become living works of art and attain longevity, these unhealthy attitudes need to be brought to light and replaced with healthier lifestyle attitudes.

While planning for this section of the book, we questioned how we could best teach, challenge and address "the body" with a fresh approach. No doubt there are plenty of books on the market and new ones released every year containing diets to follow, exercise routines to try, and low calorie recipes to cook, so we will not be going in that direction. We chose to address key unhealthy lifestyle attitudes that we believe play the largest negative roles in our lives today. We then provide healthy lifestyle attitudes to take care of our bodies from a wise balanced approach.

A large component of our physicality lies in our sexuality. One of the reasons we exist in the first place comes from the natural human desire to connect and procreate. The place in our bodies that is humming with creativity, so to speak, is centered in our sex drive. Some people have been raised to be ashamed of their sexuality, instead of celebrating it. We have chosen to address this issue and to bring a conscious, balanced, and healthy perspective towards sexuality.

UNHEALTHY LIFESTYLE ATTITUDES

Year after year, more and more entertainment-based products are released on the market coaxing us into a sedentary lifestyle. Grabbing some fast food and "vegging out" on the sofa for an evening's entertainment after a long hard day's work seems much more enticing than the alternative of taking time to make healthy low calorie dinners, and hitting the gym, or taking a walk. Balance and time management are the key. The occasional fast food meal is okay, but if we choose this route day after day, we fall into the lifestyle habit of abusing our bodies. Resting is healing, and entertainment can be stress relieving and inspiring, but resting without adding intentional physical movement will catch up with our health over time. But, statistically we have to ask, "Are we over resting and over eating?"

According to the World Health Organization, obesity is spreading in pandemic proportions across the globe. There are 1.5 billion people who are overweight worldwide and of those individuals, five hundred billion are obese. The forecast is that the number will increase to 2.3 billion overweight and seven hundred billion obese in the next few years. Morbid obesity continues to maintain the largest growth. With an obesity rate now escalating to more than thirty-five percent of Americans we have to query, "How high will we allow the rate to go until we collectively begin to make conscious, mature choices to turn the odds back in our favor?" The Center for Disease Control and Prevention says, *"American society has become 'obesogenic,' characterized by environments that promote increased food intake, nonhealthy foods, and physical inactivity. The medical cost of obesity in the United States has reached an estimated $147 billion annually."* Once thought to be a North American problem, nations around the globe are finally bringing their countries individual issues into worldview.

Argentina enacted an "Obesity Law" in August 2008, to help battle eating disorders, such as overeating, anorexia, and bulimia in their country. All high calorie foods must carry a warning label, and all diets advertised in the media must be backed by a health professional. Public and private health insurance companies are required to cover all forms of eating disorders. The Italian Society of Obesity was formed to address the growing problem in Italy's contemporary society. Their statistical data states, *"The spread of overweight and obese in Italian society reveals that the phenomenon has reached a dimension that albeit not as serious as in other Western countries constitutes a serious threat to public health and to the national budget."* Unhealthy lifestyle choices have even begun to affect Okinawans, once thought of as the healthiest group of people on the planet with more centenarians than any other location. Health expert, Andrew Weil, who has made three trips to the island, reported his findings in his book, *Healthy Aging, "Sadly, I must report that Okinawan's longevity is now beginning to diminish as more of its people move to Naha (the islands capital city) and other population centers, eat Western food, including fast food, and begin to live like the rest of us."*

The not-for-profit, International Association for the Study of Obesity is a thirty-thousand-member organization comprised of fifty-three national and regional associations around the world representing fifty-five countries. Their mission statement is as follows, *"To improve Global health by promoting the understanding of obesity and weight-related diseases through scientific research and dialogue, whilst encouraging the development of effective policies for their prevention and management."* They report that, *"Obesity poses one of the greatest public challenges for the twenty-first century with particularly alarming trends in several parts of the world. The prevalence of adult obesity has risen three-fold in many countries since the 1980's and the epidemic is spreading at particularly high rates in children."* The bitter irony is as some nations fight obesity the opposing problem of world hunger still affects 870,000,000 people. And, for the first time in our history, there are more overweight people on our planet than there are those going hungry.

According to a June 2008 article written by Kelley Hollard in the *New York Times*, obesity related problems are costing companies forty-five billion dollars a year. To address the problem many large corporations throughout North America have implemented mandatory monitoring of their employee's health after having been advised that increasing preventative practices is cheaper than treatment costs for obesity. Corporations in Japan have resorted to measuring workers waists and passing out dieting guidance information. The sad truth is many of us have chosen a very dysfunctional relationship with our own bodies. We abuse them by ingesting too many of the wrong foods and by choosing a sedentary lifestyle over an active one. In essence, our modern conveniences have convenience'd us right into a possible early grave.

UNHEALTHY LIFESTYLE ATTITUDES

Unhealthy Lifestyle Attitude #1: CHOICE OVERLOAD

Could it be our expanding waistlines, lost workdays, and escalating healthcare costs are the direct result of choice overload? Robert Holden PhD, author of, *Happiness Now* points out that our choice overload is everywhere. In days gone by we used to face the simple question,

"Would you like cream or sugar in your coffee?" Where as in today's world, if we take a look at Starbuck's alone, we are faced with choice overload. At their coffee houses around the globe, Starbuck's touts over eighty-seven thousand different coffee combinations. And that is just one coffee house. Our food choices and opportunities are everywhere we turn. If we want food from Japan, India, Thailand, Mexico, etc., no problem, it is right around the corner or within driving distance. If we feel like having cake, no problem, we can choose to purchase a cake of any size, form, and shape from a bakery, a grocery store, the bakery in a grocery store, an ice cream cake store, a cupcake store, on the Internet, a restaurant, a vending machine, a drug store, and on and on. Faced with these infinite choices, unless we have the proper discipline in place, we may find ourselves in a food trance running around like toddler's feeding the, "I wants."

Unhealthy Lifestyle Attitude #2: MORE, MORE, MORE…

Could it be our addiction to decades of "China Cheap" is responsible for our expanding waistlines? With the seemingly endless availability of just about anything tangible we desire at a relatively cheap price due to it's "made in China" label, we as a culture continue to want more, more, and more for our money. "I got it for only…" has become part of our everyday language. Are we so accustomed to getting "more for our money" that we demand more in all areas, including portion size? How can anyone blame us for wanting to consume some of these delicious foods, especially after being inundated with multi-million dollar advertising campaigns? For example, Hershey's alone spends two hundred million dollars a year promoting their tasty treats while fruit and vegetable advertising amounts to a mere two million dollars a year.

In the documentary film, *Super Size Me,* Morgan Spurlock educates the viewer on the portion size today versus portion size in the 1950's. One of his comparisons focused on drink and popcorn sizes offered at movie theatres. In the 1950's, a popcorn serving size amounted to three cups equaling 174 calories and a Coca-Cola served was around 6.7 oz. equaling seventy calories. Today, our popcorn averages twenty-one cups and a whopping 1700 calories. A 32 oz. Coca-Cola is 398 calories and that is not even the biggest size offered. Too often eating delicious high calorie foods is seen as being nice to ourselves. Small portion size and moderation is a good thing, but the problem comes when we are overly nice to ourselves with these foods. We are even overly nice to our pets by treating them to an obesity epidemic as well.

Yes, food is necessary for survival. We need nourishment and should be overjoyed and thankful for the food on our tables, but the lack of control to limit portion size and food quantity is out of hand. A study by the *American Journal of Preventive Medicine,* reveals the standard for plate size has gone up from ten inches to twelve inches. And, when those in the study group were given larger bowls and spoons, they consumed more food rather than taking the leftovers home.

Unhealthy Lifestyle Attitude #3: FASTER IS EASIER

There is any number of specific causes as to why we, as a world community, are dealing with a lack of caloric balance. How we manage our time plays a huge factor. Oftentimes, we are exhausted from a long day at work, so what is easier, faster, and tastier wins the decision hands down. Drive-through windows usually take five minutes to get our food where as making a home cooked dinner takes time to plan, time to go through a grocery store, and time to fix the meal. Our cars can take us to our desired location much quicker than walking even if it is a block away. Therein lies the problem. We can get stuck in a mindless rut of unhealthy choices if we do not take the time to consciously stop and plan out a healthy meal. Taking a few hours to plan balanced and healthy meals for the week can help solve time management problems, and can be a fun family activity. And, planning meals can be much more cost effective than simply grabbing "cheap" fast food.

Unhealthy Lifestyle Attitude #4: EMOTIONAL BINGEING

Emotions tend to control our eating habits. The medical community warns us our emotions are becoming increasingly responsible for our health crisis. How often do we have a bad, sad, or stressful day then turn to high calorie carbs such as ice cream, cookies, and cakes to nurse our emotional wounds of the day? During an emotional crisis we nearly never reach for healthy food choices such as an apple, or a salad. One can hardly blame us for turning to tasty treats to lick our wounds just to feel better, but treating ourselves can add up in caloric intake if we are not able to move from childish wants to adult responsibility. Once again, not aiming to be perfect, but instead to retrain ourselves to care for our bodies as a living work of art.

Unhealthy Lifestyle Attitude #5: THE COLD HARD TRUTH

Oftentimes, we live in a bubble and do not have a clear perspective as to what is going on outside our realm of existence. We may be operating under the assumption that our own bodies are not THAT out of shape, but when put to the test, we may find we actually have a very high body fat percentage and other health issues. The hard facts are becoming increasingly visual all around us. Service industry professionals say larger seating accommodations are in demand across the board from restaurants, to airlines, to ferries. Ambulance drivers are suffering back problems from having to lift patients who are increasing in size. Ambulance companies have had to order larger ambulances and gurneys to accommodate the ever-increasing commonality of three hundred to five hundred pound patients. Coffin manufacturers reveal there is a growing demand for double over-sized coffins.

Chungliang Al Huang, founder and president of the Living Tao Foundation whose intention is to help support a healthier, more creative and productive way of living says, "Many people treat their bodies as if they were rented from Hertz- something they are using to get around in but nothing they genuinely care about understanding." Yes, we are guilty of taking our bodies for granted. We run them into the ground until they begin to scream at us, and then we depend on medical professionals to fix our physical misuse behaviors through bottles of cure-all prescription pills, plastic surgery, heart surgery or lap band surgery. Professor Min Lee, Associate Professor at the Harvard School of Public Health says, "I think most people would rather not be physically active, so instead of asking how much should I do, most people want to know how much can I get away with?" The Center for Disease Control reports that twenty-five percent of us are sedentary and that sixty percent do not exercise regularly.

Unhealthy Lifestyle Attitude #6: AN UNFULFILLED LIFE

With all the numerous factors that have the possibility to come into play, we have to address low self-esteem, disappointment, and regret. There are those of us who are angry and resentful having faced utter devastation regarding past career or personal life choices and experiences. A lost opportunity with a romantic relationship, a college degree that took us into a job we now realize is not a good fit but we feel stuck, or an unexpected divorce can be paralyzing. Some are jealous and downright angry of other's financial freedom and life opportunities. We may not be happy with how our lives have played out thus far, but if we continue to let this negative mindset rule our emotions, the wear and tear will damage our physical bodies and our relationships. The fact of the matter is we need our physical bodies to exist and as dim as life may seem at times, there is always hope, ample life skills, and help available to turn most situations around.

Unhealthy Lifestyle Attitude #7: POP CULTURE AND SOCIAL PRESSURE

According to *Seventeen* magazine, ninety-one percent of teen girls feel anxiety about their looks. Doctors on two islands in Fiji reported to the BBC that after the introduction of television, poor body image issues started to develop: eleven percent of school girls admitted to vomiting to control their weight, sixty-nine percent had gone on diets and seventy-four percent believed they were "too big or fat." On the Northwest coast of Africa in Mauritania, the pressure to be thin falls on males. And although frowned upon by the government, the practice of "gavaging" or force-feeding women with high-fat camel's milk and couscous in preparation for marriage still exists. The larger the young girl gets, the more desirable she is seen to her rail-thin, future husband prospects.

Throughout the ages, pressure from society and cultural traditions have ruled waistlines. When food was scarce, a robust figure was "in," showing that one could afford food. In present day, we are bombarded with airbrushed, super fit body images from multi-million dollar ad campaigns selling products. The key to being at peace about our own physique lies in finding what weight feels healthy and right for ourselves, and then striving to maintain our ideal weight in a healthy balanced manner. A clear perspective and balanced living will help us to not allow these often times unhealthy pressures to cause us undue stress, and to put our health at risk in order to comply to these social "norms."

Unhealthy Lifestyle Attitude #8: DIETING

Dieting is one of the leading causes for weight gain. "Last meals," before starting a diet program, can amount to five thousand calories or more if we are not careful. These last unhealthy meal binges can be so tasty and enjoyable that starting a weight loss program can be seen as boring. So, we continue the dance of being lulled into unhealthy binge eating until we deem ourselves ready. The mind games we play with ourselves in dieting can be extremely dangerous. We want results fast because we hear of fad diets that give us quick results. Starving ourselves most often causes us to binge eat when we go off these diets, because we restrict calories to such an extreme that we are left feeling "starved." And so the vicious cycle continues.

Actor, Dennis Quaid believed he developed what he calls, "manorexia" from gaining and losing weight for film roles. In the film, *Wyatt Earp,* Quaid played Doc Holliday. In order to give an accurate portrayal of Earp, he dropped forty pounds by running five miles daily and consuming a mere nine hundred calories. Playing former President, Bill Clinton, Quaid ate fast food burgers and fries everyday to gain an extra thirty-five pounds. According to *Men's Health* magazine, Quaid said these practices caused him to develop body image issues and that he would, "Look in the mirror and still see a 180 pound guy even though I was 138 pounds." Quaid sought treatment to help with his problem. The National Association of Anorexia Nervosa and Related Disorders estimated in an August 2013 article that, "twenty percent of people that suffer from anorexia will die prematurely."

Unhealthy Lifestyle Attitude #9: DANGEROUS BEHAVIORS

There are many preventable diseases, disorders, and deaths brought on by dangerous behaviors. According to a September 12, 2013 article in the *New England Journal of Medicine*, overdoses of addictive opioid prescription drugs such as Oxycontin, Vicodin, etc. are the second-leading cause of accidental death in the US. The most jaw-dropping data revealed a more than six hundred percent increase in opioid prescription use between 1999 and 2010. The American Society of Interventional Pain Physicians testified before congress that Americans are being "over-prescribed and over-medicated." The US accounts for four percent of the world's population, yet we are consuming more than eighty percent of the world's opiate painkillers and other potentially dangerous benzodiazepine drugs such as Xanax and Klonopin. In recent years, the *CMA Journal* reported that in some parts of Canada opiate drug use has increased by 850 percent. These "legal" drugs are killing more people than heroin, cocaine, and methamphetamines combined.

According to the Centers for Disease Control and Prevention (CDC), *"Excessive alcohol consumption is the third leading cause of preventable death in the United States. Tobacco use, poor eating, and exercise habits top off the list."* The CDC also states, *"Sexually transmitted diseases amount to twenty million reported new cases yearly and carry the potential threat to an individual's immediate and long-term health and well-being."*

Unhealthy Lifestyle Attitude #10: IT WILL NEVER HAPPEN TO ME

Denial. How many of us at one time or another have said, "Oh, that will never happen to me" only to find down the road "that" does happen to us? Or we may flippantly judge other people when instead we should be taking an honest look in the mirror and addressing our own unhealthy lifestyle practices. We may convince ourselves that our bodies can handle our destructive behaviors but given time, our unhealthy lifestyle practices WILL catch up with our health and longevity.

Unhealthy Lifestyle Attitude #11: LACK OF PHYSICAL MOVEMENT

Every January gym memberships escalate, but it is widely reported that as many as four out of five gym memberships go unused. Dr. Michael Roizen, Chief Wellness Officer of the Cleveland Clinic says, *"Disuse atrophy is the use it or lose it theory of aging. And it is true for your memory, your sex organs, your muscles, and especially your bones. If you don't challenge these systems and keep them in good working order, they become unreliable - - fast."* The Presidents Council on Fitness, Sports, and Nutrition says that only one in three kids are active on a daily basis; less than five percent of adults participate in thirty minutes of physical activity everyday; and only one in three adults receive the recommended amount of physical activity each week. Dr. James Levine, who specializes in activity studies at the Mayo Clinic says, "Excessive sitting is a lethal activity."

Unhealthy Lifestyle Attitude #12: ALL WORK AND NO PLAY

And the dialogue goes like this, "I'm exhausted. I'm so overworked. There's too much to do at work to take a vacation. We have too many expenses to pay for a vacation. There's too much responsibility at home to find time for a vacation." In North America, an average nine days of paid vacation time goes unused every year. As the economy continues to recover, the fear of losing our jobs is real for many of us, but some companies are closing their doors, forcing workers to take time off. The effects of stress are taking a large toll on our bodies and our home life. Stress produces cortisol, the leading cause of abdominal fat, our body's ability to fight infection goes down, our arteries take a beating, and we lose sleep causing a plethora of additional health concerns. Study after study shows the need for rest and recreation is vital for emotional, physical, and mental well-being. In John De Graaf's documentary, *Running Out of Time,* he revealed, *"Women who don't take regular vacations are anywhere from two to eight times more likely to suffer from depression, and have a fifty percent higher chance of heart disease. For men, the risk of death from a heart attack goes up a third."*

Unhealthy Lifestyle Attitude #13: PROCRASTINATION

"I should. One day I will. When I have time I will. I'll be fine. One day I'll get my teeth cleaned, my eyes checked or see about a spot on my skin that looks questionable. One day I'll eat better and I'll start getting more exercise." And so we tell ourselves over and over again until years have passed and no action has been taken. A *Psychology Today* magazine article titled, *"I'll Look After My Health Later, The Cost of Procrastination"* was written by Dr. Timothy A. Pychyl who is an associate professor of psychology at Carlton University in Ottawa where he specializes in the study of procrastination. His colleague, Dr. Fuschia Sirois, revealed, *"Procrastination was associated with higher stress, a greater number of acute health problems, the practice of fewer wellness* behaviors, and less frequent dental and medical check-ups. Stress was associated with poor health and less frequent wellness and health-care behaviors, which in turn were related to poor health."

Unhealthy Lifestyle Attitude #14: LACK OF HEALTHY LIFESTYLE EDUCATION

Luckily as a child I (Claudia) grew up on farm fresh foods at home, which helped me to form a bond with a plethora of "Garden of Eden" foods. Being a southerner, we also had our delicious calorie-laden foods including homemade desserts. Nothing in this world comes close to tasting as good as my mother's chocolate and vanilla pinwheel cookies or my Aunt Blanche's sour cream pound cakes, but we all know one cannot live on sweet treats alone. Going off to college was an eye opening experience for me, as I packed on the freshman fifteen pounds within the first two months. Left to my own devices, I soon realized my mother's wisdom in portion control, exercise, and why I should not eat nightly overloaded bowls of ice cream.

How many of us are aware that when we eat in restaurants we consume twenty percent more calories than we would if we were to eat a home cooked meal? Or that just one tablespoon of mayonnaise contains an average one hundred calories and eleven grams of fat, and the average sandwich contains two tablespoons of mayo? Or that what we thought was a low calorie salad contains fifteen grams of fat and two hundred calories just counting the two tablespoons of salad dressing alone? Or that in order to gain one pound we have to eat 3,500 extra calories from what we are burning, and in order to lose a pound we have to work off 3,500 calories? With these facts, we can see how easy gaining a pound a week can be if we consume an extra five hundred calories a day for seven days.

Unhealthy Lifestyle Attitude #15: IMPROPER HEALTH CARE

Researchers at the Mayo Clinic studied 405 medical articles on medication adherence written over a twenty-year period. They concluded that approximately fifty percent of people do not use their medications properly or at all, and mostly not at all. Nonadherence results in approximately 125,000 deaths every year in the US alone. The World Health Organization (WHO) states that fifty to sixty percent of people around the world do not take their medicine as directed. Hippocrates touched on this issue in his book, *Decorum*, over two thousand years ago, "Keep a watch… on the faults of patients, which often make them lie about the taking of things prescribed. For through not taking… they sometimes die."

We know our bodies better than anyone else does, and when we notice a new ache, pain, or negative change we must pay attention to the signs and symptoms our bodies are giving us, and consult a health professional as soon as possible. The problem is many people are given warning signs, but only a small percentage actually does anything about them until it is too late.

I (Claudia) had a dear doctor friend who sensed something was wrong in his body for many months. He took great care treating his patients day after day, and year after year, but when it came to his own health, he waited to consult a fellow physician or to order any tests. He had great health care coverage and access to medication and testing daily, but still he waited. Before he passed away, he told me he knew something was wrong for a long time and that he should have done something about the signs, but he just did not want to face possible bad test results. His absence is felt by a tremendous amount of people.

HEALTHY LIFESTYLE ATTITUDES

Dan Buettner traveled the world as an explorer and researcher for *National Geographic*. During his travels, he began noticing large groups of centenarians in various regions of the world. The National Geographic Expeditions Council and the National Institute on Aging agreed to fund his extensive research project titled, *The Blue Zones: Lessons for Living Longer From the People Who've Lived the Longest*. Buettner identified five Blue Zones where, "People have the greatest life expectancy and where more people reach age 100 than anywhere else." They include, "The interior of Sardinia, a remote peninsula in Costa Rica, a Greek Island, a Japanese archipelago, and a community in southern California." Buettner concluded in his research that lifestyle attitudes and practices of the centenarians remained consistent throughout each of the five regions. A few of the prominent ones include; remaining sociable and physically active, having a purpose for living and a spiritual connection, and eating plant-based foods.

The majority of us want longevity with quality of life. In order for us to attain priceless quality of life, we must choose to embrace healthier lifestyle attitudes to take proper care of our physical bodies if we are to live balanced alongside our mind, spirit, and emotions. Altering our language from the common verbiage, "I'm dieting" to instead saying, "I'm practicing healthy lifestyle attitudes" is a great way to kick start our new school of thought.

Healthy Lifestyle Attitude #1: PERSONAL BODY KNOWLEDGE

When I (Guy) was in my early forties, I sometimes felt raciness in my system when I went to bed. I never really thought much about it as I have always been blessed with pretty good health. Around this time I was doing some work in California, and went into a drug store with a friend. While waiting for her to pick up a prescription, I noticed a blood pressure machine. Being a little curious, I thought it would be interesting to see my readings. The results were very high so, needless to say, I repeated the test. The second test came out even worse. A retired male nurse, who was watching me from the corner of his eye, came over and started chatting with me. As we were walking out of the store, he put his arm around me and said, "Young man I saw your blood pressure readings and they were way too high for someone your age. You seem like a nice man with a lot ahead of you. Please make me a promise, that when you get back to Canada, you will make an appointment with your family doctor."

Not to sound overly dramatic, but this man seemed sent from above. He looked like a retired hockey player, which got my attention. I followed up immediately on his advice. After the doctor asked me to check out my family history, I discovered that many of my relatives around the age of forty were also diagnosed with high blood pressure. I made changes in my diet and have been on a regimen of blood pressure lowering medication ever since. It took a year for my blood pressure to get back to normal, but it has been stabilized for well over a decade.

Most of us know our vision should be 20/20 and ideally we need dental cleanings twice a year. Past these stats, most of us are not aware what health tests we need performed or what our health numbers should be. We put together a list of the top ten practices to implement preventive health, to better understand our current health status, and to help catch critical changes in our bodies that may be telling us we have a heart condition, high blood sugar levels, problems with sexual health, inflammation, cancer, or a risk of stroke. We compiled this list by combining advice from the article, *"5 Health Stats You Should Know"* by Dr. Michael Roizen in the January 2014 issue of *Prevention* magazine with suggestions found on the Mayo Clinic, MD Anderson, *Harvard Health Publication* and *Life Extension* magazine websites alongside advice from Dr. Perry Chapdelaine of General, Alternative, and Preventive Medicine in Brentwood, Tennessee.

1. **Complete Blood Count:** (CBC Panel) The best low cost test for overall body condition and health status. Reveals blood cell levels.
2. **Cholesterol and Triglycerides:** Checks triglyceride (blood fat) levels as well as good (HDL) and bad (LDL) cholesterol levels.
3. **Blood Pressure:** Measures maximum and minimum pressure of the hearts blood flow. Normal is 115/75.
4. **HbA1c:** Measures blood sugar levels and tells us if we are at risk for diabetes.
5. **Vitamin D-3:** Correct levels are vital to our immune system to help fight off disease.
6. **C-Reactive Protein:** (CRP) Measures life-threatening inflammation in the body.
7. **Homocysteine:** High levels of this amino acid are associated with many illnesses.
8. **Comprehensive Metabolic Panel:** (CMP) Monitors liver and kidney function as well as electrolytes and blood proteins.
9. **Waist Circumference:** Our waist measurement should be half or less our height in inches.
10. **Yearly Physical Exams:** Annual check-ups and consultations with our primary care doctor can catch early warning signs and will help increase our longevity.
    A. For Women: Papanicolaou (Pap) tests yearly. Follicle Stimulating Hormone (FSH) measures fertility status. Mammograms, bone density, progesterone, estradiol, and testosterone levels after forty.
    B. For Men: Prostate-Specific Antigen (PSA) testosterone and estradiol levels after forty.

Healthy Lifestyle Attitude #2: HEALTHY PANTRY, HEALTHY FRIDGE, HEALTHY BODY

The well-known adage, "We are what we eat" has been around surprisingly since 1826. What a visual we would all be, if the food we ate on any given day, were hanging on our bodies for the entire world and ourselves to see. This awareness might serve as a pleasant surprise at how healthy some of us eat, but for others, it might be an eye opening experience as to why we are struggling with our health and weight. If we were to examine what foods we have in our fridge and our pantry, what would they say about us? Are we abusing or are we nourishing our bodies for longevity? Stocking our shelves with more nutritious foods will help prevent those late night junk food binges and early morning sluggishness. Here are a few suggestions:

1. Shop for groceries on a full stomach. We tend to buy more healthy foods and less unhealthy snacks. Read the nutrition labels on food products. Know what is going into our bodies. The first ingredient listed has the highest content.
2. Drink half our height in water ounces for a daily-recommended amount. Ex: If we are sixty inches tall we would drink thirty ounces a day. We may feel hunger, but our bodies may actually be thirsty for water.
3. Shop mainly in the outlying grocery aisles (fruits and vegetables). The middle aisles contain processed, packaged foods.
4. Shop for whole-wheat grains. Some packages can be deceiving, so read carefully.
5. Aim for no more than 1500 milligrams of sodium per day. Too much salt is taxing on our kidneys and forces our heart to work harder.
6. A protein serving size should fit in the palm of our hands, about the size of a deck of cards.
7. Use a 10-inch plate instead of a twelve-inch plate. Less food fills a ten-inch plate.
8. Shopping challenge. Do not go down the aisles that contain junk foods if we feel vulnerable. Try new healthy foods. Before checking out at the grocery store, challenge ourselves to look in our grocery cart and take out any unhealthy foods we may be tempted to buy.
9. Eliminate or limit fried foods. Research shows high heat fried foods contribute to arteriosclerosis.
10. When craving crunchy foods like potato chips, try crunchy healthy foods instead such as carrots, apples, or almonds.

Healthy Lifestyle Attitude #3: GRAB A BUDDY AND GET MOVING

One of my (Claudia) favorite college professors started our first class of the semester by having all of her students stand up and hug four different people in the class. She went on to explain that we were all away from home for the first time and in order to increase the odds of us remaining in college, we should connect with each other and get four hugs a day minimum. She was brilliant. I still challenge myself to get my four hugs in a day with family and friends and I would venture to say most of my friends from college still do the same. Connecting with a workout buddy can have the same effect. Studies show we are more likely to stick with a workout routine if we have a buddy to hold us accountable and to help celebrate our achievements. This time spent together can help us talk through and get through life's challenges. Physical movement is often touted as one of the most effective ways to prevent or get out of depression. Gary Small, MD, director of the Memory and Aging Research Center and the UCLA Center on Aging said, "Exercise not only increases blood flow to the brain, it releases endorphins, the body's very own natural antidepressant. It also releases other neurotransmitters, like serotonin, which lift mood," in an article titled, *"Can Exercise Cure Depressions"* on the PsychologyToday.com website.

For overall cardiovascular health, The American Heart Association recommends, "At least thirty minutes of moderate-intensity aerobic activity at least five days per week, and moderate to high intensity muscle-strengthening activity at least two days per week." So find a workout buddy, brainstorm together what work out routines to try and vary the exercise regimen to keep our interest going. Make the focus about getting stronger and healthier rather than getting skinnier. Community centers have affordable daily rates and monthly plans, as do local YMCA's. Hire a trainer to remain motivated and to map out appropriate exercise routines as well as short-term and long-term goal planning. Seek out team sports, such as curling or softball to join. Also, challenge ourselves throughout the day to make lifestyle changes: take the stairs instead of the elevator, park our cars farther from the door so we have further to walk, and ride a bicycle instead of driving a car.

Healthy Lifestyle Attitude #4: 80% FULL

When I (Claudia) was eight years old, my father came home with the news that we were moving to Okinawa for a three-year tour of duty. I did not know what to expect at first, but I quickly grew to love living on the beautiful island. I vividly remember the Japanese food, as I had never been exposed to Asian food before. I rarely saw meat in the plant-based Okinawan diet except for an in the ground full pig roast luau party my family and I attended. In school, I took, "culture class" where I learned the Japanese language and traditions. It was there where I was first introduced to the term, "Hara Hachi Bu" meaning to eat until 80% full that the Okinawans have embraced for thousands of years. When the 2002 book, *The Okinawan Program: How the World's Longest-Lived People Achieve Everlasting Health—And How You Can Too* by Bradley J. Willcox, D. Craig Willcox and Makoto Suzuki became a best seller, I was reminded of the islands lifestyle wisdom and learned more about other practices that contributed to their longevity; drinking calcium rich water and embracing "Ikigai" - a reason to get up in the morning.

Physiologically speaking, when we stop eating at 80% full, our stomachs have time to tell our brains we are done eating. Our bodies can still work on repairing and rejuvenating itself rather than overtaxing our system and sending the majority of its energy to aid in digestion. When we are too full, we not only become lethargic and tired but we also stretch our stomachs, and have to eat more and more to feel satiated.

Healthy Lifestyle Attitude #5: THE DAILY FIVE

One of the most effective programs touted for maintaining proper nutrition and health is to eat the daily five; three meals and two snacks a day. After waking up from our slumber, breaking our eight to twelve hour fast with nutritious foods is vital. Studies show eating breakfast jumpstarts our metabolism and can provide valuable energy to keep us moving throughout the day. And if our largest meal occurs in the morning, we have ample time to burn off the calories.

Eat breakfast like a king, lunch like a prince, and dinner like a pauper.

Adelle Davis

Starting the day off with a glass of water containing a dash of cayenne pepper and the juice of one lemon is a great toxin-fighter. Try eating oatmeal with blueberries and walnuts, and a piece of whole-wheat toast or an egg white omelet, turkey sausage, and sliced tomatoes. A midmorning snack such as an apple and a small handful of almonds will keep our engines running and our minds clear. Dieticians see combining a protein with our fruit as the perfect digestive combination. A balanced lunch of protein and vegetables will keep our energy going rather than loading ourselves down with a high carb meal. An afternoon snack of peanut or almond butter on a piece of string cheese with a handful of blueberries, will tweak our blood sugar. For the lightest meal of the day, our dinner could include a salad, lean protein cooked in a small amount of olive oil, and steamed green vegetables.

Healthy Lifestyle Attitude #6: AVOID PANIC MEALS

We have all had moments when we find ourselves starving and in a panic to get something to eat. I (Claudia) found myself in that very situation when I was around twenty-two years of age. I had been hired to work at the downtown Dallas Neiman Marcus store to model clothing in their famous "Zodiac Room" for the day. I did not plan ahead or make time to eat all day. By the time I finished the booking at 3p.m., I was starving. On the way out of the store, I ran into the gift shop and grabbed some chocolate covered cookies as I was pressed for time to get to my next job. As I was driving, I downed a few cookies to stave off the hunger, but was watching the road and not really looking at the container. The next thing I knew, I felt something tickling my arm. I looked down to see ants crawling all over my arm, my lap, and what looked to be hundreds in the container. I could not pull over fast enough and dispense of the ants. Of course the next day when I worked at Neiman's, they refunded my money and were very apologetic as their customer service is the best in the market. They even joked that eating chocolate covered ants was seen as a delicacy in some cultures. The lesson turned out to be a great visual reminder to challenge myself to be better prepared in order to avoid panic meals.

Grocery shopping on the weekends and planning out healthy meals for the week is a great way to avoid panic meals. There are a plethora of healthy meal planning guides on the Internet that can be found before leaving home or in magazines at the grocery checkout. Adopt the practice of keeping a list of healthy foods close by and healthy snacks in our fridge and pantry to serve as a reminder when trying to quickly decide what to eat at home.

Healthy Lifestyle Attitude #7: PRACTICE PREVENTIVE MEDICINE

Philip M. Tierno Ph.D., clinical professor of microbiology and pathology at NYU Langone Medical Center found, *"As many as eighty percent of infections are transmitted via contact like sneezing, coughing, or touching surfaces that have been sneezed or coughed on. And then touching your mouth, eyes or nose, which are the conduits of viruses into the body."* Many hospitals have adopted the motto, "Cover Your Cough, Clean Your Hands" with instructions to cough or sneeze into a tissue or into our upper sleeve to help prevent the spread of diseases. An easy way to remember how long we should effectively wash our hands is to sing the, *Happy Birthday* song while washing with soap and warm water.

There are a few additional practices known to help prevent us from getting sick: avoiding inflammation, keeping our digestive systems healthy, and making sure we are not low in Vitamin D3. Inflammation in the body is a major contributor to many diseases. Stress causes inflammation. An easy daily practice to help prevent stress from occurring is to plan to arrive at our destinations five minutes early. Our digestive health is sixty to seventy percent responsible for our immune system. Taking a daily probiotic will help keep good bacteria in our systems. Studies show that every cancer patient is low in Vitamin D3. During our yearly check-ups, is a great time to make sure our levels are normal. Sitting in the sun for fifteen minutes daily will produce Vitamin D3 naturally, but if time or weather does not allow, a daily supplement is recommended.

Healthy Lifestyle Attitude #8: CURB THE CARBS AND SUGAR

Needless to say, if we wanted to find a book on sugar addiction and its dangers, we would be hard pressed to choose from the vast amount on the market. As with most food items when consumed in small doses, sugar can be safe, but with greater availability and presence in a large majority of foods items, sugar has become dangerously toxic. High fructose corn syrup, sucrose, fructose, and other forms of sugar make up the seventy-seven pounds of sugar we each eat on a yearly basis. The American Heart Association recommends no more than six teaspoons daily for a woman and no more than nine teaspoons for a man because, "Excessive consumption of sugars has been linked with several metabolic abnormalities and adverse health conditions." Type 2 diabetes is directly related to sugar intake and is the fifth leading cause of death.

My (Guy) former college roommate, Scott Stebbins, started cutting back significantly on his sugar intake about four years ago. He could not believe how quickly the emotional and physical benefits kicked in. He found he was much more focused, his energy level was higher and more consistent, he was less moody, and his low level depression went away. He also noticed his knee pain cleared up as well as his skin blemishes and his allergy symptoms were less severe.

Paying attention to how we feel when we eat certain foods can be a tremendous awareness tool. Foods that contain simple carbs or "empty" calories do not have a lot of nutritional value and they spike our sugar levels, leaving our bodies screaming for more food. That is why when we have a bagel, a donut, or a soda pop for instance, we find we are ravenously hungry a couple of hours later.

Healthy Lifestyle Attitude #9: TAKE CONTROL OF HEALTH ISSUES

In *The Disease Delusion*, Dr. Jeffrey Bland explains, *"While advances in modern science have nearly doubled our lifespans in only four generations, our quality of life has not reached its full potential. We're masking illnesses with pills and temporary treatments, rather than addressing their underlying causes."* Keeping a health file on each of the members of our household is the first step in taking control of our health issues. We know our bodies better than anyone else. If we have a sign or symptom come up, write it in our file and make an appointment with our general practitioner as soon as possible. When seeing a doctor, take notes and ask questions such as, "What could be the underlying cause of the problem?" Request a print out of all test results and file them away when arriving back home. Study and research the wording on each printout, and investigate what each test and test result means. Compare results year after year to catch pertinent changes. When a doctor wants to prescribe medication, ask what lifestyle changes can be made instead of taking a drug. When given medication, talk to our doctor and the pharmacist to know exactly what the drug is and why we are taking it, to better understand the treatment and possible side effects.

When my (Claudia) mother was being treated for cancer in Houston, Texas at MD Anderson, I started a notebook to record everything the doctors said, all the medications that were given to her, all the tests that she had, everything she ate and all her vitals. As her primary caregiver, I became part of the team of doctors as they often consulted with me to determine how mom might respond to additional forms of treatment. Because we were keeping track of her vitals on an hourly basis, when her temperature spiked (indicating infection), we were in the emergency room within minutes. Her primary doctor, Dr. Larry Kwak, named by *Time* magazine as one of the most one hundred influential people in the world in 2010, believed staying on top of mom's healthcare was key in saving her life.

Healthy Lifestyle Attitude #10: VACATIONS, DAYCATIONS, AND STAYCATIONS

> *Every now and then go away, have a little relaxation, for when you come*
> *back to your work your judgment will be surer; since to remain constantly*
> *at work will cause you to lose your power of judgment. Go some distance*
> *away because the work appears smaller and more of it can be taken in at*
> *a glance, and a lack of harmony or proportion is more readily seen.*
>
> Leonardo da Vinci

Taking intentional time for ourselves can come in many forms and lengths of time. Vacations are becoming more affordable with more low cost travel websites in the market. Create a vacation account. Instead of buying that coffee, soda, fast food snack, or item we can live without, put the money we would have spent into the account. Staycations and daycations are quickly becoming part of our lexicon. Staycations can be entertaining and relaxing in the sense that we can plan to do fun activities in our own town without the stress and added expense of travel. A quick pick-me-up or daycation can give us a day of rest and relaxation. Checking into a local hotel for a day and getting spa services and pool/hot tub time can be rejuvenating. Last minute hotel discount pricing can be found on the Internet at sites such as Hotwire, Priceline, etc. Hotels have also started offering daycation pool, spa, and dining packages without having to book a room. Look into getting massage therapy to release toxins and to reward our hard worked bodies at low cost massage schools, neighborhood massage centers, or hire a recommended masseuse who can come to our homes. Schedule a professional facial or buy a high quality home facial product from a cosmetic store, a dermatologist or plastic surgeon's office. Treating ourselves to a manicure or pedicure, whether male or female, is a good "once in a while" body care idea. Planning vacations, staycations, and daycations ahead of time will help to hold ourselves accountable to do more than just vegging out and watching TV during our time off.

Healthy Lifestyle Attitude #11: LIMIT PITY-PARTIES

The Byrd's classic song, *Turn! Turn! Turn! (To Everything There Is A Season)* taken from the biblical book of Ecclesiastes sings about, "There is a time to dance and a time to mourn…" Grief is necessary to process our emotions and to heal. The million-dollar question is, "When is it time to move on?" Setting aside time to express grief, pity, and sympathy for ourselves is necessary, but we need to eventually move on as well. Wallowing in self-pity for extended periods can stifle living. If our grief enters the trauma zone, additional outside therapy and/or engaging a close circle of friends can aid our recovery. Part of grief recovery is getting to the stage where we must get on with our lives and learn to "carry on with a limp." There will always be scars as we travel through life, and as Billy Graham says about the wisdom of grief, "I never trust a person without a limp." True wisdom and love are matured through the trials of life.

Healthy Lifestyle Attitude #12: SET PERSONAL BOUNDARIES

Stephanie Marlin, a Spanish and English teacher friend of ours, recently conducted a survey of her students social media practices to see how many hours a day they were spending on social media: texting, emailing, posting on Twitter, Instagram, Facebook, etc. She was shocked to find the average time came out to be between six and eight hours a day on top of homework and television viewing. Some of the students said they are regularly up until 1 or 2:00a.m. As with many teachers across North America, Stephanie is concerned with the lack of physical exercise students get within the school system, as she believes there is a strong correlation between good grades and overall health. She often tries to get her students outside to play a sport or to take a walk when the curriculum allows. The National Sleep Foundation found that, "Children sleep better when parents establish rules, limit technology, and set a good example."

As technology increases, so will sedentary activities that taunt our family members and us to remain glued to a chair and a screen. We have to challenge ourselves to set personal boundaries and take care of our physical selves throughout our day. For instance, never take phones to the dinner table or watch television while eating. By establishing these practices, we eat slower, we are more aware of the food we are consuming, and we participate in priceless family time. Turn off electronic devices when getting into bed to get seven to nine hours of rest and rejuvenation, which is vital to our health and well being.

Healthy Lifestyle Attitude #13: FAMILY, FRIENDS, AND LAUGHTER

On the front page of the March 5, 2014 *USA Today* newspaper, the caption, *"Loneliness Can Be Deadly"* caught our attention. Psychologist, John Cacioppo, the director of the Center for Cognitive and Social Neuroscience at the University of Chicago reported, *"Having good relationships with a few people is one of the keys to happiness and longevity. The stresses and challenges of life are more easily endured if we can share them with someone in whom we can confide and trust."* *Robert Waldinger, director of the Harvard Study of Adult Development, an on-going seventy-five-year study says, "Loneliness is subjective. You can be lonely in a crowd, and you can be lonely in a marriage. It doesn't necessarily have to do with how many people you are with each day. It's whether you feel connected."*

We are social beings by nature as we have pointed out throughout this book. When we feel connected in meaningful ways, we feel hopeful, depression is minimized and heart conditions, blood pressure, and other health issues can be better managed. Cultivating and maintaining meaningful relationships is just as important as maintaining physical movement.

> *Laughter is the sun that drives winter from the human face.*
>
> Victor Hugo

Philosophers and great thinkers down through the ages have written often about the benefits of laughter. Today, there is a myriad of research to back up this school of thought. The MayoClinic.org website writes, *"A good sense of humor can't cure all ailments, but data is mounting about the positive things laughter can do. Laughter enhances your intake of oxygen-rich air, stimulates your*

The Masterpiece Within

heart, lungs, and muscles, and increases endorphins that are released by your brain. The long-term effects of laughter will improve your immune system, relieve pain, increase personal satisfaction, and improve your mood."

Healthy Lifestyle Attitude #14: DIVINE VANITY

You never get a second chance to make a good first impression.

Will Rogers

What impression or story does our physical presence tell others when we walk into a room? Maybe we are standing up straight with shoulders back, appearing educated, sophisticated, friendly, happy, hard working, and well-groomed with good self-esteem. Or, maybe we have bad posture, our clothes are unkempt, and our body language says we are angry, out of shape, arrogant, exhausted, and beat down by low self-esteem from the world. Whatever message we emote from day to day, there is no denying our body stories play a large role in our lives. What kind of physical story do we want to tell the world? Does our current story differ from what we would like it to be? There is no time like the present to change or to keep improving our story and there is certainly nothing wrong with a healthy dose of vanity. We should not place pressure on ourselves to strive for perfection as we have stated many times, but instead strive for excellence. As Michael J. Fox said, "I am careful not to confuse excellence with perfection. Excellence, I can reach for; perfection is God's business."

Healthy Lifestyle Attitude #15: STAY CURRENT

In the twenty-first century, the latest and greatest in medical and health advances is a mere Google search away. National and local morning talk shows often have health segments designed to educate their audiences. Major networks over the years have kept health and lifestyle syndicated programming as part of their daytime and evening line-ups with the likes of, *"The Doctors, Dr. Oz, The Biggest Loser,"* and *"Extreme Makeover,"* which can help educate and inspire us to make better lifestyle choices.

312

In 1894, the US Department of Agriculture (USDA) published its first dietary recommendations to the nation. Over time, the food pyramid came into being. As statistics came in as to how food affects our bodies, adjustments to the pyramid have been made. As part of the updated pyramid in 2014, for the first time exercise was added as a component. The daily requirements are broken down as follows:

1. Exercise: Adults should be physically active for at least thirty minutes most days of the week, children for sixty minutes. Sixty to ninety minutes of daily physical activity may be needed to prevent weight gain or sustain weight loss.
2. Grains: Half of all grains consumed should be whole grains. (6oz)
3. Vegetables: Vary the types of vegetables you eat. (2.5 cups)
4. Fruits: Eat a variety of fruits. Go easy on juices. (2 cups)
5. Milk: Eat low-fat or fat-free dairy products. (3 cups)
6. Meat and Beans: Eat lean cuts, seafood, and beans. Avoid frying. (5.5 oz.)
7. Oils: Most fat should be from fish, nuts, and vegetable oils. Limit solid fats, such as butter, margarine or lard. Keep consumption of saturated fats, trans fats, and sodium low.
8. Choose foods low in added sugar.

SEXUALITY

> *Most people don't realize that sexuality is a completely integrated part*
> *of their personality as much as actualizing in education or interpersonal*
> *relationships. Sexuality is very much a part of who we are, how we present*
> *ourselves in the world, what we do, and how we think of ourselves.*
> *Our adequacy and our self-esteem are tied up in our sexuality.*
>
> Gary Null; *Get Healthy Now*

For some we have saved the best for last, have we not? If you have been leafing through our book and were checking out the various topics our bet is this was one of the first sections you turned to. Congratulations you are normal!

In all my (Guy) years as a counselor and minister, sexuality may be the most recurrent topic discussed. Even in my unofficial sessions with people who find out my profession, sexuality is consistently one of the most frequently brought up subjects. Almost everyone wonders what is "normal" in terms of sexuality. Is it any surprise given we are bombarded with sensual images everyday of our lives through the media, pop culture, advertising, and everyday living? And yet, much of the bombardment is just an indicator that at the core of our being we are sexual creatures. We believe a clearer perspective and balance in the area of sexuality needs to be brought to light. If we gain an understanding of our sexuality, we will be much healthier in celebrating and managing our sexual desires.

> *"We are all born sexual creatures, thank God, but it's a pity so many people despise and crush this natural gift."*
>
> Marilyn Monroe

THE SAGES VIEW OF SEX

When one studies major philosophies, psychology, and the five great religions there is general agreement that there are primarily three reasons for having sex: procreation, pleasure, and intimacy.

Procreation

We cannot miss the obvious, as the human race would cease to exist without sex in the equation, but far too many people stop at procreation as the sole reason for sexual relations and overlook its additional benefits.

Pleasure

The sexual experience at its best is nurturing, loving, and enjoyable. As far as we know from studying nature, we humans are the only animals where both male and female are designed to enjoy the sexual experience. For men, obvious physical enjoyment comes from the penis even though it has more than one use. For women, the clitoris' only function seems to be that of pleasure.

Intimacy

Since we are physically designed to be integrated people, it only makes sense that the sexual encounter has the potential to draw people closer in an intimate relationship. In Jewish teaching, whenever people have sex everything is mystically intertwined as they bond their bodies together as one, not only physically speaking but spiritually, emotionally, and mentally. In a healthy sexual relationship, wholeness can be supplemented and inner healing can occur through sex. However, when a relationship leans toward dysfunction and promiscuity, sex can leave the involved parties with emotional baggage, mental distress, a weakening of one's core values, and possible sexually transmitted infections (STI).

DIFFERENCES IN THE GENDERS

Before we move on, please understand these are general rules about the genders. There are always exceptions to the rule and varying degrees of tendencies involved. When it comes to sexuality, there are three areas that seem to stand out regarding genders and their differences: self-esteem, sexual desire, and romance.

Self-Esteem

Women tend to lean more towards relationships when it comes to finding and developing their self-worth and self-esteem. For men, self-esteem tends to come from being results or goal oriented. Thus the tension in the bedroom where men can usually be satisfied by the mere sexual act while women value the experience more when an emotional connection has been made. Women tend to come more from a relationship perspective due to higher levels of estrogen while men tend to come from a goal perspective because of higher levels of testosterone. Sex for men is often seen as a release from tension while for women, more often than not, it is seen as a way to build a strong relationship. This is not to say that women do not enjoy the physical

315

act alone, or that men are not influenced by the depths of an emotional connection, but their starting points tend to be different.

Hollywood understands this difference when reviewing their sales data year after year. Women tend to gravitate more toward romantic styles of entertainment, whereas men tend to gravitate more toward action and adventure. Looking back at popular television shows over the years, one can see the differences in the roles of each gender, from *Modern Family* to *Home Improvement* to *Sex and the City*. When it comes to how the genders view sex, Billy Crystal nailed it in the film, *City Slickers*, when he said, "Women need a reason for sex and men just need a place."

Sexual Desire

From a pure physical make up, men and women tend to become aroused in different manners. Men are primarily aroused by simply looking at someone they find attractive, where women can also be aroused by someone they find attractive but emotional connections such as kindness, a warm touch, and having someone pay attention to them seems to be the stronger motivator. This is not to say men cannot be aroused by an emotional response first, we are simply addressing average starting points. Why is it that men buy almost ninety-nine percent of visually erotic materials, and women buy well over ninety-five percent of romance novels with no pictures to enhance the read?

Men are non-cyclical when it comes to sexual desire; a man's sex drive tends to be steady and constant. What most men do not understand is that a woman's sex drive can vary in a pronounced way throughout the month. Women are cyclical in nature because of their twenty-eight day menstrual cycle. The fact that women release only one ovum a month and men generate sperm every day shows how differently we are wired. Women generally have a thirty-six hour peak period for getting pregnant during the second week of their cycle, while men are fertile throughout the month. In most cases, week two is the peak week for sexual desire when a mature egg is released (ovulation) and makes its way through the fallopian tube to be fertilized.

Once a woman hits menopause, where their cycle has ceased and the risk of getting pregnant is not a factor, sexual satisfaction can actually increase. As men age, their testosterone levels can plummet, causing low sex drive while their estrogen levels can increase causing prostate trouble. Women can experience low progesterone, estrogen, and testosterone levels, which may cause numerous issues. Yearly visits to our gynecologist, getting regular medical tests, and hormone replacement can help with these issues.

Romance

When it comes to defining the word *romance* there tends to be differences with the genders. We asked couples for their definitions of romance and found the answers to be pretty standard. Men tend to view a romantic day as one that ends in sex while women tend to view a romantic day as one that has emotional intimacy. For men, romance implies sex is anticipated; for women, sex may be desired but it is not the necessary end result.

Romantic foreplay for a man is often defined as the moments in the bedroom leading up to an orgasm. Preferred foreplay for a woman is often defined as the "pre-bedroom" warm-up such as acts of kindness and intimate conversation over a romantic dinner prior to bedroom foreplay. Open communication as well as understanding and appreciating that there will be differences is the key to sexually fulfilling relationships.

WHAT IS NORMAL?

When discussing sexuality with Larry Lindoff, one of Edmonton, Alberta's most sought after family and relationship counselors, he said, *"I've been counseling for over thirty years and one of the main concerns for people in the area of sexuality is whether they are normal or not. This concern is the same now as it was when I first started my practice."* Even though we have more education and information about the biological and technical aspects of sex than ever before in history, questions still abound. As Lindoff reiterated, *"People have many questions especially in the areas of monogamy, frequency, and fantasy. It probably doesn't help that we are bombarded with pop cultures fixation on sexuality and that in the workplace the topic of sex has worked its way into casual conversation around the water cooler."* So what is normal?

Monogamy

From a physical perspective, monogamy is still the safest for staying healthy and not contracting sexually transmitted infections. Overwhelming research confirms monogamous relationships are the most beneficial for our emotional, mental, and spiritual health. *The Kama Sutra in Hinduism; Tantric Sex from Buddhism, the Song of Songs,* and *Proverbs in the Bible* all extol the virtues of monogamy. But what is often neglected to be emphasized from these ancient teachings is that couples are also expected to take time to satisfy, be intoxicated, be captivated, be delighted beyond measure, to make sex a priority, and to give each other access to their bodies in pleasing one another. Jay Leno on the *Tonight Show* interviewed the late actor, Ricardo Montalban. Leno was congratulating Montalban on his fifty-plus-year marriage. He told Leno his secret was found in this quote from ancient Chinese or Buddhist wisdom, "A great lover is not one who tries to satisfy many different women, any dog can do that, but a great lover is one who can satisfy the same woman for a lifetime."

Monogamy is a gift we give to ourselves. We are not denying that sex with numerous partners can be physically pleasurable, but over the long haul, the feelings of loneliness and emptiness begin to set in regardless of the bravado some may claim. When we develop a monogamous relationship, we put ourselves in a place to help enhance our sex lives. We learn each other's likes, dislikes, preferences, and subtleties in a mutually trusting environment. What people really yearn for is the soul connection or mystical union that sex can provide. Why is it that in the older translations of the Bible, or Shakespearean English, sex is referred to as, "knowing someone?" The implication, of course, is the high level of intimacy involved.

Frequency

How often do we think about sex and how often do people have sex? This may be the billion-dollar question with no conclusive answer. Dr. Michael Roizen and Dr. Mehmet Oz, in their book, *YOU: The Owner's Manual,* found that, "Fifty-four percent of men think about sex several times a day, compared to nineteen percent of women." The *ABC News* show, *"Lifeline,"* did a segment called, *"Do Men Really Think More of Sex Than Women?"* They followed a happily married couple around for an entire day. Their conclusion was not hard and fast numbers but they ended the story with these words, "The lesson for the day was that men may be from Mars and women from Venus, but apparently Martians think a lot more about sex."

So, how often do people have sex? Almost every major North American magazine from *Time* to *Vogue* has covered this subject in countless issues. The median average seems somewhere between once and three times a week for most monogamous couples. New couples seem to have more sex, but when life throws curves such as illness, children, or work related issues, the frequency goes down. Sexual desire varies from person to person regardless of gender so therein lies a contributing factor with the differences in frequency. "Normal" is finding a level of mutual-satisfaction.

Fantasy

Most of us wonder if fantasy or erotic thoughts are healthy, unhealthy, normal or deviant? So much of our angst comes from how we define terms and semantics. We are amazed at how many people outside the church culture know this one scripture from Jesus' famous, "Sermon On The Mount" (Matthew 5:28), "But I say to you that anyone who looks at a woman to lust after her has already committed adultery with her in his heart." What troubles us is how often this scripture is misinterpreted, creating questions, and impossible standards, while fanning the flames of guilt for far too many people. The common misinterpretation some churches give is, "He or she who looks at another person with any sexual thought or fantasy has committed adultery and is on the fast track to Hades." If we are being realistic about this conclusion, then those of us in the church have ceased to give people authentic hope of being human.

Because I (Guy) have been asked to give dozens and dozens of workshops on "*Sexuality and the Bible,*" I challenged myself to study many highly respected theologians' thoughts on the intent behind this passage. I came to the conclusion that Jesus gives us an insight on sexuality that is quite freeing rather than guilt ridden.

Defining Lust

In our studies, we were amazed at how almost every older Bible commentary would define the word "look" but not the word "lust" from Matthew 5. Commentaries seem to avoid the word like the plague. The word for lust that Jesus mentions has very little to do with harmless sexual fantasies. This word comes from the Ten Commandment word to "covet." Covet or lust is a verb defined in biblical dictionaries as follows, "*Lust is a seeking to acquire what is wrongfully yours. A passion to possess. To try and obtain what doesn't belong to you. To set the heart upon possessing. To have an inordinate desire to acquire. Inordinate means with no restraint, a fierceness of purpose or excessive in nature.*"

Jesus was saying if we look upon a person we know and have access to in a lustful way, they are off limits if they are in a committed relationship, or if we are in a committed relationship. If we begin to make plans or scheme how to seduce that person and act to attain that person sexually, we have crossed the line into lust, whether that person agrees to have a sexual encounter with us or not.

This is vastly different from a harmless erotic fantasy we may have about having sex with someone, but with no intent to act upon the fantasy. And, it is also different than simply seeing an image or being attracted to a person who crosses our path that we would never meet in real life. Not to sound trite, but it is impossible to have a relationship with an image or a person with whom we have no contact. These kinds of erotic fantasies simply need to be managed not eliminated. They are damaging only when the fantasy takes precedence over developing real relationships.

Defining Chimera

Another type of sexual fantasy someone may have can be referred to as a "chimera" fantasy. This fantasy is erotic in nature the same way lust is, but chimera is a fantasy with no intention to act upon. The origins of the word chimera come from Greek Mythology. Chimera was a creature with a lion's head, goat body, and serpent's tail. The creature existed only in imaginations, yet he could feel real. Over time, Chimera has evolved into being defined as having unrealistic sexual thoughts or imaginations that one would never act upon. Lust has to do with real situations, where chimera is a fictional scenario that comes into our minds regardless of how they are triggered. Hollywood gives up some good examples of the differences between chimera and lust.

City Slickers

Billy Crystal plays Mitch Robbins who is engaging in "locker room" talk with one of his friends on a trail ride while watching a beautiful woman riding a horse in front of them. They are questioning if they could have a sexual liaison without their spouses ever knowing, would they do it? Mitch says he would not be unfaithful period, but his buddy leans the other way. Mitch says to him: *"Can't you just look without always trying to hop in the sack with a woman? The difference between us is when I look at a beautiful woman I see a fine piece of art like at an art gallery. I appreciate the beauty and leave it on the wall. I don't try and rip the picture off the wall."*

The Quick and The Dead (Louis L'Amour version)

Sam Elliott plays Con Vallian, a cowboy in the Wild West. He is watching over a family as they move from the east to their homestead out west. They are in "Indian country" and a place full of lawless cowboys. He falls for the wife of the family, Mrs. McKaskel, played by Kate Capshaw. Con tries to seduce her until she makes it clear she is happily married. Being the gentleman he knows he should be, Con articulates the difference between harmless erotic fantasy and damaging lust. *"I'll stop chasing after you, but I won't stop looking because you are one handsome woman. Another time, another place Mrs. McKaskel, I'd of chased you down until you dropped. I don't take what's not mine."*

Derailed

Actors Jennifer Aniston and Clive Owen play Lucinda and Charles, who decide to consummate a flirtatious affair but are stopped when a man breaks into their hotel room raping Lucinda and beating up Charles. After the incident, Charles, who is married, tries to track down Lucinda to see if she is okay. When he finds her they agree the affair is over after the intense assault. In his thinking, Charles is relieved he never committed adultery when he says, *"Listen we didn't sleep together."* Lucinda sees through this and says: *"We were attacked. Just because we didn't have sex, doesn't mean we didn't cross the line. We went to the hotel, we started to do it, and we didn't stop at the conscience of our heart."*

Erotic Images, Literature, And Masturbation

When it comes to the topic of pornography the question emerges, "Is there a difference between erotica and pornography?" For most there is a distinction between the two. Erotica is generally defined as a combination of art and celebration of human sexuality. There are variations of pornography from soft-core to hard-core. Hard-core pornography clearly crosses a line, which is potentially harmful. The research is quite varied on what harm soft-porn does or does not produce.

One of America's most extensive research efforts known as *The Meese Report*: The Attorney General's, *"Commission on Pornography,"* was overseen by Surgeon General C. Everett Koop. Nine experts in their fields representing the medical community, psychologists, and religious leaders were brought together to research the effects of pornography. The commission's aim was not to end all porn, although for some of the team that would have been a worthy goal. What they could all agree upon was the need to eliminate what was defined as hard-core porn: the images or literature that involved children, animals, degrading scenes, scenes that involved or implied physical injury, and anything that appeared as non-consensual. Soft-porn with images or individual pictures of a couple having sex were considered quite mild compared to what they were trying to eliminate. The commission could find correlating links between hard-core porn and people's behavior; the effects of soft porn were not conclusive. Admittedly this is a sensitive issue and will have to come down to personal conviction and honesty for each of us. There is a fine line between erotica, soft porn, and hard-core porn and these lines can often appear blurred. Similar to how soft liquor can be handled by many, but someone with alcoholic tendencies might find a lite beer damaging, porn of any sort for someone with sexual addiction tendencies may never be healthy. If porn begins to affect people in areas of unfaithfulness, excessive loss of money, work performance, or even preferring pornography to relationships, then there is cause for concern.

There have been numerous studies on the subject of masturbation. Most men, ninety percent plus, self-stimulate on a regular basis meaning from a minimum of once a week to as much as two or three times a day. Sue Johanson, of the widely acclaimed, *The Sunday Sex Show* says, "Ninety-nine percent of men masturbate and the other one percent are lying." The findings with women vary a bit in the numerous studies we researched. The Kinsey studies found that sixty-two percent of women have masturbated in their lifetime. Other studies are as high as seventy to seventy-three percent. The levels of frequency for women compared to men are vastly different as well. Women who masturbate on a regular basis tend to perform the act between once a week, to two or three times a week. As in any study, there are some men or women who masturbate multiple times a day. When one combines all the studies together one thing is clear, men masturbate about four times more often than women.

For some, masturbation is a non-issue in terms of morality, but for others there is still the question of whether it is healthy or harmful. This is where the distinction between lust and chimera can be beneficial. I (Guy) have had many counseling sessions with people, mostly men in all age ranges, about this subject. A few years ago I counseled a deeply religious divorced man who was not in a current relationship. He came to my office and as he put it, "I'm ready to cut it off and become a eunuch because I can't escape the constant thoughts of sex, naked women, and masturbating almost everyday."

He was not the first person to express these concerns in the counseling room. Like many church-going people who are sincere in their faith, he felt like he had committed some kind of heinous sin. He believed God had written him off, because he could not turn his sexual desires completely off. This responsible man held down jobs, paid child support, wanted to get married again, and was "saving himself" sexually for marriage because of his spiritual convictions. When he learned that the majority of conservative theologians do not see masturbation as a sin issue and that his fantasies were of the chimera variety, his spiritual growth accelerated.

A sliver of conservatives, usually leaning heavily into the extreme fundamentalist camp, still view masturbation as wrong, but the majority do not. William Shedd, a conservative Presbyterian says, *"It may be a gift from God, especially when regular marital sex is not available."* Dr. Lewis Smedes from Fuller Theological Seminary in his best selling classic, *Sex For Christians*, says, *"Let us begin with a couple of indisputable facts. First, masturbation is not physically harmful in anyway. On this, all medical experts agree. Second, the Bible nowhere deals directly with masturbation. There are no injunctions against it. The Bible's silence is not because it was unknown. It is certainly not because the Bible is squeamish about sexually explicit topics. Masturbation is not inherently wrong or sinful. In the main, it is a common experience for most people and should be viewed as a normal part of life. We can emphasize its value in providing a potentially healthy genital outlet when sexual intercourse is not possible. We simply must not lay impossible moral burdens upon people, especially when we have no specific teaching against it."*

Dr. James Dobson was given sage advise from his father as a teen as recorded in his *Focus On The Family* video series, *"We were riding in the car, and my dad said, 'When I was a boy, I worried so much about masturbation. It really became a scary thing because I thought God was condemning me for what I couldn't help. So I'm telling you I hope you don't feel the need to engage in this act, but if you do, you shouldn't be too concerned about it. I don't believe it has much to do with your relationship with God.' What a compassionate thing my father did for me. He was a very conservative minister who never compromised his standards of morality. He stood like a rock for biblical principles and commandments. Yet he cared enough about me to lift from my shoulders the burden of guilt that nearly destroyed some of my friends in the church."*

ENHANCING OUR SEX LIVES

Educating ourselves on issues we have already covered, and getting to a comfort level where we can talk to our partners about our expectations and apprehensions can be the starting point to enhance our sex lives. In this day and age, there are many educational outlets to answer almost any question around sexuality. Romance novels, movies, and erotic literature have helped many understand how to please their partner and add to each other's sexual fulfillment. There are many books and tastefully produced CD and DVD series covering everything from technique to communication. *The Better Sex Video* series is popular and tastefully produced. The well known *Joy of Sex*, having sold eight million copies, and *The Art of Sensual Massage* have found their way into countless bedrooms.

Understanding The Orgasm

The *Calgary Sun* conducts an annual weeklong sex survey. In their 2008 survey, one of the topics was, *"No Orgasm? Who's to Blame?"* Almost one hundred percent of the men, and around twenty-five percent of the women in the survey said they had an orgasm every time they had sex with their partner, which is consistent with every study we came across. According to a *BBC* report, thirty-three percent of women reported never having an orgasm during sex and ten percent had an orgasm almost every time. These results were similar to a *CNN* report called, *"The Big O: Fireworks,"* which said that twenty-five percent of women had regular orgasms, thirty-three percent never had an orgasm and seventy percent seldom had orgasms on a regular basis. Sue Johanson repeatedly encourages her viewers to remember that for most women, orgasms are not the pinnacle of the sexual experience to the same degree it is for men, and some women orgasm only through masturbation. *The Calgary Sun* survey concluded with the following quote from Vancouver based sex therapist, David McKenzie, "You are responsible for your own orgasms, not your partner's."

Health Benefits

A study of over thirty-thousand men, which covered an eight-year period of time published in the *American Medical Journal Association* (JAMA), revealed that men with the most frequent ejaculations of twenty-one or more times a month were one-third less likely to get prostate cancer than the group who ejaculated four to seven times a month. An Australian study conducted by Dr. Graham Giles found, "Increased ejaculation may allow the prostrate gland to clear itself of carcinogens or of materials that form a substrate for the development of carcinogens." A Canadian study at Queens University found that men having sex three or more times a week may cut stroke and heart attack rates by almost fifty percent. But, having sexual encounters with multiple partners can increase a man's possibilities of prostate cancer by forty percent.

In her book, *Sex: A Natural History*, Joann Ellison Rodgers reports that for women sex and masturbation can help prevent cervical infections, relieve urinary tract infections, improve cardiovascular health, lower the risk of type-2 diabetes, and help work against insomnia. A study by *The Journal of Gynecologic and Obstetric Investigation* concluded that women who are sexually active during their menstruation were fifteen times less likely to develop endometriosis than women who abstained during their periods. The contractions in the uterus during orgasm may help flush away menstrual debris from the uterus. Sexual activity may also help the production of estrogen, which can act as a painkiller and reduce the pain of PMS.

Numerous ongoing studies continue to confirm the health benefits of sex; improved cholesterol levels and increased blood circulation. A couple can burn between 150 to 230 calories while having sex, which is equivalent to fifteen minutes on a treadmill. Having an active sex life also produces endorphins, which is our body's natural pain and stress fighter. Having sex and orgasms encourages the release of oxytocin, known as the "love hormone," and because of its bonding properties, encourages sudden generosity towards one's partner.

Having the ability to lead long, vibrant physically and sexually active lives lies primarily in our choices. "You control more than seventy percent of how well and how long you live. By the time you reach fifty, your lifestyle dictates eighty percent of how you age; the rest is controlled by inherited genes," Dr. Michael Roizen and Dr. Mehmet Oz report in the multi-million selling book, *YOU: The Owner's Manual*. They also advise, "Your house and body are both important investments. They both provide shelter to invaluable personal property. And they're both places you want to protect with all your power."

CHAPTER 21

WORKBOOK CHALLENGES VIII

GET TO KNOW ME

1. My current nutritional lifestyle is? Healthy____ Unhealthy____ Somewhere in between____
   How can I manage it better?_____

2. My unhealthy eating habits are?_____
   _____

3. On the average, I get ____ hours of sleep per night? Is that enough? Yes_____ No_____
   How can I manage more, if needed? _____
   _____

4. What toxic lifestyle attitudes can I change? 1. _____
   2. _____   3. _____

5. Do I have a healthy attitude towards sex and sexuality? Yes_____ No_____
   If no, what can I do to improve my attitude? _____

PRACTICAL POWER TOOLS

1. To become more self aware, create your own accountability logbook.
    Breakfast _____
    Lunch _____
    Dinner _____
    Snacks _____
    Vitamins _____
    Physical Movement _____

2. Review unhealthy and healthy lifestyle attitudes. Choose one from each category that applies to you.
    Unhealthy Attitude: _____
    Healthy Attitude: _____

3. Create a personal healthcare file. Place your test results, doctor contacts, and personal health history inside.

4. Make a list of any negative sexual attitudes that caused unnecessary guilt in your life.
    1. _____
    2. _____
    3. _____
    Now write ways you can revisit those attitudes in a healthier way.
    1. _____
    2. _____
    3. _____

BRAIN MEDICINE

1. I respect my body
2. I make time for rest and rejuvenation
3. I practice healthy lifestyle attitudes
4. I have time for consistent exercise
5. I honor my sexuality

PERSONAL BRAIN MEDICINE

1. _____
2. _____
3. _____
4. _____
5. _____

People tend to have an all-or-nothing attitude when it comes to healthy living. But if you can put these tips into practice even eighty percent of the time, you're still going to be successful.

Bob Greene, Exercise Physiologist

LIFE SKILL #5

MAKING A DIFFERENCE

People are illogical, unreasonable, and self-centered. Love them anyway. If you do good, people will accuse you of selfish ulterior motives. Do good anyway. If you are successful, you will win false friends and true enemies. Succeed anyway. The good you do today will be forgotten tomorrow. Do good anyway. Honesty and frankness make you vulnerable. Be honest and frank anyway. The biggest men and women with the biggest ideas can be shot down by the smallest men and women with the smallest minds. Think big anyway. People favor underdogs but follow only top dogs. Fight for a few underdogs anyway. What you spend years building may be destroyed overnight. Build anyway. People really need help but may attack you if you do help them. Help people anyway. Give the world the best you have and you'll get kicked in the teeth. Give the world the best you have anyway.

Kent M. Keith, *The Paradoxical Commandments*

CHAPTER 22

THE WISDOM IN LOVE

We are visitors on this planet. We are here for ninety or one hundred
years at the very most. During this period, we must try to do something
good, something useful, with our lives. If you contribute to other people's
happiness, you will find the true goal, the true meaning of life.

H.H. The 14th Dalai Lama, *The True Meaning Of Life*

I (Claudia) take great pride in being a "hands on" aunt with my nephew and four nieces. In July of 1998, I flew to Colorado a few days prior to my nephew Zak's forth birthday. At the time, I was reading a book that included some really cute idea's children had about what heaven must be like. One afternoon I was playing in the sandbox with Zak and decided to get his take on the subject. When I asked him, to my surprise, he put his head down, stopped playing in the sand and sat quietly thinking rather serious for a good while. Not wanting to push him, I let Zak take his time. After what seemed to be nearly five minutes, he looked up at me, presented a big smile, and to my delight said, "It's all about love Aunt Claudia." Of course my heart melted hearing a small child about to turn four coming up with something so profound. I will never forget that moment. As a matter of fact, I think about Zak's words often and share them with as many people as I can.

Is life really all about love? Think for a moment, what our lives would be like without love. Would we really have meaning or a zest for living? *For Love of the Game*, another Kevin Costner film helps answer the question. Costner plays aging MVP baseball pitcher, Billy Chapel who falls in love for the first time in his life as he approaches his forties. Right before he is to pitch the last game of his career, his girlfriend of four years, Jane, played by Kelly Preston, breaks up with him. He is heartbroken. Of course in Hollywood fashion he pitches the game of his life, a perfect game. His teammates help him celebrate his victory, but the real love of his life, Jane is nowhere to be found. Chapel ends the night alone in his hotel room. In what should have been one of the happiest moments of his life, he sits on the edge of his bed and weeps. The emptiness and loneliness consumes him. His "perfect game" seems almost trivial in the big picture. Chapel feels the depths of his lost love in his loneliness as he realizes nothing can replace love.

The scene of Chapel crying in his hotel room shows the power of life's most basic need…love. When we do not feel loved, we feel alone and empty, regardless of our accomplishments or the accumulation of material possessions. When we lose our sense of feeling loved, we often lose our sense of hope. When we lose our sense of hope, a deep depression can set in and our behavior can be altered in negative ways. When our loneliness and lack of hope or love reaches an all time high, suicidal thoughts may begin to consume us. Yes, life really is all about love and loving relationships.

The Miracle in the Andes, tells the story of Nando Parrado and the 1972 plane crash of his Uruguayan rugby team, family members, and team supporters. Their chartered plane crashed in one of the highest mountain ranges and most remote areas of the Andes in South America. After a handful of days waiting for a rescue plane, the survivors realized they might never be found unless someone took a chance and went down the mountain to look for help. Parrado was the healthiest of the passengers, so he volunteered even though his odds of survival were slim. Parrado had no idea where to look for help other than trekking down the mountain and hoping he would somehow find human contact.

As Parrado began the journey, he found himself on the ledge of a mountain inches away from death, starring down into a valley tens of thousands of feet below and seeing nothing but snow and ice. While Parrado gazed at the majestic mountain scenery, facing his death and the death of his family and friends, he had an ah-ha moment that changed his life forever. He realized the parties he attended, the women he bedded, and the rugby glory he experienced did not seem important anymore. The only thoughts flooding his mind were those of the people he loved, the people who loved him, and how empty life is when love is not paramount. Parrado said: *"The opposite of death is love. How had I missed that? How does anyone miss that? Love is our only weapon. Only love can turn mere life into a miracle, and draw precious meaning from suffering and fear. For a brief, magical moment, all my fears lifted, and I knew that I would not let death control me. I would walk through the god-forsaken country that separated me from my home with love and hope in my heart."*

Parrado knew if the rescue did not work, he and the remaining survivors would be buried forever never to be found in this beautiful, yet desolate part of the Andes. He said at that pivotal moment, everything was still and he caught himself starring into what he called "the ancient silence." In other words, the dead souls of those who had perished in the Andes, cried out but were never to be heard. Parrado was successful in his rescue efforts, saving the lives of sixteen passengers. Today, he lives his life telling his story around the world, reminding anyone who will listen, that nothing is more important than relationships and love, and making a difference with our lives. Nothing.

THE POWER OF LOVE

Well-known and loved actor, Michael J. Fox is as recognized for his activism with Parkinson's disease as he is for his positive outlook on life. In 2009, Fox went around the world interviewing fellow optimistically minded people on an *ABC* television special titled, *Adventures of an Incurable Optimist*. Among the places he traveled was the small Himalayan Kingdom of Bhutan, bordered by India and China. Since 1972, the nation's wealth has been measured in happiness not economic development. Bhutan's, "Gross National Happiness" campaign promotes that happiness comes down to relationships, and the campaign is said to have made the country of nearly one million people one of the happiest places in the world to live. The people of Bhutan believe loving one another begins on a family level, which in turn spreads to the neighborhood, then to the community, and eventually to a national level.

So how do we keep our hearts open to love and to loving one another? How do we consciously get out of our own heads and our self-consumed existence? Consistent practice. Making a difference is the final life skill in *The Masterpiece Within.* We strongly believe that practicing this life skill is the very soul to becoming a living work of art. We do acknowledge if one practices the principles of the first four life skills, a person can achieve a certain level of temporal success, but mastering these life skills alone will not bring the depth of satisfaction our souls seek. If we are going to truly become a living work of art, we must be a person committed to living a life devoted to loving and serving our fellow man. When we incorporate making a difference as the major key to becoming a living work of art, we begin to sense a confirmation in every cell of our being that tells us our lives are significant. We discover and experience what C.S. Lewis referred to as the "deeper magic."

The Sand People of the Kalahari Desert, the oldest of the tribal peoples in South Africa, embrace the concept of the "small hunger" and the "big hunger" in their culture. The small hunger has to do with life's basic daily needs like food, shelter, and housing. Taking care of life's basic needs can fill the small hunger rather easily. The big hunger refers to the sense of internal satisfaction we experience only through significant caring relationships with one another and the Creator. The big hunger begins to be met when we seek to love those in our sphere of influence. The deeper we are willing to go in being a loving, caring person, making it a part of our DNA, the deeper the level of satisfaction we provide for our big hunger.

If we are to impact our world for good, and experience the deeper magic or to fulfill the big hunger, we must be people who hold love as the highest value around which we build our lives. We need to regularly ask ourselves questions such as, "What am I living for? Why do I do the things I do? Am I a person committed to love? Does my life make a difference in my sphere of influence?" Albert Einstein understood the importance of these questions when he was lecturing to a group of fellow scientists. He challenged them to value love before technology when he said, "Concern for man and his fate must form the chief interest of all technical endeavors - never forget that in the midst of your diagrams and equations."

MIND YOUR P'S and Q'S

Some of us may have heard the phrase "mind your P's and Q's" as children when our parents wanted us to exhibit good behavior while in public. Or we might have heard little league coaches remind their young players to mind their P's and Q's as they stepped onto a baseball field so they would remember what they were taught in practice. In developing a lifestyle of love, we have discovered certain fundamentals or P's and Q's to which most difference makers adhere. We have taken the letters P, Q, R, S, T to create an acrostic of the five essential qualities that effective change agents seek to possess.

1. **P assion:** Loving people in our life bliss
2. **Q uiet Time:** Prayer, meditation, and reflective study
3. **R elationships:** Building regular intentional relationships
4. **S ervice:** Volunteering
5. **T o Thine Own Self Be True:** Integrity

1. Passion

The quickest way to become a person of influence with our lives is to connect with people who share similar life passions. We see this with professional athletes or music artists all the time who give motivational talks to schools. When students, who respect these celebrities, hear encouraging words to avoid drugs, alcohol, and destructive behaviors and instead concentrate on their studies, many do as advised.

My (Guy) dad was brilliant in motivating me when I was younger. I was a little sports fanatic who fought him for the sports page as soon as I found out a sports page existed. When I was struggling with percentages and division in math, my dad pulled out the newspaper and went straight to the baseball statistics. To this day, because my dad tuned into my natural passion, I can figure out my batting average percentage in slow pitch as I am running to first base. As someone who has served in "people helping" vocations most of my life, I have found the principle of connecting with people through their passion areas opens their hearts for me to be an effective change agent in their lives. The second quickest way to connect to others is to be exposed to passionate people who care about noble causes. Whether we have similar life interests or not, we are naturally drawn to passionate people.

Olympic gold medalist, Scott Hamilton is the most passionate and optimistic person I (Claudia) have ever been around. Anyone who has watched televised World and Olympic ice-skating events has seen and heard Scott's passion for the sport. His excitement is contagious and makes one want to go right out and lace up a pair of skates. Even in the film, *Blades of Glory*, Scott was asked to play a tongue-in-cheek version of himself exuding passion and excitement over the sport. From commentating, right down to the simplicity of a beautiful sunny day, Scott exudes passion for life. He often uses the quote, "The only disability in life is a bad attitude." He of all people has every right to have a bad attitude about life and sink into a corner with a twenty-four hour pity-party, after having battled cancer on numerous occasions. Instead, he chooses a more positive path daily. He and his wife, Tracie, live every day with passion and bright smiles on their faces. Scott's passion fuels his desire to make a difference in the world. He is involved directly with numerous charities, including his own, "Scott Cares," which is in line with his desire to see cancer wiped out in his lifetime. His website, chemocares.com, served as a tremendous educational tool when helping my mom heal from cancer. My husband, Rodney and I will always support anything in which Scott and Tracie are involved.

In his book, *The Great Eight*, Scott says, "*Focus on building up others, and your own sense of self-worth will improve. Some call these random acts of kindness. But the truth is, acting unselfishly is not random at all. Instead, it is a conscious, concerted effort to make the world better by making someone else's life better. The bonus: you will be happier by doing it.*"

2. Quiet Time

People who make a difference on a regular basis tend to be people who have a daily quiet time. Why is having quiet time so valuable? When we quiet our souls, meditate, or pray, we get in touch with the core of who we are, which in turn strengthens our noble value system. The more we practice our quiet time, the more we begin to prioritize the things that really matter in life, preparing ourselves to make wise loving choices.

I (Claudia) have been on the road for long stretches with many music artists over the years. One artist that consistently impressed me with his quiet time routine was Steven Curtis Chapman.

He is one the most authentic Christian music artists I have ever encountered. Not only did I witness him embracing this practice on a daily basis, but many times each day. During his usual twenty-minute quiet time breaks, he would read, pray, and spend the last few minutes in quiet thought. Whenever anyone came to me looking for Steven, whether it be a promoter, journalist, radio personality, or concert volunteer, each and every time I knew exactly where this dedicated artist could be found... in a quiet corner. To this day he remains one of the most generous, calm, and tender men I have ever known. I have to believe his consistent quiet time practices over the years have helped him tackle life's struggles better than most, considering the daily whirlwind of a busy music artist's responsibilities and most especially the grace in which he and his wife, Mary Beth, handled the loss of their young daughter.

3. Relationships

If we wait for people to come to us or for circumstances to come our way to make a difference, we may be waiting a long time. Becoming a change agent has to be an intentional decision. Giving with our checkbooks or volunteering in a charity's office is a start, but the most effective change agents tell us that building meaningful relationships with those in need has the most impact. We have found in our own lives that when we make time for others, we not only plant positive seeds in people's lives, but those to whom we give may be inspired to become a person of service as well. If we want to be humanitarians at heart, then it is not good enough to say we are, or to serve others every now and then, we have to embrace giving as a lifestyle.

One of my (Guy) biggest frustrations as a minister was seeing people volunteer for a worthy cause once every year or two, or going out of their way once in a blue moon to help someone in need. What I have observed is if we only serve on occasion or when it fits into our schedule, we may fool ourselves into thinking and talking as if we give back all the time. I would often challenge myself, and the members of our congregation in Calgary to seek out one or two ongoing relationships with people outside the church walls, who were in need of some extra love and care. The challenge was to get together with these people once or twice a week through a visit, phone call, e-mail, or anything of their choosing, to show them love and support. The personal and spiritual growth of the congregation, once this concept was embraced, was amazing to watch. Seeing and hearing stories about how people's lives were impacted on a long-term basis fueled even further giving.

One person who participated in the challenge was a woman named, Kerri Griffin, who wanted to be a source of support and encouragement for moms with small children. She thought it would be a good idea to have a group where moms could encourage each other in their family lives, to have adult conversations and to help each other realize that they were not alone in this demanding stage of life. She did not know how to get a group started, so we brainstormed and prayed together and that's when the idea of starting a crafts group for young moms was hatched. The group started small with two or three ladies that Kerri had already spent time with and then blossomed into a group of a dozen or more women. The psychological and emotional benefits of this group were off the charts. In many cases, relationships with their husbands improved and most of the women were able to see the motherhood phase of their lives as a huge blessing rather than an intermission until their real lives started again. The life long friendships that were formed are still continuing today. This "self-help group for young moms" became a lifeline for many of the women and the spin-offs were of a huge benefit to each of their family units.

Maybe Kerri and her group did not solve world hunger, but this community of women became more involved in making their sphere of influence a better place to live. They began to see that taking care of their families and serving their community was as noble a calling as someone nominated for a Nobel Peace Prize.

4. Service

Dr. Karl Menninger was asked, "What would you advise a person to do if he felt a nervous breakdown coming on?" Since psychology was his profession, most people expected him to reply, "Consult a psychologist." To their astonishment, he replied, "Lock up your house, go across the railroad tracks, find someone in need, and do something to help that person. Generous people are rarely ill people."

Most people are well aware of Vince Gill's musical talent, but in and around the Nashville community, Vince has become even better known for his humanitarian efforts. For years, his nickname has been "Benefit." He not only created his own highly successful charity events, but he also generously volunteers his time and talent to help others with numerous events from fundraisers to funerals. What an inspiring tender heart he has. Vince says, "When all is said and done the only thing you'll have left is your character."

In 2006, Vince became the recipient of the Academy of Country Music Humanitarian award. According to the ACM website, "*The Humanitarian Award recognizes artists who serve others, have a generous spirit, and help build the dreams of those in need. Gill was selected by a special blue-ribbon committee comprised of executives in the country music industry as well as local and national philanthropic leaders for his ongoing community service and charitable giving of his time and talent.*"

Vince is a stirring example that being a humanitarian is not just a now and then occurrence, but making a difference can be embraced as a lifestyle. What people also admire is how much fun he has with his generous spirit. He genuinely cares about those he is helping and generously and joyously engages in conversation with them rather than strictly socializing with event organizers. His example proves even further that when we consciously choose to make an emotional connection with those we are helping, our change agent skills advance at an accelerated rate.

5. To Thine Own Self Be True

Integrity! William Shakespeare's following words from his famous play, *Hamlet*, captures the importance of integrity. These words were Polonius' last bit of advice to his son, Laertes, "This above all: to thine own self be true, and it must follow, as the night before the day. Thou canst not then be false to any man."

Alcoholics Anonymous placed Polonius' advice on the sobriety birthday coins they give out to those celebrating each successful year in recovery, to serve as a reminder to live out the values of the AA program and to enhance the longevity of their recovery. In minding our P's and Q's, the "T" represents how important integrity is in living consistently by our core values. Living a life of integrity is at the very soul of making a difference, and provides credibility and personal empowerment. As we choose to love others, our integrity gives us the wings to impact lives.

One of my (Guy) favorite professors was Dr. George Maslany at the University of Regina, in Regina, Saskatchewan, Canada. Dr. Maslany was very passionate and entertaining in his profession and maybe even more passionate about educating workers in the people caring industry to become the best psychologists or social workers they could be. There is one class in particular that I will never forget, which covered the relationship between a counselors' level of integrity and the ability to influence a client with the greatest impact. He was not expecting his students to be perfect, but he did expect us to achieve a high level of competence before becoming employed. Dr. Maslany's message was:

"If you are not a practitioner of your materials, clients will instinctively sense the disconnect and not take your counsel with a high level of seriousness. If you are going to be a family counselor it would be a good idea that you are committed to your own family. If you are going to be an addictions counselor it would be a good idea that you're not a problem drinker or drug addict but at least a recovering addict. If you are going to be a conflict resolution counselor it would be a good idea if you are practicing conflict resolution principles in all your relationships. If you want power in the counseling room you will come across with more impact to the client when you're practicing what you are seeking to get across. Even if the client doesn't initially take your counsel, there is a good chance it will eat away at them and be of some benefit at a later date."

As we seek to become difference makers, we must keep in mind that each and every loving gesture or act of kindness we perform will not go unnoticed. Dallas Willard, author and professor of philosophy at the University of Southern California, said, "Casual connections in society and history are hard to measure." He was saying this in the context that in endeavoring to be a change agent we may not see the seeds of change in people's lives for months or years or maybe not ever in our lifetimes. The situation is similar to the elementary school teacher who seeks to inspire her students to love education, to follow their dreams, and to develop certain social skills that will last a lifetime. How often do these elementary school teachers see or hear feedback about the depth of influence they have had on their students? Rarely, if ever. Yet, the foundation for many students' lives was forged in the classroom early on through their relationships with loving teachers. As Scottish author and poet Robert Louis Stevenson so eloquently advised, "Don't judge each day by the harvest you reap, but by the seeds that you plant."

We would certainly be made up of a completely different planet of people if making a difference was presented to us and embraced from an early age. Maria Shriver would say she has had the great fortune of being raised under this exact school of thought. At the dinner table beginning at a very young age her father, Robert Shriver Jr., and her mother, Eunice Kennedy Shriver, would ask their five children what they were doing to make the world a better place. Even after she and her brothers accomplished a feat in an area of public service, their parents would not let up on the importance of making a difference. Rather than allowing them to wallow in their accomplishments and shower them with praise, their parents immediately challenged their children to get to work on their next humanitarian project. Public service was constantly taught to be the most noble of professions. Maria's parents could not be accused of being slackers themselves. Her mother founded the Special Olympics and her father founded the National Head Start Association as well as helping his brother-in-law, John F. Kennedy, start the Peace Corps. The familiar Scottish proverb rings true for the Shriver family, "Charity begins at home, but shouldn't end there." Maria and her four brothers, Bobby, Timothy, Mark, and Anthony all continue to work primarily in public service.

> *Service is the rent we each pay for living. It is not something*
> *we do in our spare time; it is the very purpose of life.*
>
> Marion Wright Edelman;
> Founder of The Children's Defense Fund

CHAPTER 23

EVERYDAY HEROES AND ANGELS

I don't know what your destiny will be, but one thing I do
know: the only ones among you who will be really happy
are those who have sought and found how to serve.

Albert Schweitzer

Julia Martin of tiny Carvel, Alberta, Canada just outside of Edmonton is the greatest everyday hero and angel I (Guy) have ever witnessed. Her son, Jerry, is one of my first true life-long friends whom I met in college when I was seventeen years old. Julia passed away in 2001 after a lengthy battle with cancer. Her funeral, one of the most amazing services I have ever attended, was held in her home church where I used to work as a teen. The church held about four hundred people, but the packed crowd inside and the chairs set up outside more than doubled the attendance. What was unique about her funeral was that fifty percent or more of those in attendance were not members of her church or even regular church attendees. These were people many of whom initially had an aversion to even darken the door of a church that Julia loved and cared for over much of her lifetime.

Julia, as we mentioned previously in sustaining spiritual growth had opened her home to anyone in need for over fifty years. She invited addicts, troubled teens, rejected spouses, and those down on their luck to stay as long as needed at the home she and her husband shared. These visits could range from overnight to a couple of months. Julia had this unique ability to love people without judgment, yet she so kindly and gently gave what could be seen as direct and sharp advice. She planted spiritual seeds of hope in pretty much everyone she met.

The senior pastor of her church did a scary thing for some funerals. He opened the mic to anyone who wanted to pay tribute to Julia's memory. He suggested that people speak for only a minute or two and after ten minutes or so he would carry on with the service. I have been to a lot of good funerals in my day, but the open mic portion of this service lasted over an hour with most people respecting their minute or two. People from every walk of life and economic background imaginable got up to speak as the line began to overflow into another part of the church. Julia had touched every age, gender, race, religious or non-religious background one could think of. The common refrain was how we all were better people, because of Julia's influence and how we had all drawn closer to the God she loved. Julia was the most non-preachy church going lady I have ever met, yet the most spiritual.

> *"A wise woman who was traveling in the mountains found a precious stone in a stream. The next day she met another traveler who was hungry, and the wise woman opened her bag to share her food. The hungry traveler saw the precious stone and asked the woman to give it to him. She did so without hesitation. The traveler left, rejoicing in his good fortune. He knew the stone was worth enough to give him security for a lifetime. But a few days later, he came back to return the stone to the wise woman. 'I've been thinking,' he said, 'I know how valuable the stone is, but I give it back in the hope that you can give me something even more precious. Give me what you have within you that enabled you to give me the stone.'"*

Unknown

My (Claudia) mother, Mary Church, is the person who taught me the importance of giving and receiving love. She served as a great example in the art of loving people not only within her family but also with friends and total strangers. Throughout my life, my mother has been a social butterfly striking up conversations with people wherever she went. On more occasions than I can count, I would ask who these people were she was talking to and how long they had been friends? Expecting her to give me an answer in years she so often said, "Oh, I just met them with you today, honey." On any given day throughout my childhood, mom set a great example of making a difference, whether she volunteered to help a friend with their children, their yard work, to pick up food for them at the grocery store or medicine at the drug store, to give them a ride to the doctor, to take them to get a haircut or to lunch, to give them a few much needed dollars, or to just listen when someone needed a friend. If I had not witnessed in person her acts of kindness, I would have never known about them because never once have I heard her brag about helping anyone.

One day while sitting next to mom during the first month of her cancer treatment at MD Anderson Hospital in 2008, mom surprised me when she said something about her type of cancer. As no one in my family had battled cancer and the fact that mom had just found out she had cancer, I asked how she could possibly know so much about the treatment for lymphoma. She told me that she had taken her neighbor, Ruby, to all of her cancer treatment appointments the previous year and that she too had lymphoma. Mom then told me stories of the different people she had spoken to while in the waiting room and that now she realized how much it must have meant to them to have someone to talk to as they battled cancer. Even during the darkest days of mom's eight month fight against the disease, she never complained, she never shed a tear for herself, and she never missed an opportunity to engage in conversations with nurses, doctors, fellow patients, or their family members and to ask them how they were doing.

When talking with her one evening about a year into being cancer-free, I asked where she had been all day, because I had tried calling many times to check in with her. She reluctantly revealed, *"Well, I was just cleaning the house this morning and it occurred to me that maybe someone at the cancer center where I used to take Ruby might be alone and need someone to cheer them up. So I got in my car and went over there for most of the day. I sure hope I helped a few people find their smile."* Yes, she is that sweet, kind, giving, and loving. I am truly blessed to call her my mother. I can say the same for my father, Claude Church who is just as sociable and giving. He donates much of his time to honor fellow military veterans and has won awards for his volunteer work with disabled veterans at the V.A. hospital in Dallas.

Everyday heroes and angels seek to empower those in need, not to fix or enable them. Enabling or trying to fix others without encouraging them to embrace responsibility or to incorporate life skills will never heal a person's heart, particularly if they are enmeshed in a negative or hopeless direction. Many humanitarian organizations have referred to the ancient Chinese proverb, "Give a man a fish and he will live for a day. Give him a net and he will live for a lifetime," to emphasize the importance of empowerment in giving aid or resources.

Yes, there are isolated circumstances where all we can do is give to others with no expectations of them bettering their life conditions, but in most circumstances the best way we can represent ourselves as an everyday hero or angel is to empower or teach another person or community skills to stand on their own.

How often have we heard someone say, "I was able to achieve this or accomplish that because someone believed in me." This is the very essence of what everyday heroes and angels do. Benjamin Disraeli put it this way, "The greatest good you can do for another is not just share your riches, but reveal to them their own." In the book, *Me to We*, humanitarians, Craig and Marc Kielburger advise, " 'You' is charity, 'We' is partnership. Pride can sometimes become an issue when your offer is interpreted as pity. No one wants to lose face. When you respect the feelings as well as the input of the people you are trying to help, the result can be an empowering experience for everyone involved."

Professor Muhammad Yunus was shocked by the devastating impact loan sharks had on the poor in the villages of Bangladesh, so he decided to turn the situation around, and empower the poor. Yunus teamed with Grameen Bank to help people keep their dignity and gain self-respect at the same time by offering $27 to $42 no interest loans primarily to women. His financial model proved to be a success with a ninety-seven percent loan payback rate. In 2006, Yunus and Grameen Bank were awarded the Nobel Peace Prize for their efforts to create economic and social development. This financial model has been adopted for programs in fifty-eight countries including the US, Canada, France, the Netherlands, and Norway. The Yunus Centre's website states their ultimate goal, *"The total eradication of poverty from the world. Grameen, he claims, is a message of hope, a program for putting homelessness and destitution in a museum so that one day our children will visit it and ask how we could have allowed such a terrible thing to go on for so long."*

Everyday heroes and angels do not always receive the accolades, awards, or press celebrities or those on a global stage might get for their humanitarian efforts. Most everyday heroes and angels do not give to others in order to receive praise or a statue, yet everyone appreciates some form of validation or gratitude on occasion.

There are certain organizations that have honored everyday heroes and angels for decades, but around 2005 more and more organizations began jumping on board to honor everyday heroes in North America and beyond. *People* magazine honors everyday heroes and angels in their *"Heroes Among Us"* pages of their magazine and website. *USA Weekend* magazine and the, *"Hands On Network"* teamed together to create *Make a Difference Day*, an annual event that takes place on the fourth Saturday of every October. Every year millions come together in their communities. Neighbors helping neighbors, making this day the largest single day of volunteering around the world. *CNN* created *"CNN Heroes"* which honors ten everyday people who are changing the world. Viewers are encouraged to vote for their favorite hero on the *CNN* website and the winner is announced during a televised award's ceremony the weekend of Thanksgiving.

When someone gives to us in small or grand ways, expressing our gratitude both verbally and with a written thank you note goes a long way. Thank you notes not only acknowledge the giver's graciousness, but the appreciation they receive often fuels further giving.

My (Claudia) brother-in-law, Todd's younger brother, Jason, passed away at the age of fifteen following a three-month battle with leukemia and because his parents were so devastated, as any parent would be, I volunteered to help make his funeral arrangements. While at the funeral home, the director asked if we wanted to use their chapel for Jason's service. I asked if I could see it before deciding. As we were about to walk in, I saw an open coffin in the chapel and a minister speaking at the podium through the window. I said, "Oh, there's a service going on." As I looked closer, I realized no one was attending the service. I asked the funeral director what was going on. She said, "This man had no loved ones, so as a courtesy we're giving him a service." The fact was hard to fathom that not even one single person in a town as big as Dallas would be inspired to come and pay their last respects. I have thought of this moment many times, but it was not until the last few years that I began to truly understand how this could occur. The answer was there for me all along. "He had no loved ones."

When we choose to open our hearts and give love to others, we naturally draw people in like flies to honey. When we choose to close our hearts, people will respond accordingly to the metaphorical wall we have built to keep them out. The more open, loving, and accessible we are, the more full and enriched our lives will become.

Giving of ourselves for the greater good of mankind not only makes a difference in people's lives, but thanks to various studies and research, there is now scientific evidence the giver benefits as well. Linda P. Fried, M.D., director of the Center on Aging and Health at Johns Hopkins reports from their study, "What we found is a 'win-win' for everyone involved. Giving back to your community may slow the aging process in ways that lead to a higher quality of life in older adults." Dr. Jorge Moll's research at the National Institute of Neurological Disorders and Stroke found, "Something in our brains shaped by evolution allows us to feel joy when we do good things."

In his study, Moll discovered through magnetic resonance imaging that giving stimulates the mesolimbic area of the brain, which stimulates the release of dopamine causing a euphoric sensation. The subgenual region of the brain is also affected when serving mankind. The area is responsible for releasing oxytocin, the hormone that plays a large role in increasing cooperation and trust in humans. The Corporation for National And Community Service revealed from their research that the human heart actually grows stronger due to charity work. They found when those who suffered from coronary disease or a recent heart attack had volunteered, they decreased their depression and despair, therefore reducing their risk of subsequent heart attacks and increasing their life expectancies.

There are approximately one million charities in North America. Choosing a charity to put our blood, sweat, and tears into can be overwhelming. So where do we start? Sir Paul McCartney has these wise words to say, "Some people say to me there are so many issues, we don't know which ones to support. I say don't freak out – just choose one that appeals to you and get on with it. They all connect."

ONE LITTLE LIGHT

I (Guy) grew up around five underground potash mines in Saskatchewan, Canada. The mines can go down as far as a kilometer or more (a little over a half a mile). One day my family and I went on a private tour of one of the mines. Our guide drove us in a jeep-like vehicle through all the underground tunnels and showed us how potash is mined and how the tunnels connect together to cover over 4,700 kilometers (around three thousand miles).

At one point, the guide stopped the jeep at a crossroad in the tunnels and said, "I want to show you all how black the darkness can be down here." He turned out the jeep lights and instructed us to turn off our helmet lights. I have never seen such darkness or blackness. Then the guide lit a match and said, "Isn't this amazing! Look how much we can see with one little light. I never get tired of showing this to people." We could see the outline of each other and about a quarter of a mile down where each of the four tunnels led. That one little light was a comfort to each of us as we were able to see each other and the path, which lead us back to safety. Many times in my life, I am reminded of this potash mine experience and the power one light/one life can produce.

> *As we let our light shine, we unconsciously give*
> *others the permission to do the same.*
> Nelson Mandela
> 1993 Nobel Peace Prize winner

CHAPTER 24

WORKBOOK CHALLENGES IX

GET TO KNOW ME

1. On a scale from 1 to 10, my current generosity level is? _____

2. What loving and giving act for another do I perform on a regular basis?_____

   _____

   How does giving make me feel?_____

3. What loving and giving act does someone else do for me on a regular basic?_____

   _____

   How does this act of kindness make me feel?_____

4. How can I better serve my community in which I live?_____

   _____

5. What is one act of kindness I have done in my lifetime that made a significant impact on someone's life? _____

   _____

6. Who do I know in my life that is an everyday hero?_____
   What can I do to acknowledge their efforts?_____

   _____

PRACTICAL POWER TOOLS

1. Brainstorm ways you can give back. Start by participating in something around your area of passion. For example, if you love sports sign up to coach a little league team. If you love art, sign up to teach an art class at your local community center. Challenge yourself to give back in small ways on an ongoing basis such as volunteering in a nursing home once a month, or at your favorite local charity's annual fundraiser event.

2. The term, *Pay It Forward* has become part of our culture's lexicon. Starting today, make a deliberate choice to make paying it forward part of your lifestyle. Think of three or four acts of kindness you can do throughout the coming week, and if and when the party acknowledges your act, encourage them to pay it forward. And, when someone does something kind towards you, thank him or her and let him or her know you are going to pay it forward.

3. Organize a social gathering and have those you invite bring with them a touching story of how someone was an everyday hero. Brainstorm ways to give back as a group and set a plan in motion before the gathering is over.

4. Take a service walk around your community or around your place of employment and make mental notes or actual notes on ways you can make a difference. If you see a person that needs a helping hand or an encouraging word do not hesitate to do something or say something nice. If you feel a little shy about taking a service walk alone, take along a friend. When going on these walks be prepared with granola bars, cookies, a couple pieces of fruit, some spare change, or other items to give away that say you care.

5. Acknowledge an everyday hero amongst your friends, family or community. Most people like to give without fanfare. Yet, when we quietly acknowledge their act of kindness this will encourage their hearts and quite often refuel then to keep on giving. Take them to lunch, send them an encouraging email or handwritten letter, make a phone call or send an encouraging text, give them a gift card to a restaurant, movie theater or their favorite store. Ask to go along with them on one of their next "making a difference" outings.

BRAIN MEDICINE

1. My heart is open to love
2. I am conscious of other's needs
3. I am blessed and thankful
4. I make time to give of my time
5. I make a difference

PERSONAL BRAIN MEDICINE

1. _____
2. _____
3. _____
4. _____
5. _____

I have one life and one chance to make it count for something... My faith demands that I do whatever I can, wherever I am, whenever I can, for as long as I can with whatever I have to try to make a difference.

Jimmy Carter

2002 Nobel Peace Prize winner

and 39th US President

CHAPTER 25

THE MASTERPIECE PLAN

It had long since come to my attention that people of accomplishment rarely sat back and let things happen to them. They went out and happened to things.

Leonardo da Vinci

For twenty-five years, from 1492 until 1517, the world experienced some of the most monumental moments in history. During these two and a half decades of the Renaissance period, Christopher Columbus discovered the Americas setting off a wave of immigration previously unseen by the world. Michelangelo created three of his most famous works of art: the *Pieta*, the *David*, and the masterfully painted ceiling of the *Sistine Chapel*. Leonardo da Vinci painted one of the most talked about, studied, and reproduced religious paintings in history, *The Last Supper*. During this time of cultural rebirth, Da Vinci also painted what is considered as the greatest portrait of all time and the most valuable painting in existence, the *Mona Lisa*.

Similar to the *David*, the *Mona Lisa* took a number of years before its completion. Da Vinci worked on the masterpiece intermittently from 1503 to 1506. Believing the painting remained unfinished, he continued refining the work from 1515 to 1517 before he passed away in France in 1519. With all the time Da Vinci devoted to creating his *Mona Lisa*, he was convinced she was never truly finished. He is quoted as saying, "I believe I have never finished a single work." We can liken working on our own masterpiece within to how Da Vinci saw most of his artistic masterpieces, continual works in progress, not completely perfected over a short period of time but instead, continually fine-tuned.

I (Guy) am convinced the older we get and the more life lessons we learn, attaining the life we imagine is about constantly refining our life choices. Music legend, Neil Young, wrote in his 2013 memoir, *Waging Heavy Peace: A Hippie Dream*, about his personal life, his career path, and how hard he has worked to avoid artistic complacency. Young has sustained a successful career spanning generations of fans. He has managed to remain relevant by holding fast to the attitude that his life and music can make a difference in people's lives. He explains that the premise for his record, *Rust Never Sleeps*, was how things in the material world do not last and how we need to keep refining what does matter. Similar to how Young explains avoiding the trap of complacency, we must put our choices under a microscope and refine, refine, and refine to keep our own inner masterpiece alive and relevant.

In the summer of 2010, I (Claudia) decided to take my nephew, Zak, and my two nieces, Sydney and Hannah, to spend a few days exploring where their grandparents were from and to meet relatives in western North Carolina. My dear sweet cousin, Diane Matheson, who had taken her daughter, Brooke, to a gem mine the day before, mentioned someone had found a 1,686 carat emerald, selling for over a million dollars the previous year. The kids were alight with excitement over the possibility of discovering their own buried treasures, so Diane and I made plans to take them the next day. Once at the mine, deep into the Carolina woods, we all began digging with our tools in the creek area. Hours passed sitting in the middle of nature before any of us took a break. As I made the round trip journey to get us all something to drink, I began to notice the intense concentration and enthusiasm of everyone within view, including my family members. The hope in finding a rare gem was palpable!

Once back to digging in the creek, I shared my discovery with our group. Brooke, who was twelve at the time, mentioned how calm she was "creeking" when normally in school she can hardly sit still. Before we knew it, our prospecting careers were coming to an abrupt halt with the setting of the sun. Our hard day's work proved fruitful with topaz, rubies, sapphires, garnets, aquamarines, tourmalines, quartz crystals, and yes, a few small emeralds. Some of our gems were recognizable with the naked eye, but to our surprise when we consulted the mine's gemologist, she taught us the most valuable gems in our buckets were the ones covered over with years of hardened dirt and rock.

Driving back to our hotel, the kids, mud-soaked and exhausted, fell asleep from their hard day's work. I could not help but smile looking at them, not only for the love I have for them, but for how inspiring their hope was to watch throughout the day. The thought occurred to me, if we could all summon that much determination, HOPE, and patience in ourselves and chisel away the years of damaging effects life has placed upon us, what a priceless treasure we would reveal. What a tremendous difference our presence could make in the world.

> *Who would make sure that the statue of David is still standing? Or,*
> *that the Mona Lisa is still smiling? Who would be their protectors?*
> Professor Frank Stokes in the film, *The Monuments Men*

ABOUT THE AUTHORS

GUY SCHOLZ

Guy is a three-time Canadian best-selling author and national award-winning journalist. His first book, *Gold On Ice: The Story of the Sandra Schmirler Curling Team* was a runaway bestseller as the top selling non-fiction book written by a Canadian in 1999/2000. Guy's follow-up books, *Between the Sheets: Creating Curling Champions* and *Between the Sheets: The Silver Lining,* working with Olympic Silver Medalist, Cheryl Bernard as his research assistant, were used by the vast majority of Olympic curlers in the 2006, 2010, and 2014 Olympic Games. His upcoming books include, *No Regrets: The Tim Thomas Story* and *Pint: Richie Hall's Life Lessons From The Gridiron.* He is an ordained minister, certified social worker, communications manager, blogger, and semi-pro athlete winning over forty Bonspiels in the US and Canada as well as a USA National Arena Curling Championship in 2014. For over three decades, he has conducted numerous workshops in over two hundred communities throughout North America. Guy splits his time between Nashville, Tennessee, and Calgary, Alberta.

CLAUDIA CHURCH

Claudia has worked in the entertainment arts for over three decades. After receiving her degree in Fashion Merchandising she traveled the globe as a fashion model working with top agencies such as Ford, Elite, Kim Dawson, and Karin Models. As a country music artist, she achieved chart success and received rave reviews in publications such as *Billboard* and *People* magazine for her self-titled CD, released on Warner/Reprise Records. Her live performances have taken her around the world including over a dozen USO shows in Bosnia-Herzegovina. As an actor, Claudia has appeared in short and long form films, prime time television series, and over one hundred local and national commercials. A natural born teacher with a zest for helping others achieve their goals and dreams, she has conducted numerous workshops and coached many in the entertainment arts throughout North America. Claudia currently resides in Nashville, Tennessee.

SPEAKING ENGAGEMENTS, PRIVATE COACHING, WORKSHOPS, AND SEMINARS

Guy and Claudia are available for speaking engagements, private coaching, workshops, and seminars. For more information visit, themasterpiecewithin.com or contact them at:

Guy Scholz
Guy@themasterpiecewithin.com

Claudia Church
Claudia@themasterpiecewithin.com

To order additional copies of this book or for group sales, visit themasterpiecewithin.com or balboapress.com.